WRITING
TO THE POINT

Fourth Edition

WRITING
TO THE POINT

Fourth Edition

WILLIAM J. KERRIGAN
Fullerton College

ALLAN A. METCALF
MacMurray College

HBJ

HARCOURT BRACE JOVANOVICH, PUBLISHERS

San Diego   New York   Chicago   Austin
London   Sydney   Tokyo   Toronto

ISBN: 0-15-598313-X

Library of Congress Catalog Card Number: 86-80752
Printed in the United States of America

To the Instructor

It really works.

That is the lesson those of us in the English department at MacMurray College learned, more than a decade ago, when we took the first edition of *Writing to the Point* into our freshman composition classes.

There were seven of us in the department at that time, with widely differing backgrounds and approaches. Some were traditionalists, some innovators; some liked to lecture on grammar, others encouraged students to talk about their feelings; some emphasized mechanics, others structure, the reading of literature, or creative expression. We met weekly, as we still do, to argue for our respective emphases and to reach some understanding of what everyone else was doing.

But when *Writing to the Point* came along, we were amazed. Unlike the other attractive texts we had used for a year or two and then discarded, it actually made a difference in our students' writing—a palpable difference.

With *Writing to the Point,* we saw our students—good, fair, and indifferent—making a point and generally adhering to it; supporting that point with usually relevant particulars; and, most of the time, making clear connections from paragraph to paragraph and sentence to sentence. Moreover, we found ourselves able to talk about writing with a consensus and precision previously impossible, not just with students but also with colleagues.

In the first year or two, we were still suspicious. Our initial inclination was to quarrel with the dogmatic certainty and authoritarian persona we found in the book, even as we instructed our students to follow along. We knew there were many different ways to write well and many competing theories about the teaching of writing. How could Kerrigan presume to know?

But he did. The evidence mounted, year after year: in testimonials from students, like one who took the course in 1977 and recently said, "That book saved me in college" (she went on to get A's in later courses); and in papers written by transfer students, who turned out to be far behind our Kerrigan-trained students in simple expository writing. We the faculty, too, found ourselves consciously improving our own writing through one or another of Kerrigan's lessons, as we had never done when using other writing books. And so we took Kerrigan to heart.

New faculty as they joined us went through the same initiation. At first came the shock of having to follow a stern and unfamiliar method. Then followed the shock of seeing students learn it. And finally, after a year or two, came the realization that the Kerrigan method is unusual only in its approach and style, not in its content. What it teaches is what anyone would want in expository writing: unity, coherence, detail.

The approach of *Writing to the Point* is holistic. But it is holistic in a far different sense than the approach in those textbooks which simply offer chapters on the word, the sentence, the paragraph in the belief that the parts will somehow add up to the whole. In marked contrast, *Writing to the Point* has an organic unity. Each element intimately relates to the whole; in fact, the book begins with the whole (the thesis of the theme) and then shows how to develop the whole so that every detail relates to it.

And we gradually learned that, despite its insistence on a very specific method, *Writing to the Point* offers both instructor and student room for individuality and creativity, even while ensuring that any student who can write a sentence (the starting point) will both learn and apply the basic principles of expository writing.

The flexibility is such that no instructor need abandon techniques that have worked in the past. Those who value prewriting will find ample opportunity to call for it, especially with Steps 1 and 4; those who favor rewriting will find occasion at every step, but especially in the chapter on "Correcting the Theme." (Kerrigan calls it "correcting," a term less daunting and more familiar to the student than "revising"; but the chapter requires, and demonstrates exactly how to undertake, thorough revision.) Sentence combining, though not treated at length, has a moment of special emphasis in this book. Grammar and style may be incorporated as the instructor wishes at many appropriate points of connection. Readings of fiction or nonfiction will be grist for the mill.

What makes this book different, then? What makes it work? The answer to both questions is the same. Kerrigan set out, not to make a textbook, but to teach writing. A man of much practical as well as academic experience (as the autobiographical vignettes scattered through the book will attest), he hit upon the first steps of his method while struggling to make the principles of exposition clear to composition classes at Iowa State in the 1950s. For two decades, there and at Fullerton College, he improved on the method, and finally in the early 1970s, at the suggestion of a student, wrote it as a book.

Writing to the Point, then, is an actual course written down—a course actually taught to students like yours and mine, good, fair, and indifferent. Consequently, its style is deliberately and strikingly oral: not just making use of "I," "you," and contractions, but also with emphasis supplied by italics and repetitions not usually found in writing. The result is a book that students can read, even as Kerrigan teaches them how to write (and read) the kind of formal prose with which they are less familiar.

Furthermore, because it reflects actual teaching, *Writing to the Point* has a structure quite different from that of a textbook that proceeds from an idea; it meets the psychological needs of students, not just their logical needs. It has the pacing of an actual course. So instead of chapters of equal size devoted to each of the six steps, Kerrigan makes some short, some long, according to the need of the student and the place in the course. He puts Step 1 in a short, simple chapter, to provide a confident start. Step 2, which needs much attention, requires a chapter three times as long. Immediate relief follows in the short, simple chapter on Step 3; that is succeeded by the longest chapter of all, on Step 4, which appropriately emphasizes the importance of going into detail. Then, instead of continuing with the last two steps, Kerrigan interpolates three chapters, two shorts and a long, to exemplify and review Steps 1 through 4. Psychologically, the student comes to realize that the earlier steps must be thoroughly learned before the mystery of Steps 5 and 6—those that do the most to make a student's writing look professional—can be revealed. In practical terms, these chapters give the student time to write a few themes incorporating Steps 1 through 4 before going on to 5 and 6.

Finally, after Steps 5 and 6, four chapters remain. They contain further exemplification and practice for those last two steps, just as Kerrigan provided for the earlier steps after introducing Step 4. But these last chapters also do more. They complete the incremental, almost unnoticeable stages of development from the amazing simplicity of the early lessons to the complexity of writing an argumentative theme or a research paper. Thus, at the end, by sure degrees, the making of an effective expository writer is complete. And the lesson will not be forgotten.

If the book is an actual course, what is left for the instructor to do? The question answers itself in the reading. At each stage the student needs practice in doing the steps—in class discussion as well as in homework. The instructor is needed to provide intelligent, precise criticism of the student's writing, just as Kerrigan provides for the examples in the book. Step 1, for instance, asks students to write a sentence of a certain kind. The class needs discussion of many such sentences so that students will have a sure sense of which ones work.

One of the virtues of *Writing to the Point* is that it has no pointless, supernumerary exercises. For the most part, the students' assignments are simply to write themes or parts of themes, or to improve on themes already written. If there is opportunity for further assignments, the instructor can then simply ask for more of the same, because the way to learn writing is by writing.

Moreover, the Kerrigan method doesn't get dull. Each set of sentences X, 1, 2, and 3 is a stimulating intellectual challenge for the instructor as well as the student: a triumph if all the sentences stay on the point, an exercise in revision if they do not. Each theme is a similar exercise in virtuosity. The method is simple, but its application to the actual matter of writing is endlessly challenging, and the visible development of students into sure practitioners is a recurring satisfaction. And Kerrigan's book itself offers challenges to conventional nostrums about teaching writing, challenges that stimulate thinking anew each time the instructor guides a class through the Kerrigan experience.

This book does not attempt everything. It does not attempt to teach grammar, style, or the research paper, for example. Students who have trouble writing a grammatical sentence, or wish to improve the flow of their prose, or need the rules of research documentation, will have to turn to books designed for those purposes. But important lessons on all three topics appear in *Writing to the Point* just where experience shows students are most ready for them.

To Kerrigan's own years of teaching, this Fourth Edition adds the wisdom of more than a decade of using all three earlier editions at MacMurray College.

Those at MacMurray who helped me in this revision included both new and experienced instructors, with a combined 54 years of teaching *Writing to the Point*. Equally helpful were five reviewers from other institutions, who gave the draft of this revision the painstaking scrutiny it needed—and the benefit of their similarly long experience with the Kerrigan way. The result is a far better edition than any solitary reviser could have produced.

Yet this Fourth Edition will not at first glance seem different. My intent was not to make a new or different book, but to help an already excellent book live up to its fullest potential. There are changes, sometimes many changes, on almost every page, but my aim is simply to bring out the true Kerrigan that was already latent there.

In preparing this edition, I was assisted by MacMurray colleagues Richard McGuire and Philip Decker, with whom I have shared Kerrigan since the first printing of the First Edition; Elizabeth Crowley and Robert Seufert, who joined us during the Second Edition; and Ulrike Jaeckel, who came along for the Third. Eugene Laurent, who had also been with us for the first, died just before work began on the revision; this edition is dedicated to his insightful championing of the Kerrigan method. My heartfelt thanks go to them all, and to the magnanimous, relentless outside reviewers: Sister Ritamary Bradley, St. Ambrose College; Sherre Owens Smith, University of Toledo; John N. Snapper, Grossmont College; Scott Cawelti, University of Northern Iowa; and Vicki Goldsmith, Northern Michigan University, who also deserves credit for material introduced in the Third Edition that is incorporated here. At MacMurray College, much-appreciated help has come at crucial times from Jeff Decker, Edwin Ecker, Richard McFate, and Teri Metcalf. At Harcourt Brace Jovanovich, my special thanks go to Paul Nockleby, who brought us all together, and to Bruce Daniels and Merilyn Britt, who guided the book into its final shape.

Finally and happily, I acknowledge the help of the man who started it all, William J. Kerrigan. This is my own revision, but it remains quintessentially his book. It has been a great pleasure to make the acquaintance of a person who is almost as fascinating as the persona of the book, a man who might be called the Nikola Tesla of English composition. After you read the book (and Chapter 9), you'll know what I mean.

Allan A. Metcalf

From the Preface to the First Edition

. . . The course in this book is highly structured and teaches highly structured writing—which is just what students want and certainly need. Far from restricting students, the tight structure soon frees them to say what they really want to say. Their themes become as individual as their handwriting. And students endowed with gifts of expression find at last a form in which they can put those gifts to meaningful use.

In fact, what will please you most—as it pleases me most—is that on completing the course students will be enthusiastic about their own writing and the good, solid sense it makes when they reread it.

William J. Kerrigan

Contents

Chapter 14

CONTRAST   *161*

Chapter 15

THE ARGUMENTATIVE THEME   *171*

Chapter 16

THE REAL WORLD   *179*

Appendix I

THE SIX STEPS   *197*

Appendix II

CHECKLIST FOR REVISION   *198*

Appendix III

SEVEN FORMS OF EXPLICIT REFERENCE   *199*

Appendix IV

SEVEN RULES FOR CONTRAST   *200*

Index

201

WRITING
TO THE POINT

Fourth Edition

Chapter 1

STEP 1

Step 1 is simple. But before we begin with Step 1, I'd like to say something helpful about the method in this book. It *is* a method, a step-by-step method— and that is what makes this book different from others you may have used. The book itself, as you'll see at once, talks directly and familiarly with you, instead of formally to your instructor; so it is not so much a book as a conversation.

Now the method taught in this book has proved useful to everyone from grade school students to graduate students in English. (As a matter of fact, one excellent writer, the head of a college English department, told me gratefully that he had learned some things of value from it.) But what you'll really like to hear is that out of the thousands of college students who have studied this method, not one has failed to learn to use it. And after learning it, not one has failed to write themes that, as both the student and the instructor could see, were quite acceptable—better than the student imagined possible. You too, at this point, can't imagine how much more impressive and effective your writing will become after you put this simple method to work.

I suspect that what lies behind this method is my experience with swimming. Efforts to teach me to swim, beginning back in my grade school days, had time after time proved utter failures. In crowded municipal pools, in small private pools, and in swimming holes in rural creeks, my friends told me to do this and do that, gave me one piece of advice and then another, held me up as I waved my arms and legs, put water wings on me, demonstrated for me again and again. No use. I couldn't learn to swim a stroke or to keep myself up in the water for one second.

But one day when I was in my twenties and was paddling my hands in the water in the shallow end of a pool—while other people swam—a friend of mine got out of the water and said, "Walk out there ten or fifteen feet, and turn and face me on the deck of the pool here. OK. Now raise your hands above your head, take a deep breath and hold it, close your eyes if you want to, and just lie face down in the water. You absolutely can't sink. Then, when you're out of breath, stand up again."

I followed his directions and, to my surprise, I didn't sink.

"Now," he said, "when you lie down again in the water, just kick your feet up and down. You'll come right to me at the edge of the pool."

I did as he told me. When my hands met the side of the pool and I stood up again, I realized that after years of vain effort, I had—in less than five minutes—learned how to swim.

It was the simplest kind of swimming, to be sure; and I need not take you through the steps that followed, in which I moved my arms, lifted my head to breathe, and developed various strokes. Let me say only that today I have an acceptable swimming technique.

When it came to teaching theme writing, then, I wanted a method like that—a method that was going to work for all students, good, fair, and indifferent. What was needed was a set of simple instructions that any and every student could follow, that would lead—like "lie face down in the water"—to automatic success. Other writing textbooks contained plenty of good advice, but not a method of organizing the advice so that it would lead step by step to a successful theme. So I had to figure out the instructions myself. The foolproof method I developed is fully contained in this book.

But before turning to that method, I have a few more helpful words. First, remember that it guarantees that you will write acceptable themes. That is because it is automatic: it relies not on any special skill of yours, but on what you already must know if you are able to read and write. It does not depend on your having good ideas, a good vocabulary, or good expression. For that reason, it cannot guarantee that the themes you produce will be literature. (To produce literature you would ordinarily need to have done a lot of reading and writing, besides, of course, having been born with unusual gifts.)

But after all, what call will there ever be for you to write literature? In your government class, in your psychology class, in your biology class, if your instructors require you to write a paper, what they will want is a decent, clear, orderly, detailed explanation of something, not a beautiful personal essay. Similarly, in later life, when you have to write a report for your employer or employees, for your customers, or for your colleagues, the people you write for will not expect a masterpiece. But they will want a clear explanation of something they need to understand. To teach you to do that kind of writing is the modest but useful purpose of this book.

Some of you, however, will protest that you do intend to write literature later on. Good for you! If so, you will find this book a solid foundation for it. Meanwhile, if we are all to achieve the modest goal of this book, you will have to do some work—though I must keep assuring you that it will be work that you, whoever you are, *can* do, if you can read these words. Remember that the fundamental secret of swimming was revealed to me by my friend in a flash. But I did not immediately become a decent swimmer! No, it required hours of practice in the pool. We learn to swim by—and *only* by—swimming; we learn to skate by skating; and you—as you don't recall but I'm sure believe—learned to walk by walking. It should not surprise you, then, that we learn to write by writing.

So first of all, you'll have to apply your mind to the instructions that go with each step in this method. You can understand the instructions; they're not as hard as the rules of football, basketball, pinochle, driving a car, or making your own clothes. And you can follow a football game, play cards, drive, or make your own clothes, can't you? But you probably won't understand the instructions without some effort—they're not as simple as "touch your right ear."

Believe me when I tell you, however, that what you *don't* understand in this book you won't need in order to write an acceptable theme. You'll get the main ideas, all right. Sometimes you'll go along, maybe even for several pages, saying, "This stuff is too deep for me. I don't know why it's in here anyway." Right! That material is here because *some* students will find it helpful for the kind of theme *they* write. But it needn't worry you.

So if you're occasionally baffled by something as you study the six steps, be patient and do not become discouraged. Your first puzzlement, for example, may come later in this chapter, where I compare a certain sentence to a magnet. You may say, "I don't think I really see the point. And especially I don't see whether I'm supposed to be learning something here or not." Go right on and don't worry. The magnet—or whatever else you don't understand—isn't essential.

At the same time, don't be timid. If you don't understand something, give it at least a second try before going on to the next thing.

Besides understanding as much as you can, you'll have to write themes to show yourself you can apply the rules—and to get practice, of course. Actually, a dozen practice themes of about three hundred to five hundred words should be enough to make you a decent writer.

"But," you object (and this will be only the first of your objections), "that's just the point: I can't write a theme." Have no fear. Just follow the instructions, simple step by simple step, and you'll automatically be writing a theme before long. "Just take a deep breath and lie face down in the water."

"But," you may object instead (you're very good at objections), "I already know how to write. I got A's on my themes in high school." Excellent. You are the rare student, then, on whom nothing in this book will be wasted. You'll understand everything. And being sensitive to good writing, you'll know how much more you'll have to work to reach professional level. Whether your goal is the Pulitzer Prize for literature or for investigative reporting, through the six steps you'll discover strengths in your writing that you had never imagined possible.

I'll make a bargain with you. I can't give you clear directions and at the same time answer all your objections. But I promise to answer your objections later on, when the answers won't get in the way of something else; and I'll also give you the reasons behind each step.

Let's look at one more objection, though, and a partial answer to it. It's related to the one I just mentioned. Particularly if you feel and have been told that you already write well, the method that follows may at first strike you as cramping your style by (a) keeping you from saying what you want to say and (b) forcing you to do meager, bare, thin, mechanical writing. But if you're patient, you will find that the very opposite is true. The method we are about to begin will allow you to employ your talents more fully than ever before.

I'd like to tell you something now, before we begin Step 1, and ask you to remember it throughout this book. Will you? It is this: the method you are about to follow is not something new. It is simply a description of the basic things all effective writers do today and did yesterday and hundreds of years before that. And I want you to keep in mind that they do them and did them not because they're the right way to do things according to some English teacher, but because they're the main way—the necessary way—of helping *readers* to follow what a writer is saying and to get a clear picture of it.

STEP 1

Write a sentence.

"Well, nothing could be simpler than that," you say. All right, but be sure that it's a *sentence*, because everything depends on that. The following, for example, are *not* sentences: "If I won the lottery"; "The pleasures of a cattle ranch"; "Where gold mining is profitable"; "Why we should study anthropology." No, a sentence makes a definite statement—without any why's or where's or if's to depend on. A sentence has *two parts* (a subject and a predicate) telling us that somebody (or something) *is* something—or *was* something, or *does* something, or *did* something.

Somebody)   (is or was something.

Something)   (does or did something.

For instance, "The child is crying"—can you see that somebody is *doing* something in that set of words? That's what makes it a sentence. Notice that same thing in the following sentences.

Power corrupts.

Colors affect mood.

Oxygen is essential for life.

Henry Ford was an innovator.

My mother is a resourceful woman.

I learned self-reliance on a cattle ranch.

Richard Nixon was a misunderstood president.

Orderliness makes work easy.

If you still have trouble recognizing a sentence, and being sure you're writing one yourself, don't cheat yourself by thinking you can just go on to the next paragraph and come back to this problem later. The ability to recognize a sentence is absolutely necessary in this course, because anything *but* a sentence will no more work as Step 1 than water will work as gasoline in your car, or a piece of string as a spring in a clock. (A little book that teaches this skill is *Writing in College* by William J. Kerrigan [New York: Harcourt Brace Jovanovich, 1976].)

But perhaps you'll grasp what I mean when I tell you that *the statement you write for Step 1 is not a title or heading of any kind*. Sometimes when students write their statement for Step 1, they write a sentence, all right, but show that they think of it as a title by writing it with capital letters—for instance: Oxygen Is Essential for Life. No! The sentence in Step 1 is not a title or heading, nor is it an introduction. Don't let me leave you with any such idea. It's going to be a sentence in your theme—a definite, complete statement of something you know about. In fact, it is, in miniature, your whole theme.

So, write a sentence.

Any sentence? Well, theoretically yes, any sentence. But for your purposes here I must be more specific. First, this original sentence that you're writing for Step 1 ought to be short and simple: "Uncle Ben is a perfectionist"; "Cigarette smoking is dangerous to your health"; "Keats was a Romantic poet." As you will see later, if the sentence in Step 1 isn't short and simple, you'll be in trouble when you reach Step 2.

Second, the sentence is to be a statement (called a declarative sentence), not a question or a command. That is, it is not to be a question like "Why is cigarette smoking dangerous?" or "Was Keats a Romantic poet?" Nor is it to be a command like "Don't start smoking" or "Practice writing at least one paragraph a day."

Third, be sure your sentence for Step 1 makes only one statement, not two or more. Don't try to use a sentence like "Smoking is dangerous and expensive." That's two statements: one that smoking is dangerous, the other that it's expensive. For Step 1, say that it's dangerous or say that it's expensive, but don't say both.

Let me explain that each new step casts light on the preceding steps (if a step can be said to cast light). So if you ask whether Step 1 can be any sentence that meets the conditions I've given, let me say for now that you will soon be able to tell very well that some sentences will suit your purposes while others will not. For instance, the sentence "Dogs bark," which is as short and simple as they come, would not prove very useful to you. Also, as you'll see when I discuss Step 2, sentences that tell how something looks (description), what happened (narration), how to make or do something or how something works (process) will not suit your purpose either. Nor, at this stage, will you want to employ *contrast* or *comparison* in your Step 1 sentence, because it will mean added complications later.

Most important of all, you will discover that your Step 1 sentence needs to be a sentence you can say much more about—for that is what you will have to do in the succeeding steps.

But let's cross all those bridges when we come to them. Meanwhile, we've made Step 1 more specific.

STEP 1

Write a short, simple, declarative sentence that makes one statement.

ASSIGNMENT

Do Step 1 as your first assignment, and the writing part of this lesson is done. Do it right now, and keep it in your notebook for further consideration.

You will of course want to check, in class or on your own, to make sure that what you have written for Step 1 meets all the specifications: Is it a sentence? Is it short? Is it simple? Is it a declarative sentence? Does it make only one statement?

Next, since the written work for this lesson is so short and easy, you can spend some time rereading what you've read so far. The first thing to make sure you've gotten out of what you've read is that, just as by following my friend's simple directions I couldn't *not* swim, you, by following my directions, can't *not* write an acceptable theme. You're bound to succeed. Or, if you already write well and think that this work is too simple for you, just be patient and consider the following story.

When I was a young child, an older cousin of mine presented me with a simple bar of iron and told me that I could do lots of tricks with it. Being a bright little boy, however, I was quite skeptical about the powers of an old piece of iron! But in a few minutes I learned that that short, simple iron bar had an amazing property: it was magnetized! And I certainly could perform with it tricks I had never imagined possible. Well, in somewhat the same way, the short, simple sentence of Step 1, though seemingly almost powerless, has certain wonderful qualities that, once you've begun to suspect they're there, you could spend years exploring.

All the first half of this chapter, which you've been asked to reread, is actually a preface. But if I had called it a preface, you probably wouldn't have read it; so I smuggled it into this first lesson because I think that knowing you're going to succeed—can't *not* succeed—is the biggest extra help this book can give you. The second thing you should get out of this chapter is all I've said about Step 1 itself. Go over that part thoughtfully, because every word will prove helpful. Reread this whole lesson carefully—now or later—before going on to the next one.

Chapter 2

STEP 2

This chapter is quite long, perhaps too long to be digested as a single meal. I have therefore divided it into sections, each of which you can regard as a single lesson. There is no writing assignment until the very end, but to be prepared for it you will need to reread each section carefully, doing your best (which is good enough for me) to make sure that you are following what I'm saying. Of course, you may not be *interested* in following it; just remember that it wasn't intended to entertain you, but to teach you something that you're going to need to know.

Your instructor or a friend will come in handy here if you have questions or objections. But let me anticipate one possible objection from readers who already have had some successful experience in writing and who worry that their creativity is being stifled. Remember that Step 2 is only Step 2. In it we do not begin the theme proper or even get into the first paragraph of the theme itself.

A. A NEW KIND OF THINKING

Step 2 will ask you to do a kind of thinking you've probably never done before. (Steps 4 and 6 will ask you for still other new kinds of thinking.) But it is a kind of thinking that everyone can do—with a little effort. Still, it is easier *not* to do it; through laziness, you may try to cheat yourself by juggling Steps 1 and 2 so as to avoid that thinking. It won't work, so you might as well make the effort. Granted, this book has promised you automatic success, but not *automated* success! You can't push a button and have a theme pop out. Lifting weights, you know, will certainly increase your muscular strength—but not if you just leave them in the corner and never lift them!

In the same way, then, the method presented here will be a successful method for you, but only if you *use* the method. And to use it, you will have to pay a reasonable amount of attention, exert yourself to achieve a reasonable

7

amount of understanding, do a reasonable amount of thinking, and perform a reasonable amount of work. So promise yourself that you'll be honest with Step 2.

STEP 2

Write three sentences about the sentence in Step 1.

This basic version of Step 2 contains a couple of traps, so I'm going to have to reword it in a minute. Meanwhile, let me define "three sentences." "Three sentences" means three short, simple, declarative sentences, each making only one statement—just as in Step 1. Mind you, they must be *sentences*. So far, so good. But here is the trick, stated in this more complete wording of Step 2.

STEP 2

Write three sentences about the sentence in Step 1— about the whole of that sentence, not just something in it.

You ought to reread Step 2 a couple of times so that you're familiar with it. Let me clarify its instructions by example.

Suppose my sentence in Step 1—let's label it sentence X—is "Studying consists in teaching yourself." Next, Step 2: I have to write three sentences about that sentence. And let's say that for the first of my three I write, "There are many subjects to be studied." Think about it: "There are many subjects to be studied." Read sentence X again: "Studying consists in teaching yourself." And now my sentence 1: "There are many subjects to be studied."

Do you find anything wrong? Do you understand, with certainty, that I have not really followed the instructions in Step 2? If you do see that, you have grasped—believe me—the whole essence of composition. And of course you're right: "There are many subjects to be studied" is about studying, all right, but has nothing to do with the fact that studying consists in teaching yourself. In other words, that attempted sentence 1 is not about the *whole* of sentence X; it is just about something (studying) *in* sentence X.

This is a time to return to Step 1 for a moment. (We will go back many and many a time—because what we learn about Step 2 also tells us more about Step 1.) Remember that we said Step 1 must be a sentence, and a sentence always has two parts:

Somebody)   (is or was something.

Something)   (does or did something.

In following Step 2, then, to write about *the whole of* our sentence X, we must write about both parts of it: somebody or something, *and* what somebody or something is or was, does or did. The problem with "There are many subjects to be studied" is that it is about the first part of the sentence X only. Sentence X says:

Studying)   (consists in teaching yourself.

Look again at our sentence 1: "There are many subjects to be studied." Is it about the first part of sentence X? Certainly, for it is about studying. But is it also about the second part of sentence X? Does it say anything about *teaching yourself*? No, it does not. And thus it fails the test for Step 2.

Now before continuing to the next paragraph, please reread the first part of this lesson, from the beginning to this point.

After you've reread up to this point, it's natural for you to want an example of a series of sentences in which the writer has followed Step 2 correctly. All right, how about this:

X   Studying consists in teaching yourself.
1.   It consists in applying yourself for a length of time to a lesson you set before yourself.
2.   It consists in explaining the points of the lesson to yourself as if you were explaining them to someone else.
3.   It consists in drilling and testing yourself until you are sure that you have mastered the lesson.

I think you'll agree that those sentences 1, 2, and 3 are truly about the whole of sentence X. In fact, *each really restates the idea of sentence X in some particular way.* Sentences 1, 2, and 3 can be more specific about the first part of sentence X ("studying"), or about the second part ("consists in teaching yourself"), while keeping the rest of sentence X the same. That is, for sentences 1, 2, and 3 you can concentrate on the subject, the first part of the sentence:

X   Studying)   (consists in teaching yourself.
1.   Studying mathematics)   (consists in teaching yourself.
2.   Studying psychology)   (consists in teaching yourself.
3.   Studying government)   (consists in teaching yourself.

But the development of sentences 1, 2, and 3 usually goes best when you concentrate not on the subject but on the predicate—not on the *something* ("studying") but on *what that something is or does* ("consists in teaching yourself"):

X   Studying)   (consists in teaching yourself.
1.   It)   (consists in applying yourself for a length of time to a lesson you set before yourself.
2.   It)   (consists in explaining the points of the lesson to yourself as if you were explaining them to someone else.

3.   It)   (consists in drilling and testing yourself until you are sure that you have mastered the lesson.

Can you see that these sentences 1, 2, and 3 are about the whole of sentence X? For setting a lesson and requiring application (the material of sentence 1) are what a teacher does, so that doing these things yourself, at home, is being your own teacher—teaching yourself. In the same way, explaining is what a teacher does; drilling and testing are, too.

You may have noticed that the sentences 1, 2, and 3 in this example were somewhat long. Yes, they were—and if you noticed, good for you. I deliberately made them long so you would slow down and read them carefully. In a more short and simple form, you could write:

X   Studying)   (requires teaching yourself.
1.   It)   (requires setting a schedule for yourself.
2.   It)   (requires explaining the lesson to yourself.
3.   It)   (requires self-testing.

It should be clear to you by now that Step 2 won't work if you've been careless in doing Step 1. If you write a sentence X and then find that you have great difficulty writing sentences 1, 2, and 3, take a good look at your sentence X. Sometimes the problem lies there. You may have put the topic where the *is* or *does* belongs, and really stated nothing that the topic is or does. Obviously this will make it impossible to restate in some particular way what the topic is or does. Here's an example of the error I'm talking about. A student picks a topic, "Dodge City," and throws it into any old sentence: "I live in Dodge City." That sentence makes a statement not about what Dodge City is or does, but about what the writer does. And how many ways can you say that you live in Dodge City? Dodge City should come first, then be or do something:

X   Dodge City looms large in the American imagination.
1.   Its history symbolizes the exciting conflicts of the Old West.
2.   It is the romantic setting of many a Western movie.
3.   Its atmosphere attracts tourists from across the nation.

Each of these is really a statement about Dodge City, and, even more important, each is a particular way in which Dodge City looms large in the American imagination.

Before I try to clinch my point with some more examples of sentence X followed by sentences 1, 2, and 3, let me say one thing. Examples of right ways and wrong ways to do Step 2 may seem to you to go on and on here, with one just suggesting another, and you may begin to ask, "What's all this leading to? What am I supposed to get out of all this?" The answer is that you have already gotten out of this chapter what you're supposed to get; you have already caught on to Step 2. But it's tricky, so you need practice in it. That practice is what the next few pages provide. All you have to do is read it and know that it's deepening your understanding of Step 2. So let's go on with the examples.

Let's say my sentence X is "Aunt Olga has a bad temper," and let's say my sentence 1 is "Aunt Olga was born in 1914." She was born in 1914? What has that to do with her having a bad temper? Am I attempting to say that babies born in 1914 were unusually likely to grow up having bad tempers? Look at the mismatch between the second parts of the two sentences:

    X   Aunt Olga)   (has a bad temper.
    1.   Aunt Olga)   (was born in 1914.

No, my sentence 1 won't work. We'll have to cross it out and start again. How about "She loses her temper at least three times a day"? That sentence may come a little too close to just repeating sentence X, but at least it has something to do with the fact that Aunt Olga has a bad temper; it's not just some random fact (like *born in 1914*) about Aunt Olga that has nothing to do with her bad temper.

But let's take a more difficult example.

    X   To be educated, we must study anthropology.
    1.   In anthropology we study the customs of primitive peoples.
    2.   In anthropology we study the social relationships of primitive peoples.
    3.   In anthropology we study the myths of primitive peoples.

Study this example and see what you think of it. (If, after studying it, you don't understand the discussion of it that follows, don't worry. There's more for you in the material that comes a little later. But try now to concentrate on the example I've just given.) Something is wrong with this example (and I don't mean that the writer should have given anthropology its wider meaning, the study of all peoples, primitive or not; the writer's choice of the restricted meaning is perhaps legitimate, and in any case that's not what we're quarreling with). Remember that the writer's original assertion—sentence X—is that *to be educated* we *must* study anthropology. That's what sentence X is; that's what it *says*; and that—not something else the writer may have had in mind—is what sentences 1, 2, and 3 must be about. Please notice that. For in writing themes, you are dealing strictly with what you put down on paper, not with what you have in mind but do not have down on paper.

Even the way those sentences are written hints of trouble. Notice that the writer, probably with the praiseworthy aim of providing a little variety, produces sentences 1, 2, and 3 that cannot be matched with the sentence X:

    X   To be educated,)   (we)   (must study anthropology.
    1.   In anthropology)   (we)   (study the customs of primitive peoples.
    2.   In anthropology)   (we)   (study the social relationships of primitive peoples.
    3.   In anthropology)   (we)   (study the myths of primitive peoples.

"Anthropology" appears on one side of the subject "we" in sentence X, on the other side in sentences 1, 2, and 3. Matching up the word order of sentence X with that of sentences 1, 2, and 3 makes the problem clear:

    X   We)   (must)   (study anthropology)   (to be educated.

    1.   We)   (study the customs of primitive peoples in anthropology.

    2.   We)   (study the social relationships of primitive peoples in anthropology.

    3.   We)   (study the myths of primitive peoples in anthropology.

Do you see now what is missing from sentences 1, 2, and 3? Passing over any debate about what being educated means—since we can suppose that the writer expects us all to agree pretty much on that—we are still faced with the fact that in sentences 1, 2, and 3 the writer says nothing about a study of customs, social relationships, and myths being *necessary* ("*must*") *for education*. It's as if sentence X said "Oxygen is necessary for life" and then sentence 1 said "Oxygen has an atomic weight of 15.9994." What has oxygen's having an atomic weight of 15.9994 to do with its being necessary for life?

So it looks as if the writer either forgot the intention of the original statement about anthropology (its being necessary for education), or else did not really have a clear intention to begin with, but just put anthropology into any old sentence X—the first one that came to mind or looked important—and then paid no more attention to sentence X and went on to make a few statements about anthropology as a general topic. In other words, the writer seems to have ignored the very point of Step 2.

There is a way out of a difficulty like this that I haven't yet mentioned. Seeing that sentence X wasn't properly connected with sentences 1, 2, and 3, the writer in this case might have studied sentences 1, 2, and 3 to discover whether in fact they had something in common and then produced a new sentence X out of that.

    X   Anthropology is a study concerned with primitive peoples.

    1.   It is concerned with their customs.

    2.   It is concerned with their social relationships.

    3.   It is concerned with their myths.

You may say, "But what has become of the original subject? You've made up a new subject yourself." No. First of all, it was the writer, in sentences 1, 2, and 3, who left behind the original assertion that anthropology is a necessary part of an education. Second, I did not make up a new point; I got the only point I could find out of the original sentences 1, 2, and 3.

This is a perfectly acceptable procedure. In fact, each time you write sentences 1, 2, and 3, you will want to check back to make sure they fit sentence X. If they do not, you must alter them, as a tailor alters clothes, until they fit snugly. Look at the sentences 1, 2, and 3 together; ask what they add up to, what single point they support. Then ask if your sentence X states exactly that point. If not, adjust sentence X, or sentences 1, 2, and 3, until they match. So if sentences 1, 2, and 3 say that anthropology is concerned with customs, social relationships, and myths of primitive peoples—then *anthropology, concern,* and *primitive peoples* need to be in sentence X.

At this point you may object, "This seems to be more about anthropology than about writing themes!" Be patient. Our imaginary writer's sentences have to be about *something*. They happen to be about anthropology, and we have to say a little about it so as to say how the writer wrote about it. Pretend that *you* had written about it, and you'll see the point of discussing it.

So what else could this writer—or you—have done to make sentences X, 1, 2, and 3 come out all right? Well, yes, you could have kept the original assertion—a sentence X you happen to like—and figured out a series of 1, 2, and 3 that would really fit it. I could only guess what your sentences 1, 2, and 3 would then be: something, perhaps, about learning from primitive beliefs and practices that our way of looking at things is not the only way—which is one of the products of true education, certainly; then something about learning that beneath all the differences between peoples, human nature in every time and place has proved ultimately the same—another product of education, of course. You might have added the assertion that we do not get enough of those products of education from history and geography alone. Anyway, you have to do *something* to make sentences 1, 2, and 3 really say something about *the whole of* sentence X.

Personally, I think asserting "To be educated, we must study anthropology" sets up something too hard to prove. We ought not, in our sentence X, bite off more than we can chew.

There is still another possibility. The writer may still feel right in choosing both the original sentence X and the original sentences 1, 2, and 3—for reasons, however, that I won't bother to discuss now. But I'll come back to it.

Let me emphasize, before we leave this example, that one of the problems with the original sentences X, 1, 2, 3 on anthropology is that they did *not* take anthropology for the grammatical subject. Look again at our first version of sentence X:

X   To be educated, we must study anthropology.

Now *To be educated*, though it comes first, is not the subject. The grammatical subject of this sentence X is *we*—but *we* is not what the writer really thought of as the subject. As sentences 1, 2, and 3 make clear, the real subject is *anthropology*. Make that *real* subject the *grammatical* subject; put it first in the sentence; and then tell what it *is* or *was*, *does* or *did*. Well-fitting sentences 1, 2, and 3 will then follow much more naturally.

B. STEP 1 AGAIN

In this section I want to add something more about Sentence X in general. I was saying in the last section that we ought not bite off more than we can chew in sentence X. This is a reminder that each step casts light on steps that have gone before, and later on in this book you will be able to tell at a glance which sentences will suit your purposes for sentence X and which will not. For now, let's discuss another sample sentence fully. "My father was a plasterer" is not very suitable because, as you can see, there are hardly three sentences that you can write about it. You could say that a plasterer does this, that, and the other thing, but those things are true of all plasterers, and the fact that your father was a plasterer hardly enters into the matter.

True, it is possible to imagine circumstances that would not flatly rule that sentence out. For you can imagine a child's asking you, "What did your father do?" You'd say, "He was a plasterer." But then the child would say, "Oh? What did he *do*?" Then you would go on to say what he, like any plasterer, did. (Often, as we will later see, it is useful to think about sentence X as the answer to a question: "What is anthropology?" "Why is anthropology educational?" Thinking of it as the answer to a question will probably suggest at once a good series 1, 2, and 3.)

Let's take as another example the sentence "My name is Lloyd Palfy." It's not suitable for a sentence X because there's no more to be said—no series 1, 2, and 3 are possible. Oh, you *could* force yourself to say, "Lloyd is from the Welsh *llwyd*, meaning 'gray'; I was named that as a baby not because I was gray, but because Lloyd is my uncle's name. Palfy is from the Welsh *ap-alfy*, meaning 'son of Alfy (Alfred)'; but I'm not really the son of Alfy, for my father's name is Llewellyn, not Alfy. Palfy is a name given to some ancestor whose father *was* Alfy and who passed the name down to us as a permanent surname." But is that natural? When somebody asks you your name and you give it, does it ever occur to you to add an explanation like that? No. In fact, the person who came up with those sentences 1, 2, and 3 must have had a different question in mind—not "What is your name?" but "How did you get your name?" And the sentence X in response to that would be "My name is a family legacy."

Of course, having written as sentence X "My name is Lloyd Palfy," you might go on, for sentences 1, 2, and 3, to give other facts about yourself: where you live, what you do, and so forth. But if you did that, you would simply be ignoring Step 2. For remember, you wrote "My name is Lloyd Palfy," and according to Step 2 you are stuck with discussing what your name is *and nothing else*. Where you live and what you do have nothing to do with what your name is.

The moral is: be sure you are very careful about your selection of sentence X, because you are stuck with talking *only about what it says*—the whole of what it says.

You may unconsciously—or consciously, to be honest—want to avoid the work that Steps 1 and 2 involve. When you are asked to write a theme—say, about a relative—you may come up with a sentence like "Uncle Ralph is a wonderful man." That sentence is so broad and vague that it says nothing; all it does is allow the lazy writer to put down just about anything about Uncle Ralph in sentences 1, 2, and 3. Or worse, it leaves the writer with nothing more to say, no clear direction to go in. No, sentence X must be more particular and definite: "Uncle Ralph is a perfectionist"; "Uncle Ralph is a pinochle addict"; "Uncle Ralph can repair anything"; "Uncle Ralph is a hypochondriac."

Those sentences really determine the kind of thing you're going to have to say in sentences 1, 2, and 3—as "Uncle Ralph is a wonderful man" does not.

So if you're tempted to write "Aunt Jane is marvelous" as your sentence X, think again! It's not a good sentence X, because it allows you to say almost *anything* about Aunt Jane: she knits beautiful sweaters; she takes in stray dogs; she once won a beauty contest in North Dakota.

Notice that after you've said Aunt Minnie is wonderful, you're left to think how you're going to say why she's wonderful; but when you've said that Uncle Ben is a miser, a statement that pins you down, you know at once what you're going to have to say; you find that it's already in your head, and what follows practically writes itself.

A good sentence X fits the sentences 1, 2, and 3 like a well-tailored suit. It should not be a baggy clown's outfit! So when you have finished Steps 1 and 2, check the sentence X to make sure it does fit snugly, and alter it if necessary. Consider Aunt Minnie again:

    X   Aunt Minnie is wonderful.
    1.   She knows Basic.
    2.   She knows Fortran.
    3.   She knows Pascal.

Can you see that this sentence X, when you get down to it, is much too baggy and ill-fitting? Once we started listing Aunt Minnie's wonderful qualities, we see that we really meant a sentence X something like "Aunt Minnie knows computer languages." *That's* wonderful—and it's also specific enough that the reader of sentence X will know what direction the Step 2 sentences will take.

Oh, I can hear another objection. Students will say they are afraid that if they narrow down X and get specific right away, they won't have anything left to say, so they remain too general. The opposite, however, is true; if they are specific in X, they will have more direction for 1, 2, and 3. With a well-wrought, precisely pointed sentence X, the theme practically writes itself. The extra time and effort required to write a truly suitable sentence X will save time and energy later on.

There is another problem with "wonderful"—or "exciting," "boring," "good," "bad," "great," "terrible," and the like. Not only do they make a sentence X too big, but they also hide the true subject within them, so that the writer seems to be writing about one thing but in fact is writing about another. That other thing is the writer's own likes and dislikes, concealed in "exciting" or "boring": "My ten o'clock class is boring" means "I don't like my ten o'clock class." So "Aunt Minnie is wonderful" really means "I admire Aunt Minnie"—quite a different point from her knowing computer languages.

(Some students will object here that they have been taught not to use *I* in their themes, or at least to use it rarely. Whether *I* is suitable or not depends on the nature of the assignment; but in any case it is much more ego-centered to avoid *I* in this fashion, pretending that one's own reactions are somehow built into the nature of things and hold true for the world at large.)

Now I told you that Step 2 would involve a kind of thinking you'd probably never done before. You get the point, don't you? Let's see if you do. When asked to write a series X, 1, 2, and 3 about some teacher they've had, some people, despite having heard all this explanation, write a sentence X something like, "Miss López was my geometry teacher." Now either such writers understood *nothing* of what I've said—and that's hard to believe—or else they have decided that they are not going to bother with Steps 1 and 2 and are simply going to write not on a *sentence*, but on a *topic*—namely, Miss López. That's only part of sentence X, not the whole of it. Then for sentences 1, 2, and 3 they feel free to write just anything that comes into their heads about Miss López:

    X   Miss López was my geometry teacher.
    1.   She had a good sense of humor.
    2.   She gave low grades.
    3.   She was also a gym teacher.

Well, she did all those things whether she was a particular writer's geometry teacher or not; they have no connection with sentence X. The only sentences 1, 2, and 3 that I can think of that could be connected to "Miss López was my geometry teacher" would be evidence that she *was* the writer's geometry teacher: the records at Umber Heights High School, the testimony of classmates, the agreement of Miss López herself. Remember, if I say in sentence X that Miss López was my geometry teacher, then my sentences 1, 2, and 3 have to be strictly about that fact *and nothing else*.

It may be well to recall here that sentences 1, 2, and 3 repeat the idea of sentence X in some particular way. Now "Miss López had a good sense of humor" is certainly not any particular way of saying that she was my geometry teacher. Neither is the statement that she gave low grades, nor the statement that she was also a gym teacher.

You'd better reread the example about Miss López and all I've said about it until it becomes crystal clear.

Next, we can look at another kind of example—the "promise" sentence X.

    X   I want a compact car for three reasons.
    1.   The original cost is low.
    2.   It is cheap to maintain.
    3.   It gets good gas mileage.

Performance is better than promise. And so this kind of sentence X, admirable as it is in letting the reader know that three reasons will follow, does not merit our highest approval, because it fails to give any clue as to what those reasons will be. It is like a newspaper story that says only, "The president gave a speech today," without telling what the president said. No, this sentence X only *promises* to say something instead of actually saying it. So it would be better if for the same series 1, 2, and 3 we could write a sentence X that would say all that the sentences 1, 2, and 3 say, but not in the detail in which they say it. Then we would have something like this.

    X   A compact car would be economical to own.

1.   The original cost is low.
2.   It is cheap to maintain.
3.   It gets good gas mileage.

There sentence X doesn't just promise to say something—promise to give "reasons." It actually gives those reasons in one word, "economical." Then it goes on quite naturally in sentences 1, 2, and 3 to spell out ways in which a compact car would be economical.

(You will notice also that the sentence X has been tailored to fit in one other way—by removing the "I want" to get to the true subject, the compact car. The writer will develop the sentence X not with a description of desires, but with discussion of the car and its economy.)

Next we must examine a "promise" sentence that confronts us with a further problem.

X   I want to live in Atlanta for three reasons.
1.   My favorite aunt lives there.
2.   I like the climate there.
3.   I can get a good job there.

In that set of X, 1, 2, 3 the three reasons are so different that it would be almost impossible to cover them all in one summarizing sentence X. We'll study that kind of set more fully when we come to Step 5. Meanwhile, let's just say that there's nothing really wrong with it—it's not confused, illogical, or unclear—but it's not the kind of writing this book should be giving you practice in, namely, definite summarizing statements followed by explanation of what has been said.

(I am not really contradicting myself when I say that, by trying hard, I might be able to find one particular quality to cover the three reasons about Atlanta: Atlanta offers me *contentment*, for my favorite aunt lives there, I like the clement weather there, and I can get a good job there. But this is stretching it—and note how general "contentment" still is.)

Earlier in this chapter I said there was still another possibility—which I promised to discuss—open to the writer who told us that anthropology is a necessary part of education and then simply went on to tell us what is taught in anthropology, with no further hint of why anthropology is a necessary part of education. That additional possibility is this: the writer may argue, "Oh yes, these points are connected with anthropology as a necessary part of education; *I intend to show that connection later on.*"

This is an intelligent argument. The writer is not aware at this point, however, that the purpose of sentences 1, 2, and 3, as we will see more clearly later, is to give the reader an *immediate* clue to how each of those sentences is connected with sentence X. But because the writer's argument is a natural one, we'll have to reword Step 2 one more time, inserting the words *clearly and directly.*

STEP 2

Write three sentences about the sentence in Step 1—clearly and directly about the whole of that sentence, not just something in it.

You see, the writer's sentences 1, 2, and 3 may eventually prove to be connected with sentence X. But we don't know. And that's just the point. We ought to know, clearly and at once. That's why we have to put into Step 2 the words *clearly and directly*.

C. RELATING IDEAS

It is important now to explain why I said at the end of Chapter 1 that, for the purposes of this program, you are not to use a sentence X which (a) is descriptive, (b) is narrative, or (c) introduces a process. Description is how something looks. So don't write, "Mt. Hood looks ghostlike on cloudy days," or "Main Street sparkles with fresh paint." Narration is what happened or what somebody did. So don't write, "I was almost killed on my motorcycle," or "By age thirty-five my uncle built up a chain of shoe stores." Process is how to make or do something, or how something works or is constructed. So don't write, "Knitting a shawl is easy," "Use your knees right to ski well," "A diesel engine works without spark plugs," or "A coral reef is built up of the solidified skeletons of small sea animals." True, papers on such subjects are perfectly good in themselves. You will have occasions in life, certainly, to write such papers. (This very book is nothing but a long process paper.) But they are—fortunately for all of us—too easy. They usually involve only a space relationship ("to the left," "above," "further along") or a time relationship ("first," "next," "then"), with perhaps some cause-and-effect relationship involved ("This provides a contrasting background"; "This causes the steam to condense.") Thus they do not present the kind of problem that the program in this book is designed to train you to solve—the kind of problem in your writing that you are sure to meet, both in school and later in your business or professional life.

Problems in description, narration, and process writing—though we'll say something about them later—you can solve by yourself. (Extensive professional training in such matters is, of course, provided by courses in creative writing and technical writing.) This book is fundamentally concerned with problems in the relationships of ideas—problems that are part of your education as well as part of learning to write. Such problems are probably new to you, and they are what you must have practice in solving.

Perhaps you'll have a clearer idea of this distinction if I give you an example. Most of this book—the material that tells you what to do, or how something is done—I wrote with relative ease. But whenever I came to a place where I had to think up and write an example for you of something involving X, 1, 2, 3, I had to stop and do some hard thinking, and then had to write slowly and

laboriously. My point is, again, that process writing (like description and narration) is comparatively easy; it is problems in the relationships of ideas that
call for rigorous training and practice.

Thus we must rule out here any sentence X like "In June the Iowa countryside has a parklike beauty"; "Making root beer is simple"; or "A diesel engine is
easy to understand." We must rule out, too, "My father was a plasterer" if what
follows is going to tell the story (narration) of how he became a plasterer.

A statement of simple fact ("March has 31 days"), pure faith ("God loves
me"), or personal taste ("I like apple pie") also does not work well as a sentence
X, because so little more can be said about it.

The best sentence X, for our purposes, states a conclusion you have reached
that needs to be explained and that might be contradicted—a statement that
somebody else might not agree with, and that you therefore have a need to
defend. For Step 2 (and as we will see, Steps 3 and 4) requires that you *explain
further* your sentence X. So it is best to find a sentence X for which you can
imagine a reader saying, "I doubt it. Convince me"—and that is what you proceed to do, starting with Step 2. This is a procedure we are familiar with in
everyday life: "I need $50 till the end of the month"; "That coat looks great on
you"; "I need an extra week to do my assignment." (I doubt it. Convince me!)
To put it another way, the best sentence X, for our purposes, is one that *you*
would label *true* but that you can imagine another intelligent person labeling
false. In your sentences 1, 2, and 3, then, you will begin to explain why the
statement should be labeled *true*.

I have illustrated Steps 1 and 2 largely with simple statements, so that you
will not have trouble understanding the ideas as you learn the principles. But
the principles apply to much more significant discourse as well—which is why
we are bothering to learn them. Here, for example, is an excerpt from a speech
by Abraham Lincoln to Congress in 1862. See if you can label the sentences X,
1, 2, 3 (and 4, in this case):

> Fellow-citizens, we cannot escape history. We of this Congress and this
> administration will be remembered in spite of ourselves. No personal sig-
> nificance or insignificance can spare one or another of us. The fiery trial
> through which we pass will light us down in honor or dishonor, to the
> latest generation. We—even we here—hold the power and bear the respon-
> sibility.

Admittedly, after all this you are left with the task of inventing those three
sentences. How do you go about it? Well, as I said earlier, a good way to invent
a sentence X is to think of it as the answer to a question. Now, for inventing
sentences 1, 2, and 3, my answer is again—a question. A good way to go about
finding your sentences 1, 2, and 3 is to decide what questions, or what kind of
question, a reader would naturally ask after you announce your sentence X.
Then let sentences 1, 2, and 3 provide explanations or answers. If, as I have
just suggested, you have chosen a sentence X that an intelligent reader might
question, your task in Step 2 is clear: to provide answers to the question, Why
should I agree with this? In what specific ways can sentence X be said to be

true? (If you can't think of any questions a reader might ask, then you probably have as dead-end a sentence X as "My name is Nels Swenson.")

D. A CAUTION ABOUT CONTRAST

Let us return for a moment to the set of X, 1, 2, and 3 which we improved at the start of the last section:

X   A compact car would be economical to own.
1.   The original cost is low.
2.   It is cheap to maintain.
3.   It gets good gas mileage.

Now suppose that, instead of being concerned just with the compact car, we want to set it beside a full-sized car and consider the difference in cost. In that case our sentence X might state, "A compact car would be more economical to own than a full-sized car." And since, by Step 2, sentences 1, 2, and 3 must be clearly and directly about *the whole of* sentence X, we would want this series:

X   A compact car would be more economical to own than a full-sized car.
1.   The original cost is lower than that of a full-sized car.
2.   It is cheaper to maintain than a full-sized car.
3.   It gets better gas mileage than a full-sized car.

In setting two things side by side and noticing how they are different, this X, 1, 2, and 3 introduces *contrast*. And contrast has the advantage of helping us find and keep to a point. Suppose, for example, you want to write a theme about college. What can you say about college? That it has a nice view from the window of your biology lab? Somehow that doesn't seem significant. But now try *contrasting* college with something comparable, like high school. Then more significant features emerge:

X   College is different from high school.
1.   College classes meet less often than high school classes.
2.   The college year is shorter than the high school year.
3.   Classes in college take up less of the day than high school classes do.

As it turns out, our sentences 1, 2, and 3 are so focused that we can in turn revise sentence X to make it fit more exactly: "Schedules in college are different from those in high school."

Contrast is natural to human beings—and very useful in our writing. We contrast one friend with another, Republican with Democrat, tea with coffee, summer with winter, a typewriter with a word processor. We also contrast one person, institution, or activity with that same person, institution, or activity at a different time: "Sara has grown two inches in the past year," "The U.S. Postal Service is more efficient now than it was in 1960," "Driving has become less hazardous since the 55 miles per hour speed limit was enacted." Contrast, in fact, is essential to our perception of the world: if everything were the same hue, lightness, and intensity (as it is in the complete absence of light), we could not see.

Nevertheless, for the time being I suggest—as emphatically as I can without making it an absolute prohibition—that you *avoid* contrast. This is for a very simple reason: as you can see from the examples I have given, using contrast complicates the sentences of Steps 1 and 2—the very sentences that are supposed to be short and simple. In fact, contrast *doubles* the number of things you must be sure to include in your sentences 1, 2, and 3. If your sentence X is simply, "A compact car would be economical to own," then each of the Step 2 sentences must be sure to mention two things—the compact car and its economy. But if you say in sentence X, "A compact car would be more economical to own than a full-sized car," then each of the Step 2 sentences must mention not two but *four* things—the compact car, its economy, the full-sized car, and its economy.

Similarly, a sentence X that contrasts schedules in college and high school requires attention to *four* things in each of sentences 1, 2, and 3: college, its schedules, high school, and its schedules. This does *not* seem so short and simple!

Sometimes, in fact, the complicating business of contrast slips into our writing without our noticing it. Adding a *more* or a *less* or an *-er* ending is all that it takes. Look at one more version of our sentences on the compact car:

X   A compact car would be more economical to own.
1.   The original cost is lower.
2.   It is cheaper to maintain.
3.   It gets better gas mileage.

Do you see the contrast here? The *more* of sentence X, the *-er* of *lower* and *cheaper* in sentences 1 and 2, and the *better* of sentence 3 all tell the reader that we are comparing the compact car with something else—and we haven't even said what that something else is.

I recommend, therefore, that for now you hold yourself back from the natural tendency to make a contrast in your sentence X. You will do best to avoid the extra complications of "College is different from high school," "Anthropology tells us more about primitive peoples than psychology does," "Uncle Ben is more of a perfectionist than Uncle Henry," "A compact car would be more economical to own than a full-sized car." Toward the end of the book, though, when you have mastered the six steps, I will encourage the use of contrast and comparison and devote a full chapter to helping you use them.

E. REPEATING AND OVERLAPPING

No, we're not done with Step 2 yet. At the end of the chapter I'm going to give you an assignment (you can guess what it is), but before doing so, I want to clear up a possible misunderstanding. When I said earlier in this chapter that sentences 1, 2, and 3 each restate, in some particular way, the idea in sentence X, I did *not* mean that sentences 1, 2, and 3 are simply sentence X repeated in different words. That is, we mustn't have something like this:

X   Studying consists in teaching yourself.
1.   Studying is being your own teacher.
2.   In studying, you do what the teacher does.
3.   In studying, you act just as a teacher does.

These sentences 1, 2, and 3 are just a rewording of sentence X. There is nothing in any of the sentences 1, 2, and 3 that is *more particular* than the corresponding part of sentence X. In fact, in this example you could exchange sentence X with sentences 1, 2, or 3; and whenever you can do that, you have missed the point of Step 2. Any sentence 1, 2, or 3 that can be exchanged with sentence X needs to be made more particular, so that it *cannot* substitute for the X.

The importance of choosing sentences 1, 2, and 3 that are different from, by being *more particular* than, sentence X should be very clear to you now—if you have been studying this chapter and not just reading through it. But just in case some doubt remains in your mind, I'm going to give you some more sets of X, 1, 2, and 3, with explanations. These examples I've deliberately made very simple, so they wouldn't work well in longer themes. But they should work very well for my purpose here, which is to make sure you understand the principle of Step 2. So now let's start again from X.

In sentence X I make a statement. Once I've made it, there's no point in just making it again. Instead, in sentences 1, 2, and 3 I'll give three *different, particular* ways in which that statement is true. Say that in sentence X I write "A light thing rises to the top." Now I'm not just going to say that again, in different words: "A light thing floats above a heavier thing." No, after saying "A light thing rises to the top," I'm going to pretend that someone then asks me, "Like what?" And I'll answer with three *ways* in which light things come to the top. (I must remember that every way has to be stated in a complete *sentence*.) Here we go:

X   A light thing rises to the top.
1.   A cork, being lighter than water, floats on top of the water.
2.   A balloon filled with hydrogen or helium, being lighter than air, floats up into the air.
3.   Oil mixed with water, being lighter than water, will rise to the top of the water.

Now notice two things about that example. First, sentences 1, 2, and 3 do not just repeat sentence X. Sentence X has nothing in it about a cork, water, a balloon, hydrogen, helium, air, or oil. Second, although sentences 1, 2, and 3 are different from sentence X, they haven't taken us off the subject; a cork, a balloon, and oil are all *particular kinds of* "light things." And sentences 1, 2, and 3 are all different ways in which we find that "a light thing rises to the top."

But no example is as clear and convincing as one from everyday experience.

So here's one that will show you how well you already understood what I'm talking about before you ever heard of X, 1, 2, 3. You know perfectly well you can't go to a fast-food counter and just say to the people taking your order, "I want something to eat." They'll say, "Well, what?" Now you know it won't do any good to say again what you've just said, even in different words. It won't do any good to say "I want some food," or "I want some nourishment," or "I want a lunch." You've already said that! Only the words are different. So they'll say, "Yes, but like what?" So finally you'll say, "One, I want a hamburger. Two, I want some french fries. Three, I want a chocolate shake."

Notice that you haven't really *changed* what you said first. You haven't said, "No, I guess I'll have just a glass of water." You're still telling them that you want something to eat. But you've got down to three *particular kinds* of "something to eat." So here's your X, 1, 2, and 3:

X   I want something to eat.
1.   I want a hamburger.
2.   I want some french fries.
3.   I want a chocolate shake.

You use X, 1, 2, 3 every day in your conversation. It's perfectly natural. You say, "Today is certainly a typical May day." And then you go on and add to it, not by changing it, but by saying *how* it's certainly a typical May day in this, that, and the other way. You won't *repeat* that it's a typical May day, even in other words, but everybody will know that its being a typical May day is what you're still talking about as you go on to make statements about the flowers, the birds, the sky, the air, and so on.

So all I'm asking you to do is transfer this normal way of talking onto paper. What I want you to notice is that you never keep on just repeating "It's a typical May day" in other words. Do you? Do you say, "It's a typical day in the fifth month of the year. It's a typical day in the month between April and June. It's a typical day in the first month of the year with no *r* in its name. It's a typical day in the month that has the shortest name," and so on? No, you just say it's a typical May day and *then you get down to cases*. You explain what you mean when you say it's a typical May day, just as you explained what you meant at the fast-food counter when you said you wanted something to eat.

Try it yourself. You say, "Winter is really here." That's a sentence X. *Then* what do you go on to say about its really being winter? There you have your 1, 2, 3 and so on. But all that you say adds up to "Winter is really here," doesn't it? You haven't changed the subject. You haven't just repeated it, either. You've added some *particulars*, you've got down to cases, by use of details about the cold, snow, ice, icicles, overcoats, and so on. Oh, I admit that May and winter won't do for the kind of themes you're to write in this class, because they're too easy—they're descriptive. But themes are not what I'm after at this point. All I'm after is making sure that you understand *any* X, 1, 2, 3.

Now, if you understand the mistake of just repeating sentence X in your 1, 2, 3, you can easily understand the error of repeating *within* your sentences 1, 2, and 3—of having them overlap. I make the mistake of overlapping 1 and 2, or 1 and 3, or 2 and 3 if one of them really says the same thing as the other though in different words. For instance, in 2 I might say "The flowers are all blooming now" and then in 3 "The buds have finally burst into blossom." But now isn't 3 just about the same thing as 2? Your 2 has to be really different from your 1, and your 3 has to be really different from your 2. So if you write "Our government involves a balance of powers" and then "Each governmental power is posed against the others," you're guilty of overlapping, because the two statements amount to the same thing.

You have to make every one of your sentences X, 1, 2, and 3 different from every other—even as you have to see that they all make the same point. How do you do this? By making sentences 1, 2, and 3 *more particular* than sentence X, and by making each of your sentences 1, 2, and 3 tell about a different particular aspect of your sentence X. Think of sentence X as a pie, and sentences 1, 2, and 3 as that same pie cut in three slices. Each slice has the same ingredients and flavor as the whole pie; it is just a smaller piece.

And the pieces must match. Sentences 1, 2, and 3 can list three aspects of studying, three computer languages that Aunt Minnie knows, three reasons for buying a compact car; they can divide the point into past-present-future, family-community-nation, work-play-rest. Here is an example of a mismatch among sentences 1, 2, and 3:

X   Broccoli is healthful.
1.   It has vitamins.
2.   It has minerals.
3.   It helps prevent cancer.

Do you see that sentences 1 and 2 slice the pie according to the *sources* of the healthfulness in broccoli, while sentence 3 changes the topic to the *results* of eating it? Now the results might be part of the evidence for the healthfulness of the nutrients mentioned in sentences 1 and 2, and the nutrients might be the source of the health benefit mentioned in sentence 3, so there is a real likelihood of confusing the reader. No, you have to find a sentence 3 that gives another *source* of broccoli's healthfulness, perhaps "Broccoli adds bulk to the diet."

I keep saying things like "you have to" as if I were laying down the law. No. It's not my doing, but in the nature of things. When you come to write a theme, you'll quickly understand that "have to." If you learn now to avoid repeating sentence X or overlapping sentences 1, 2, 3, your whole job in writing a theme will be much easier. You'll have a clear route marked out for yourself, and you won't have to waste time because you've doubled back on your own tracks. That kind of doubling is not only time consuming; it tends to confuse you about where you really are going.

F. ANOTHER WAY TO TEST YOUR WORK

Occasionally you may write an X, 1, 2, 3 and feel uneasy about whether it meets all the requirements, even though you have carefully followed Steps 1 and 2, and have avoided repeating your sentence X or overlapping any of your sentences 1, 2, 3. In a case like that, you may want to use this extra test for a proper relationship between X and 1, 2, 3.

X is not only a more general statement than 1, 2, and 3; it can, in a sense, be said to include them. That is, the information given in sentence 1 (or 2 or 3) is always, though in more general terms, included in sentence X. The opposite is not true, as you can readily see. That is, the idea stated in sentence X is *not* entirely contained in any sentence 1, 2, or 3. Think of your X as a jar full of cookies; the jar contains all the cookies, but each cookie does not contain the whole jarful! Now, if you want to find out whether your 1, 2, and 3 are properly related to your sentence X, just ask yourself whether the idea stated in X completely covers, in general terms, everything said in specific terms in sentence 1. Then do the same with sentences 2 and 3. If anything in sentence 1, 2, or 3 is not covered by the idea stated in sentence X, it does not belong where it is.

Let's take an example. Suppose I say "X. An insect has six legs." and then "1. A mosquito has six legs." Now you ask yourself, "Does the idea that insects have six legs include the more specific idea that a mosquito has six legs?" You will agree that it does, I hope.

All right. Now if I just say, out of a clear sky, "A mosquito has six legs," you'll think, naturally enough, that I'm just making a remark about a mosquito, not about all insects. "A mosquito has six legs" (say it's my sentence 1), by itself, certainly doesn't give you the whole idea of my sentence X, "Insects have six legs." In contrast, as I've said, my sentence X would cover my sentence 1. Does that throw any light for you?

Someone may answer, "Yes. But you're certainly spending a heck of a lot of time on X, 1, 2, 3!" I am. That's because X, 1, 2, 3 is *thinking*; and if you understand it, there's nothing in the world that, given time, you can't understand.

G. A NOTE ABOUT REPETITION OF WORDS

Many students are bothered all through Step 2 by the repetition of words in my examples. Their objection to the repetition demands an answer—not just one answer, but two.

Well, first, as I said earlier, we aren't yet writing the whole theme. When we come to it, the repetitious 1, 2, and 3 will be rather widely separated. Then the distant repetition, echoing in the reader's mind, will serve as a guidepost announcing that you have come to a new part of your theme.

Second, as I'll explain at length later, repetition isn't the bad thing you've been supposing. On the contrary, it's the immediate sign of craftsmanship, and in fact the basis of all the arts. Just look around at your classroom and the building it's in, and notice the *repetition* of the windows, the lighting fixtures, the units of the chalkboard, the doors in the corridor. Look at all the examples of repetition you can find till you reach the point of saying, "Why, it's *all* repetition!" Yes, how different the product of professional builders from the tree-house that you, as an amateur, may have built as a child! Next turn to a piece of writing you may have memorized in grade school, the justly admired Gettysburg Address. See not only how both *conceived* and *dedicated* are repeated in its first few lines, but how the word *nation* occurs there three times! Lincoln knew, too, what he was doing when he concluded with the perhaps most famous repetition of all time: "of the people, by the people, for the people." Repetition of words is a valuable principle of rhetoric. What your English instructor will object to in your papers is *pointless* repetition.

Don't suppose, then, that repetition has no purpose. I use it to make my point clear, just as I'm encouraging you to use it to make your point clear. You will soon find that repetition is sometimes not only useful but necessary, if your reader is to understand the connections between ideas in your themes.

Now at last you should be ready for your assignment. Before you begin it, you may as well know that Step 2 isn't really limited to three sentences. It could be four or five or any greater number. But for the time being, three will be enough. Not two (or one)—that is not enough. "Three" in Step 2 means three or more. But unless you personally want to have more, three will be enough for most of the exercises in this book.

ASSIGNMENT

Make up as many as a dozen sets of sentences X, 1, 2, and 3. Do each set in the following form.

X Power corrupts.
1. It corrupts the powerful.
2. It corrupts the powerless.
3. It corrupts every relationship between the two.

You'll find that doing this takes work. It will especially take work—highly profitable work—if you do not restrict yourself to the simplest subjects (cars, sports), but try a few subjects like government, science, literature, or business. In any case, take the assignment seriously.

Now stop at this point and do the assignment before you read on.

Are you ready? Good! It's time to take a look at those sets of sentences to make sure you've really caught the idea of Steps 1 and 2.

I'm not a mind reader, so I don't know how your instructor will plan to review your first sets of sentences. But don't be surprised if you spend a lot of class time on them. It takes time, and some real work, to master Step 2. When you do, you'll find that your writing is already better than it's ever been before. And don't worry. It's like learning to ride a bicycle. At first you're going to fall off a few times, and you'll need support, but after some determined practice you'll be able to keep your balance and get somewhere.

Be prepared to read aloud in class your best set or sets. Then both you and others in the class will benefit by the examples heard and discussed. (Don't shrink from having your work criticized; you're in college to learn, not to make a good showing.)

Among those errors your instructor detects will be those we've already discussed but also some miscellaneous ones, the chief of which follow.

First, a sentence X may contain too sweeping a generalization: "The police are corrupt." What, all police? I know one metropolis where corruption among all public servants seems to be a way of life, but there must be honest police officers even there; and I also know another metropolitan area where I'd probably have a hard time finding any corruptible police officer.

Second, a sentence X may be wholly true, yet too broad. "College is important." Undeniably, but like "Aunt Milly is wonderful," it doesn't pin you down to a definite class of assertions. Why not go the whole hog and say "The world is wonderful"? The other extreme, the too-narrow sentence X ("My finger hurts"), we've already discussed as one that leaves too little more to be said. (If you went to a doctor about the problem, however, "My finger hurts" would become a very useful sentence X: "It hurts with a sharp pain when I try to bend it"; "It hurts with a light stabbing pain when you touch it"; "It has a dull ache even when it is not touched or moved.")

Third, sentences 1, 2, and 3 may break the commitment made in sentence X. That is, sentence 1, 2, or 3 may be completely irrelevant to the idea stated in sentence X. It's hard to say whether an appparently intelligent student hasn't studied, has genuinely misunderstood, or has simply refused to follow directions when that student reads aloud something like this:

X   Dialysis is a process of cleansing the blood used when kidneys do not adequately perform that function.
1.   Dialysis machines are expensive.
2.   Dialysis has been successfully used in the treatment of schizophrenia.
3.   Artificial hearts can temporarily take over while a damaged organ repairs itself.

There is hardly a student in the room who cannot see at once that a set like that is defective from beginning to end. But for the moment let's set aside that the sentence X just given is not a simple statement, that it is not an easy sentence to say much more about (unless you have special technical knowledge), that it is a definition of a *process*, and that sentences 1 and 2 are not about the *whole* of sentence X but about something in it. (Sentences 1 and 2 make no mention of two important parts of sentence X: "cleansing the blood" and "when kidneys do not perform.") The main thing you should notice right now is that *sentence 3* is startlingly irrelevant.

I hope you still have time before class to go over your sets of X, 1, 2, 3 to correct mistakes like these. You'll want to correct them, now or later, before you move on to Step 3.

It may seem strange that the chapter about Step 2 concludes with ten rules for the sentence of Step 1. But if I had given you these rules in Chapter 1, they would only have baffled you, for they derive from our knowledge of the requirements that Step 2 makes on the sentence of Step 1. As you progress through the book and learn more about the function of sentence X, you will find less and less need to refer back to this list; the rules will become automatic. Meanwhile, though, after a long chapter you may find it helpful to have them summarized here.

TEN RULES FOR SENTENCE X

1. Create a sentence that you can then say much more about. (Not "I live in Chicago" but "The myth of Chicago is known around the world.")
2. Be precise about your subject. (Not "Studying is hard" but "Studying projective geometry is hard.")
3. Be precise about what your subject is or was, does or did. (Not "Body-building is beneficial" but "Body-building develops endurance.")
4. Start sentence X (and sentences 1, 2, and 3) with the subject. (Not "There is a proper use for each tool" but "Each tool has its proper use.")
5. Make sure the subject is your real subject. ("Science fiction is fun" means "I enjoy science fiction"; "Dishwashing is boring" means "I don't like to wash dishes." Neither topic is capable of much development. See the next rule.)
6. Avoid topics which are merely statements of personal preference ("I like stamp collecting"). Instead, take the object of the preference as the subject of a new statement ("Stamp collecting teaches history.")
7. For now, avoid *contrast* because it introduces extra complications. (Not "Football is more warlike than soccer" but "Football is a warlike sport.")
8. For now, avoid simple *description*, *narration*, and *process* because they are too easy—and because we are learning to write expository essays. (Not "Yellowstone has hot springs," "General Lee advanced his troops into Pennsylvania," "Folding a paper airplane takes three steps.")
9. Do not simply *promise* to make a point, but *state* it. (Not "Beowulf triumphed in three ways" but "Beowulf defeated three monsters.")
10. After you have written sentences 1, 2, and 3, check to make sure that your sentence X fits them exactly. Then you will be ready to go on to the next chapter and Step 3.

Chapter 3

STEP 3

Chapter 2 was so full of good advice that you probably have forgotten most of it already. But if you don't remember everything, don't worry. Remembering all the instructions is *not* the point of this book. Learning to do Step 2, on the other hand, *is* an important part of the point. And you did learn Step 2, didn't you? Can you say it (and Step 1) from memory? If not, go back and look it up, so you can do the following assignment.

ASSIGNMENT

Memorize Steps 1 and 2 in their full final versions (pages 6 and 18).

Memorize those steps *exactly*, word for word? Yes. In my classes, I even call on students to recite the steps from memory. And not because I like the sound of my own words, but because we must agree on what we are talking about. When I say, or when your instructor says, that a certain X, 1, 2, 3 has a problem with Step 2, you need to know that the instructor means sentence 1, 2, or 3 is *not* "clearly and directly about the whole of" sentence X.

After all, I'm asking you to memorize only six steps in this whole course—much less than you may have to memorize in one week for a course in biology. There is no wasted effort in my method, but there is effort! So go ahead and memorize Steps 1 and 2, and when you know them by heart (try taping them to your mirror so you'll see them every time you look at your face), you're ready to go on.

Now that you're ready for it, you'll be glad to see that Chapter 3 is a short one. If I made it long, I'd just be going over the same ground covered in Chapter 2. That is because Step 3 runs on the same principles as Step 2. So Step 3 won't take long to learn—if you have really learned Step 2. (Would you recite Step 2 one more time, please? Good.)

29

But before proceeding, I need to introduce Step 3 with a serious warning: the theme you will write as the assignment at the end of this chapter will seem (to you) about as poor a thing as you have ever written. Were it not for this warning, you might say, "Well, if this is his idea of a theme, there's no use going on with his method. 'By their fruits you shall know them,' and look at the miserable apples his tree has produced. No, I'm going back to my own way of writing themes."

Be patient. The theme you write at the end of this lesson may seem really miserable to you. But let me tell you that though you won't be able to see it right away, what you write will have four *necessary* qualities of a decent theme. I won't tell you what they are now; you'll find out later.

This theme of yours, I agree, will lack other necessary qualities, and I'll be glad you feel that lack (without, probably, being able to put your finger on it, name it, or describe it). For the last three steps—especially Step 4—are designed to take care of that lack. Thus feeling strongly, if not clearly, the need for those steps, you will be able to take them quite seriously when you come to them.

Let me tell you a story. I learned calligraphy (which you might call printing by hand) from one of the finest calligraphers in the country, a man regarded by many people as the foremost authority on the forms of the letters of our alphabet. Can you imagine how he had me spend the first three weeks under his instruction? He had me draw lines about one and a half inches long, one after another, line after line, with a reed on old newspapers. First it was vertical lines; then he added horizontal lines; next lines slanting down to the right; then lines slanting down to the left; and finally half circles. This I did, hour after hour, day after day, week after week.

Now I could point out a number of things about that instruction. For instance, it was not what many people call interesting. If I had come to the expert expecting him to "make it interesting," he would have had no time for me, because he had better things to do—but particularly because if I could not get myself interested in my own progress in drawing those simple lines well, then any other "interest" would have been beside the point.

But what I especially want to point out is that the instruction served a twofold purpose, as I saw later. First, of course, it was necessary training to be undergone before I approached the production of actual letters. But second, it was a test—a test of my docility. *Docility* means "teachableness" and is simply the quality of being willing to follow simple instructions and to have confidence in instructors, who have been through all the learning—and perhaps much teaching—before, and just might know what they're doing. If I had not proved my docility, my instructor—who, as I said, had better things to do—would not have wasted a minute on me. Fortunately, I turned out not to be one of those beginners who, at the very beginning, "know" that the instructor is wrong.

Today I, whose talent in art is practically nil, can produce writing (what you would call printing) that the ordinary person would call beautiful. I know myself that my work is decent but certainly not excellent, and for that reason I have not identified my instructor by name—though surely it was a triumph for him to teach someone who has no speck of natural ability to produce work that the ordinary public thinks is beautiful.

So, with the moral from my story—that similarly you, whatever your talent, by patiently, docilely, and seriously following a step-by-step method, can produce writing so effective that other people will admire it—we can ascend Step 3.

STEP 3

Write four or five sentences about each of the three sentences in Step 2.

There are five comments that need to be made about Step 3. First, one of the two necessary things in Step 3 is that the number of sentences you write must be *at least* four or five. Some people, in fact, would say that ten would be a better minimum, and I would agree in theory. But four or five will be enough for our purposes. Remember, however, that while fewer than four or five will be totally unacceptable, more than four or five will be very good indeed. Don't worry that I seem to waste time in dwelling on this simple matter; just be sure that *you* always have at least four or five—no fewer!—sentences after each of the three in Step 2. (And that means each of your paragraphs—for that is what Step 3 provides—will have *five or six* sentences, counting the Step 2 sentence. It has the Step 2 sentence *plus* four or five more.)

Second, the first four or five sentences are to be about the whole of the *first* sentence in Step 2, the second four or five about the whole of the *second* sentence in Step 2, and the third four or five about the whole of the *third* sentence in Step 2. There is no need to spend much time on the meaning of "the whole of" here, for that was covered at length in the chapter on Step 2. But it is just as important as it was in Step 2! You understand, of course, that the sentences in Step 3 bear the same relationship to the sentences in Step 2 as those in Step 2 bore to sentence X in Step 1. So do not grow careless here. To help you remember that the directions "clearly and directly about the whole of" remain all-important, we will add them to the statement of Step 3:

STEP 3

Write four or five sentences about each of the three sentences in Step 2—clearly and directly about the whole of the Step 2 sentence, not just something in it.

Third, have no fear—you will be happy to learn that Step 4 is not going to be "Now write ten or eleven sentences about each of those five"! (Instead, Step 4 will show you exactly *how* to do Step 3. That's another reason for making this chapter short and moving right along to Step 4.) But notice this: sentence X and the three sentences in Step 2 had to be short and simple statements because you have to write additional sentences about the whole of the statements each of them made. Now when you come to these four or five additional sentences and realize that you are not going to have to write more about each of them, you see that they don't need to be short and simple. Nor should they be! You will have long sentences and short sentences, simple sentences and complex sentences, sentences making just one statement, others making several.

Fourth, though, as just indicated, you are to take care not to have the sentences in Step 3 a series of short baby sentences, you are *not* at this point to worry at all about the *quality* of these sentences. That is a very special matter to be taken up in the next step. Don't worry at all about whether these sentences are "good"; just take care that there are at least four or five of them and that some of them, at least, are of pretty good length.

Last of all, I am giving you the way I want you to arrange your paper on your page. First, just as you did in the preceding chapter, put down sentence X (Step 1), labeling it *X*. Directly underneath it put down sentences 1, 2, and 3 in a column, labeling them *1*, *2*, and *3*. Then draw a broken line across the page under what you've just done.

Next, under the broken line, indent as you do when you start a new paragraph and *copy down* sentence X, labeling it *X*. Under this, indent in the same way and *copy down* your sentence 1 from Step 2, labeling it *1*.

Then, without further indentation and (this is highly important) without any further numbers or letters, write the four or five or more sentences that go with sentence 1 (Step 3). Then indent, copy down sentence 2, and proceed as with sentence 1. Finally, in the same way, indent and copy down sentence 3 and its four or five sentences. You should end up with something like the sample on the following page.

Study this model for two things only. The first is its appearance on the page. Note that it names sentences X, 1, 2, and 3, and that these appear as a column. Note then that this column is followed by a broken line. Next note that sentence X is repeated, and is again preceded by the letter X. Then note that sentence 1 is repeated, with its numeral 1, and is followed at once, in paragraph form, by the four or five sentences that go with it, none of these four or five sentences having an additional numeral or letter before it. In the same way, sentence 2 is repeated, with its four or five sentences after it; and then, of course, sentence 3.

Every theme you write for this course is to look exactly like that; so do not ask your instructor, "Do you want us to have X, 1, 2, 3, and all that on our theme today?" The answer is *yes*.

The second thing you are to study the example for is that it does faithfully follow Steps 1, 2, and 3. First, it begins with a *sentence* that expresses an idea, not with a topic or title. Second, that sentence is followed by three sentences connected with the whole idea of that first sentence—three sentences that, in fact, *repeat* the idea of that first sentence, except that they do so in more particular ways. They are to sentence X like slices of pie to a whole pie—no added ingredients, no subtracted ingredients, but only parts of the whole thing. Third, each of those three sentences is followed by four or five sentences whose purpose is clearly and directly to help explain *it*. Note particularly that these sentences count up to at least *four* (not three, or two, or one!) after the numbered

X I dislike winter.

1. I dislike the winter cold.

2. I dislike having to wear heavy winter clothing.

3. I dislike the colds that I always get in the winter.

X I dislike winter.

1. I dislike the winter cold. It makes me shiver. It chaps my lips. It gives me chilblains. It can even freeze my ears.

2. I dislike having to wear heavy winter clothing. I hate to wear earmuffs. I hate to wear galoshes. I hate to wear a heavy coat. I hate to wear long underwear.

3. I dislike the colds that I always get in the winter. They stop up my nose. They give me a cough. They give me a fever. They make me miss school.

sentence they follow—making at least *five* sentences, counting the Step 2 sentence, in each paragraph.

Some students may wonder why I spell out these simple matters in such detail. The answer is that experience has shown me that I have to do so. Even with this emphasis, about half the students who do the next assignment will fail to follow the form. Will you be one of them? Let's hope not.

Each of your papers from now on is to be arranged just like the example. For though I dislike red tape just as much as you do, there are good reasons for using this arrangement. One reason is that it allows your teacher or a friend helping you—and even more important, you yourself—to see at a glance exactly what you are doing. Another is that it reminds you that you're learning a new kind of writing, a kind that you have not done before. When you get to the end of this book, you will learn how to remove the special format and still have a proper theme. But right now you must use this format to guide your steps.

It would take a lot of time to discuss some of the other, more complicated reasons for using this special form, and I should get on to the point that, while you are imitating the form of the example I've given, you will surely not want to imitate the Dick-and-Jane style of its Step 3 sentences. For while all the sentences of Step 1 and Step 2 should be simple, the sentences of Step 3 should not! But we will return to that point in the next chapter, so I won't belabor it here.

Instead, study the example to see how every sentence in the theme—each in its own particular way—repeats the original idea, namely that the writer dislikes winter. That's the real test to see whether you've actually got a sentence X—is it really the statement that's repeated, in one way or another, in every sentence from the beginning of the theme to the end?

For despite the see-Dick-run style, I repeat that the theme itself has four qualities to be found in even the best of themes. They are: (1) a thesis sentence that announces its point at once; (2) a topic sentence for each paragraph that is clearly and directly related to the thesis sentence; (3) paragraphs that are clearly and directly related to their topic sentences and are well developed; and (4) specific examples.

(Waste no time discussing your own like or dislike of winter. In this course we're studying how themes are put together, not the facts or ideas those themes contain. A composition class can too easily turn into a "discussion" class. And that perversion, besides encouraging students to place a foolish value on "opinions," leaves little time for learning composition.)

ASSIGNMENT

Choose your own subject and write a paper following Steps 1, 2, and 3 (just as the example does). Arrange it on the page in the same way as the example. Do *not* worry if it doesn't seem to be a "good" theme.

I say "your own subject," but remember that you cannot write a theme on a subject alone; a subject is just one part of a sentence; you must make a statement about your subject, and then write your whole theme *on that statement.* Perhaps you will choose the subject "high school." All right, but what do you have to say about high school? High school *is* or *was, does* or *did* something. Perhaps you will say that high school can be a good preparation for college. Fine, but remember then that your theme must be about high school *as a good preparation for college*, and nothing else. What if, instead, your sentence X was

"I went to Troy High School"? In that case, your theme could tell us nothing about Troy High School except that you attended it. Could anyone write such a theme?

Finally, *save* every theme you write until you have finished this course. Sometimes we'll look at your old themes again.

Chapter 4

STEP 4

Here, at Step 4, is the place where good students, average students, and even poor students begin to shine. They have not really appreciated how far they have come in Steps 1, 2, and 3, but when they have grasped Step 4 they themselves are delighted to find that at last they are really writing! Admittedly, as I'll say in a moment, it is not in the very next theme that they work this miracle. The breakthrough comes when they conquer a mysterious reluctance—discussed in a moment—to accept that Step 4 really means what it says.

Well, what you meet here is a long, long chapter. You will find most of the individual parts clear. But if you feel (though perhaps mistakenly) that you are one of the average or poor students just mentioned, you will find so many sections here that as you read along, you may begin to feel confused. Don't worry. Read the whole chapter anyway. And by all means do the several assignments in it as well as you can. Then, when you reach the summary at the end, don't feel responsible for understanding and remembering the rest of the chapter. All the extra things that aren't in the summary will be fine for other students, but you'll be able to write your themes—good themes—without them. If you think of yourself as a good student, of course, you won't want to miss a thing!

When you reach that summary, though, study it well, and in the assignment that follows it do your level best to carry out the instructions. You may not do well on that assignment; many people do not. But don't be discouraged. You'll find yourself doing better—and will be pleased with yourself for doing better—as you move along.

Anyway, Step 4—for everybody—is the place where the struggle really begins. For although this step is the most important of all, and although beginning writers *can* without difficulty both understand the instructions given and apply them, in nine cases out of ten they simply *won't*.

Why? I have no idea. If I could discover why, then we could proceed without difficulty. But as things stand, we must proceed *with* difficulty. For, of course, beginning writers do eventually put Step 4 into practice; there would be no reason for this book if they didn't. But for some reason, to get them to do so is like trying to open a rusty lock.

What is to be done? First, to oil the lock, we'll start with some intermediate exercises. Second, as I have always done in my classes, I'll criticize your first themes extensively. (Of course, I haven't developed ESP sufficiently to be able to do that at long distance! So if you're not using this book as a textbook in class, if you have no instructor to criticize your papers for you, you must criticize them yourself—under my direction. You can do it if you use all the seriousness and capacity for hard work that are in you. For, like so many valuable things in life, it doesn't require any particular amount of intelligence—only serious hard work.) Third, I'll divide this chapter into sections, each with an assignment at the end, so that you can consider each section a lesson by itself. Fourth, in this chapter I'll ask you to write more than one theme.

But cheer up! You'll master Step 4 in the end. Moreover, you will be pleased with your last paper or two, and you'll be pleased with yourself for having produced something sound and substantial. Besides, the material you are about to face is not necessarily dull; since it calls on you, as I said earlier, to do a kind of thinking you've never done before (but that you *can* do), it has the attractiveness of any new accomplishment.

STEP 4

Make the material in the four or five sentences in Step 3 as specific and concrete as possible.

I think "specific," "concrete," and "as possible" need an explanation.

A. BEING SPECIFIC

What do you mean by *specific*? We might get at the answer by asking what the opposite of *specific* is. Many people will say *vague*. No, not exactly; the opposite of *vague* is *definite* (and I do not find the followers of my method have any trouble with, or need special training in, being definite). *Specific* here means "special kind of" or "particular." Its opposite is *general*.

Now there is no exact dividing line between the general and the specific. A word, for example, is usually more general than some words but more specific than others. An example will make this quite clear and will also demonstrate clearly what we mean by *specific* and *general*. Briefly, the specific is *a particular kind* of the general. Thus *a drink* is more general than *tea* (a particular kind of drink). So *tea* is more specific than *a drink*; *oolong* (a particular kind of tea) is more specific still.

Or take the word *flower*, for instance. Considered by itself, it's fairly general, yet fairly specific. It's fairly general because we can think of words that are more specific than *flower*—words, that is, that name one or another particular kind of flower. Give me an example of a particular kind of flower. "Rose"? All right, *rose*. Of this pair—*flower, rose*—then, we say that *flower* is the more general and *rose* the more specific. Simple, isn't it? And now that you've seen the example, reread from "A. Being Specific" to this point.

Now that you've reread, let's carry the same example further. *Rose* is more specific than *flower*; but what is more specific than *rose*? (Our answer will be a *particular kind* of rose.) How about *moss rose*? Or *American Beauty* rose? Or, if you don't know the varieties of rose (and only a fool would expect you to put down on your paper what you don't know), why not just *red rose*?

Now for another example—one that will appeal to many readers—take the word *car*. What's more specific? You can name a make of car. More specific still? The makers of cars give their products a variety of fanciful names with which you are probably familiar; if you're not familiar with them, you can name a year, or a color, or both.

So with *book. Mathematics book* is more specific; *calculus book* more specific still; and *Randolph and Kac, Third Edition*, about as specific as you can get.

Now mind you, this is not just a more or less interesting study of words, but a matter that you'll be using in all your themes from now on. For the rule in Step 4 says that the material in Step 3 is to be *as specific as possible*; and that means that you cannot use *flower* in one of those sentences if it's possible to use *moss rose*. That may shock you. But the result of using this rule is writing that the reader can clearly understand. And let me ask at least this: do you have to be a genius to say *peppermint ice cream* instead of *food*, or *homemade root beer* instead of *cold drink*, or *dandelions* instead of *weeds*? Can only the talented do that? Or can't it be done by anyone who can order his favorite flavor of ice cream, make her own root beer, or weed the front lawn? Yes, any normal person can do it—*if that person will*.

At this point you may be thinking, "I've heard about being particular once before." Yes, more than once! You will remember that for Step 2 I told you to write sentences 1, 2, and 3 that were about the whole of sentence X but *more particular*—more specific—about one part of it. Sentence X, "Aunt Minnie knows computer languages," becomes more specific in sentence 1—"She knows Basic." That's the way Step 2 works: you move *one step* towards being more specific as you go from sentence X to sentences 1, 2, and 3.

Now Step 4 asks for the same—only much more. For Step 4 insists that the sentences of Step 3 (the heart of your paragraphs) be as specific *as possible*, not just a little more specific. Later on we'll have to examine this *as possible* at length. Meanwhile, let me anticipate an objection by saying that of course, sometimes you must use the more general word. If you're saying "He loves all flowers," you would defeat your purpose if you changed *flowers* to *African violets*. For "He loves all African violets" is simply not what you meant to say. (Note, though, that if it is not contrary to your purposes, you might *add* fairly specific names of flowers by way of *example*. But more on examples later.)

To finish our study of the general and the specific, let's go back to the word *flower* and move this time in the direction of the more general. What is more general than *flower*? I think you will say *plant*. And that's almost as general as you can get, because *greenery, shrubbery,* and *foliage* are not more general than *plant*; they just mean "collections of plants." To get to the more general we have to skip over botanists' distinctions between green plants and, say, fungi, and go to *organism* or *living thing*. Most general of all is *thing*—and it's astonishing how many students will use *thing*, the most general word possible except *being* itself, in an assignment in which they have been instructed to use words that are as specific as possible.

For *car*, a more general term would be *self-propelled land vehicle* (which would include buses and trucks), then *self-propelled vehicle* (which would include hydrofoils, dirigibles, and submarines as well), then finally *vehicle*, and, of course, *thing*.

As you become more specific, you will find more and more choices; as you become more general, the choices are fewer, till you end up with the undifferentiated *thing*. We can represent the difference as a pyramid, with "thing" at the general top and many things at the specific bottom:

GENERAL

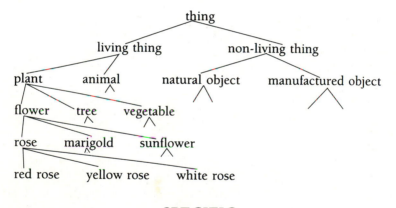

SPECIFIC

This moving back and forth between the general and the specific is another kind of thinking that you've never been called on to do. Being new, it will be a little awkward at first, but it's as necessary for you as learning to separate an egg is for a person first learning to cook.

And from now on in your reading, both of articles and of stories, you must notice other writers' use of specific words.

ASSIGNMENT

Take each of the following words and write below it a more specific word, and below that, if possible, a word more specific still. Then above it write a more general word, and above it, if possible, a word more general still. Thus for the word *man* you might list the following:

living thing
animal
man
soldier
Corporal Charles T. Schwartz

Here are the words you are to practice with: (1) vegetable, (2) song, (3) lesson, (4) chair, (5) candy, (6) soldier, (7) pen, (8) sweater, (9) employment

You'll find some of these easy and some hard to do. (Look at the next paragraph for some hints.) Finally, choose three words of your own and do the same thing. Be prepared to read your best one, or ones, aloud in class.

I find that a warning must be introduced here. Note that as you go down the list, each word is *a particular kind* of the word above it. Thus Corporal Schwartz is a particular kind of soldier; a soldier is a kind of man; a man is a kind of animal; and an animal is a kind of living thing. You must apply that test to the lists you make: is this word really one particular kind of the word above it? is *soup* really a kind of vegetable? is *plumber* really a kind of *employment*? (A plumber is a person, whereas employment is a thing; a plumber is a kind of employee, perhaps, but not a kind of employment. *Plumbing* is a kind of employment.) Moreover, noticing that the words on the list are persons and things, you cannot logically put *brave* on the list with *soldier*. *Brave* (an adjective) simply *describes* a person; it is not a person. (Unless you're using the Indian term, *a brave*, but let's not have quibbles like that.) So, if you're using it on your list, you have to use *brave man* or *brave person*.

B. BEING CONCRETE

The rule in Step 4 demands also that the material in the four or five sentences of Step 3 be as *concrete* as possible. What is *concrete*? Of course, one meaning is "a mixture of cement with gravel and sand, used in construction," but that can hardly be the meaning here. Let's first define *concrete* by stating its opposite—*abstract*—and say that concrete things are things properly speaking, while abstract things are thoughts about things. This will be clear in the following examples.

Child, chair, pencil, paper, and *room* are all concrete. The test is this: can I see it, rap on it to see what sound results, smell it, taste it, or feel it to see whether it is rough or smooth, hard or soft, hot or cold? Can I paint it a different color, weigh it on a scale, measure it with a ruler, trip over it or run against it, lift it or drop it, move it to the right or the left? If I can do all or some or even one of those things, it is concrete. So *child, chair, pencil, paper,* and *room* are all concrete.

In contrast, *freedom, justice, bravery, beauty,* and *cooperation* are all abstract. And the test is the same. Can I paint freedom a different color? Feel justice to see whether it is hot or cold? Trip over bravery? Rap on beauty to see whether I get a sharp knock or a dull thud? Smell or taste cooperation? No. In fact, you find those questions pointless or meaningless. Therefore, such words are abstract.

(Of course, any of those abstract words can be used not in its abstract sense, but to name a concrete person or thing. Thus *beauty* can be used to designate not the *quality* of pleasing the observer, but the person or thing that pleases, so that we speak of a horse, an orchid, a tennis champion's backhand swing, or a successful pass to left end as "a beauty." A judge on the Supreme Court is called a justice, and Shakespeare by "bravery" sometimes means fine clothes. You yourself, of course, know whether you are using a word abstractly or concretely; but it is not a waste of time to dwell here on an idea that may be quite new to you.)

Finally, you will notice that unlike the difference between what is general and what is specific, which is likely to be *relative*—a question of more or less (*jacket* is more specific than *article of clothing* but less specific than *ski jacket*)— the difference between what is abstract and what is concrete is *absolute*. A word is either abstract or it is concrete; there is no question of more or less. The abstract never shades into the concrete; there is a definite, clear-cut difference between them. As we have seen, sometimes in practice a word may be either abstract or concrete, depending on the way it is used. For instance, *music*—if it means the whole art of music, it is abstract; if it refers to singing or playing that you can hear or to a sheet of music that you can see, it is concrete. But it is never half one and half the other.

The next two paragraphs may or may not interest you. They are for students who have a special interest in writing; for those of you who don't, it would be all right to skip to "Back to our real business," two paragraphs on.

At this point some of you may object that the only examples I have given are nouns—names of persons and things. "What about verbs—words like *come, go,* and *eat*?" you ask. Well, the answer is that those words may be a matter of concern to you if you advance to considerations not of composition but of style (expression). Let's talk about that here. In this program you will not be required to use only specific verbs (*totter* or *stride* instead of *walk*, or *walk* or *ride* instead of *go*) or only concrete verbs (verbs designating an action you can observe rather than a relationship—*clutch, strike,* or *cheer* rather than *own, hate,* or *admire*). But it won't hurt you to be aware that some verbs are specific or concrete, and others aren't. So too with adjectives: "a good book" versus "a green book"— *green* you can see (concrete), whereas *good* you cannot. And so with adverbs: *loudly* is concrete, whereas *usually* is abstract.

By the way, you may have noticed that in this book I tend to use a lot of abstract and general verbs like *is, has,* and *does*. While there is a reason for that, let me emphasize that you are not to use this book as a model—something to imitate. It will be better for you to imitate the work of most other professional writers, who—also for very good reasons—tend to use varied, specific, even concrete verbs. Yet let me also point out that you shouldn't overdo it: using all colorful, attention-stimulating verbs in a memorandum on why your firm ought to buy a particular kind of padlock would be as much out of place as wearing your best clothes on a camping trip.

Back to our real business, which is that, in the four or five sentences of Step 3, you are to be as concrete as possible. It's important to remember that though there is a distinct division between the abstract and the concrete, for at least most abstract words there are some concrete things we can associate with them. Take the abstraction *bravery*, for instance. What persons and things can you associate with it? A soldier, perhaps; a medal; even a short account of a person performing a brave act—Mary Mestrovič dashes into a burning house, finds little Frank Palko cowering under a dining-room table, grabs him up and staggers with him to safety. The abstraction *beauty*? A young woman; the peaceful and joyous face of an aged minister; a violet; Schubert's *Serenade*.

For your assignment you are to take a certain number of abstractions and write down a concrete person or thing that you associate with each. In putting down the concrete person or thing you needn't use just one word; for instance, for *patience* you might put down "a mother feeding her child pureed carrots"; or you might even tell a one- or two-sentence story, like the one about the daring rescue I just recounted.

But before you begin I want to repeat one distinction that is often confused. *Abstract* is not the same as *general*, and *concrete* is not the same as *specific*. For instance, *virtue* is abstract and also quite general; *honesty* (a particular virtue) is more specific, but it is still abstract. *Letter carrier* is fairly specific and is also concrete; *human being* is far more general, but it is still concrete (after all, we can still see human beings, weigh them, and—if they let us—stand them on their heads). If you were given the abstraction *kindness*, you could not give *mercy* as a concrete accompaniment. Mercy is one sort of kindness, all right—it's more specific than kindness—but it's still abstract, isn't it? Test it—can you measure its length? Weigh it? Stand it on its head?

Again I must introduce a warning. For after this instruction some students will still, for example, write "punctuality" as a concrete accompaniment to *promptness*. Then they have to be asked whether punctuality is really concrete. Can you taste it, or weigh it on a scale, or paint it a different color? No, they admit. All too clearly they haven't taken the trouble to apply those tests for concreteness and have therefore come up with just another abstraction. Another matter: the words on the list are *things* (nouns)—abstract things, or, as we say, *entities*. They are therefore to be accompanied by concrete entities, that is, things or persons. They are not just descriptions (adjectives) of things. Hence, don't match *rich* with *success*. So, if your idea of success is financial, put down a concrete thing or person: *money*, or *a millionaire*. Similarly, when you go from concrete to abstract, do not put down *ready* to go with *fire extinguisher*. *Ready* is not a thing; it describes a thing. Put down an abstract noun: *readiness*.

ASSIGNMENT

Here are your abstractions; write down a concrete person or thing you can associate with each.

(1) compassion, (2) boredom, (3) hostility, (4) shyness, (5) peace, (6) nervousness, (7) democracy, (8) courtesy, (9) anxiety, (10) art, (11) diligence, (12) ugliness, (13) aviation, (14) orderliness, (15) promptness, (16) success, (17) inflation, (18) transportation, (19) confusion, (20) cowardice, (21) impatience, (22) speed, (23) industriousness.

(Before you write the matching word for *industriousness*, look it up in your dictionary. It doesn't mean a job in a factory! You will find that you yourself may be an example of industriousness—if you have been taking this lesson seriously.)

Next, can you go the other way? Can you take a concrete thing and associate it with an abstraction? (There isn't always just one right answer; you might associate a racing car with *speed*, *beauty*, *success*, *excitement*, *sport*, *wealth*, or perhaps even *transportation*.)

ASSIGNMENT

Try to associate an abstraction (keep in mind what that is) with each of the following persons and things.

(1) a taco, (2) a fire extinguisher, (3) a song, (4) a whip, (5) a flag, (6) a truck, (7) a mother, (8) schoolbooks, (9) a prayer book, (10) vitamin capsules, (11) a schoolroom, (12) a school bell, (13) a skeleton, (14) a police officer, (15) a poem.

Finally, choose three abstractions of your own and give each a concrete accompaniment; then choose three concrete persons or things and give each an abstract accompaniment.

C. GOING INTO DETAIL

No, we are not finished yet. To complete Step 4, we must give it a longer wording. We must also explain what we have added to it, and we must have exercises on what we have added.

STEP 4

Make the material in the four or five sentences in Step 3 as specific and concrete as possible. Go into detail. Use examples. Don't ask, "What will I say next?"

Instead, say some more about what you have just said. Your goal is to say a lot about a little, not a little about a lot.

ASSIGNMENT

You won't be surprised that I'm asking you to memorize Step 4. You don't have to show me (or your instructor) that you've memorized it, though, until after the new additions to Step 4 have been explained. And be of good cheer—this is by far the longest of the steps to memorize. Steps 5 and 6 are comparatively short.

Though you may not see any connection between most of the new directions in Step 4 and the shorter version we saw earlier, take my word for it that they add up roughly to the same thing as the original Step 4; the new directions are just specific ways of solving the same problem. But let's examine them one by one. First, "Go into detail."

I taught some years from a composition book, now long out of print, in which the author asserted that three-fourths of all good writing consists of details, and lots of them, and that the other fourth doesn't matter. Think about it; it's a bold assertion. I'm sure most of us think that the other fourth (which is structure—covered by Steps 1, 2, and 3—and connectedness—covered by Steps 5 and 6) certainly does matter. And I'm sure the author I speak of would have agreed that structure and connectedness do matter, because they're necessary ways of letting your readers follow what you are saying, of keeping them from getting confused. But to emphasize dramatically that, without details, writing just can't be called writing, he was willing to go so far as to say that details are the only things that matter.

That author might also have had this in mind: If you wrote a report on the lack of some safety provision in a tin mine and put in it all the details necessary for a full understanding of the point, but didn't put them in a clear order and didn't connect them clearly, an editor who didn't know anything about safety provisions in tin mines could still put your report in good order, with proper connections. But if, on the other hand, you wrote a report without sufficient details, then no matter how good the order and how clear the connections, the editor could do nothing.

So impress this on your mind: three-fourths of all good writing consists of details, and lots of them; the other fourth doesn't matter. But what are *details*? You already know one use of the term. Suppose you went into a police station and reported that you had just been held up and had lost your wallet or purse. That would be your sentence X (or sentence 1, 2, or 3). The officer at the desk would say "Give me the details," and it would be clear to you that you were to tell him your name and address, where and when the holdup took place, what the holdup man looked like, how he talked, how he was armed, how he left the scene, whether there was a car involved, whether there seemed to be other people with him, and a description of your wallet or purse and its contents, including how much money it contained.

The officer at the desk might ask you for other details, such as where you had been just before the holdup, even where you had been lately, where you were going, whether it was usual for you to be walking where the holdup occurred; and he might or might not explain how such details were relevant. (Notice, by the way, that *relevant* means "connected" or "related," and that it begins with *rel-*, just as *related* does.) The officer would not question you on such details as your mother's middle name, your favorite breakfast food, the color of your pet cat, or your ability to type; those details would be *irrelevant* (not related) to the case: they would be about you, but not about the fact that you were held up. (Does that remind you of "clearly and directly about the whole of" in Steps 2 and 3? I hope so!)

Or you're visiting a doctor, and your sentence X (or sentence 1, 2, or 3) is "My finger hurts." You won't expect the doctor to be able to do anything about it unless you give some details. Where does it hurt? What kind of pain? How long has it been hurting? What were you doing when it started to hurt? Did you put anything on the finger or take any medication?

Now suppose you're writing a theme, and your sentence 1 is "Mail service in the United States has become somewhat faster lately." (You'll notice that this involves the extra complication of contrast—contrast between service in an earlier slower time and the present faster one.) Now you can't just add "The Postal Service is trying to pick up the mail and ship it in a better way" and then go on to repeat weakly your sentence 1—"This makes the delivery faster. Mail used to be rather slow sometimes, but now it is moving with greater speed. This is an improvement that everyone appreciates. This shows progress on the part of the Postal Service."

No, the question is, *How* is the Postal Service picking up mail now? And, perhaps, what was the old way? What are the new hours of collection, and how do they make mail move faster? How fast is faster? When must I mail my letter so that by tomorrow it will reach an addressee 150 miles away? How is first-class mail now handled? Will my letter go from coast to coast in two days? What about Express Mail? If you are writing out of your head and don't know the answers to most of those questions, you obviously should have chosen a subject that you *do* know details about. Or, if you don't know enough details but do have time enough to find them, you'll have to look for them—perhaps in the library.

Understand that if you say that mail service is faster, or make any other assertion, the reader takes it for granted that you know some *facts*, or have had some experiences, that lead you to make that assertion. After all, your idea didn't just come down out of the sky. And the reader wants to know what those facts or experiences are. *Facts* are the valuable part of your paper—contrary to what you may have believed up to this time. Your *ideas*—which you express in sentences X, 1, 2, and 3—are there only to give point, meaning, and direction to your facts—to show what you think those facts add up to.

In other words, as some instructors find they must tell students, Step 4 calls on you neither just to *repeat* your ideas in different words, nor to introduce new ideas. It calls on you only to supply the *facts* that go along with those ideas, the facts that have caused you to have those ideas in the first place. You say Greg Kautz is a successful salesman? What are the figures, the sales records (facts) that make you say so? You say that Anita Hogarty is an outstanding student? What are her achievements (facts) that make you say so? You say you think you're catching cold? What are the symptoms you have (facts) that make you think so? Notice that you don't just repeat that you think you're catching cold, you think you feel a cold coming on, you bet you're coming down with a cold. But notice, too, that the sneezing, the dry or runny nose, the sore throat, perhaps fever, chills, listlessness are not *new* ideas; they all add up to the same old original idea that you voiced: catching cold. What you are doing is giving *evidence* for exactly what you say.

Look, I say "Here is one dollar." Then I say, "See, here are ten pennies, a nickel, a dime, and three quarters." It's the same one dollar; I've just spelled it out in the different coins that make it up. Really, it's as simple as that.

Are any of you out there thinking of careers as lawyers? Step 4 is excellent practice for what you'll need to say to the judge. Make your case by going into detail—while sticking to the point.

Let's take another example. Let's say I assert that my grandfather is neat. I then go on to indicate that he is neat in his person, in his habits, and in his work. That sounds like a set of sentences X, 1, 2, and 3, because I haven't gotten down to any real details yet. Up to that point, here is how the reader is unconsciously reacting: "After all, what is *neat*? I know what *neat* means, of course, but this writer's judgment about neatness and my judgment of it may be different. So what he says isn't meaningless, but it isn't yet clear in my mind what he has in *his* mind when he calls his grandfather neat. Furthermore, though I don't think he's wrong, or lying, I have no way of knowing whether *I'd* call his grandfather neat or not."

The reader doesn't know my grandfather—I do; and I have observed several things about him that have led me to assert that he is neat. If I tell the reader those several things, he or she will see clearly what I mean and will probably agree with my judgment. In other words, what the reader really wants to know are those several things I've observed about my grandfather that have led me to say he's neat.

So this is the place—and the reason—for details. First, under personal neatness, I should tell how, on rising, my grandfather shaves; checks to see that his moustache is properly trimmed; vigorously brushes his teeth, his tongue, and his partial plate; and gargles with (name the brand). He then takes a shower, including a shampoo, and finally puts on deodorant (I'd name the brand) and shaving lotion (brand?) and combs his hair. Then he steps into clean clothes and goes downstairs for breakfast.

Next, I'd go into orderliness in Grandfather's personal life: his bed immediately made, his coats and slacks always hung up, his detective novels in neat rows in the bookcases. Then his work habits: as a cabinetmaker he keeps his shop frequently swept; his saws clean, sharpened, and hung up in order; his chisels placed in the proper drawers. And his cabinetwork itself is always flawless.

Of course, I have just begun to give details on each point. And already some-one is saying, "But that takes so long, and it takes up so much space! What's the point of all that?" Of course it's long. How else do you think you're going to get your four or five—or ten—sentences for Step 3? You're not, I hope, going to just say feebly over again, in slightly different words, what you've already said—"Yes, he's neat, all right. He's even neater than my mother, and that's saying a lot. In fact, he's about the neatest man I ever met. I wish I were that neat. Everyone should be neat."

With that kind of performance—refusal to go into detail, which leaves wholly unanswered the question why you say your grandfather is neat—you're going to end up being the sort of person who in ten minutes covers half or three-quarters of a sheet, then snaps shut his notebook and announces: "I can't think of anything else to say." We must answer such a person with the point of Step 4: it's not a question of thinking of anything else to say, it's a question of saying some more about what you've just said by going into detail.

As for the other question—"What's the point of all this?"—the point is that now the reader can say, "Yes, I see what he means by *neat*. And yes, I'd agree; I'd call his grandfather neat, too." The reader can say it because in my theme I've made myself clear and convincing in the only way anybody *can* make him-self clear and convincing—that is, by going into detail.

Of course, what may be in the back of your mind is this: "Nobody cares whether my grandfather is neat. Who's interested in whether he brushes his partial plate vigorously or not?" That's a very important question, one that will be taken up at length later. Meanwhile, without saying I agree or disagree, let me give you two reassurances. First, some of the most absorbing novels in the world, novels that have entertained generations of readers, are made up in part of information just as simple as the information I have just given about my grandfather. Second, you are only practicing now. We are not going to print your theme in the school newspaper. A concert pianist doesn't invite people to come to listen to him practice scales—but he couldn't stay on the concert stage without the practice. When the football team reports for the first time in late summer, there are lots of exercises and drills before anyone gets to play a game. So in doing these exercises you are not attempting—yet—to create something important. You are practicing on simple things so that when the time comes you'll be able to do well whatever important things you're called on to do.

Finally, note that details take their place in Step 4 because, by their very nature, they are likely to be concrete and specific—more so, at least, than the general statement ("My grandfather is neat") that they are used to explain.

ASSIGNMENT

Write five to ten (or more) sentences—at least one hundred words—on the sentence "I'd hate to have you see my top bureau drawer." Give details of the mess—or the dirt, or the secrets—that you wouldn't want to show to the world. (If your top bureau drawer, like mine, contains only a neatly folded pair of pajamas, you will need to substitute another drawer—or

your roommate's. But be sure to look in a real drawer; don't make one up.)
In doing this assignment you will find for yourself what we mean by *details*
and surprise yourself with your ability to use them.

D. USING EXAMPLES

Another definition of *detail* is "short example." An example is something
taken from among a number of things like it, and used to stand for them. You
have a box of broken toys you're planning to fix. You reach into the box, take
out a little red wagon with one wheel missing, and say to someone, "See?
They're all like this." The wagon with a wheel missing is an example of the rest
of the broken toys in the box. So you could have said, "The toys in this box
are all old broken ones—*for example*, this red wagon."

Again, suppose I say, "Medicine has made many advances in the last forty
years." I may feel that I have stated my idea clearly, but since I know that
readers' and listeners' minds work better with concrete, specific things than
with abstract generalities alone, I add a few *examples* (since they tend to be
concrete and specific). Now I can't say how many advances medicine has made
over that period—maybe twenty, maybe five hundred. But I do know that just
a few of these will be enough to make my abstract general idea ("advances")
sufficiently specific and concrete for people's minds to catch on to clearly, so I
furnish just a few. (The point is that no one would, or would need to, list all
five hundred.) Those few are, of course, my examples. So what I continue with
is, "*for example*, the antibiotics, the Salk and Sabin immunizations for polio,
organ transplants, and open-heart surgery." You see, those four accomplish-
ments are taken *out of* the list of twenty or five hundred and *made to stand for*
the rest of that number. Those four, then, are what we mean by examples.

Do not, as some students tend to do, mistake an *analogy* for an *example*. An
analogy is a comparison used to make something clear. Here is an analogy: "A
green leaf is like a little food factory. It takes some raw materials, separates
them, recombines some, and thus turns out food for the growing thing of which
it's a part." Here a factory is not given as an example of a leaf. It's not being
offered us as one leaf out of a multitude of leaves, obviously. That is, here
nothing is being taken out of a list to stand for the rest of the list. One thing (a
leaf) is simply being compared to another *different* (though in some ways similar) thing—a factory—to make something about the leaf clearer.

Analogies are fine, in their place. But they get us away from the facts, and
the facts are what we want in Step 4. Your bureau drawer looks as if a tornado
hit it? (That's an analogy.) Perhaps, but what do you *see* when you look in it?
A gray sweat sock twisted around a Los Angeles Olympic Games T-shirt,
crushed into the corner. . . .

In using examples in conversation, as you often do, you usually use the word
like. "On such a short trip I think I'll take along just a few things, like my
toothbrush." Here you have in mind a list of things that probably include toothpaste, a comb, razor, lipstick, perhaps aspirin, a brush, a change of undercloth-

ing. You feel that your reader gets the point when you give one example, and might in fact be annoyed if you took the time to list all the items.

In more formal English, in addition to *like*, you may use *such as, for example*, and *for instance*. Be sure you punctuate them correctly. When your examples are items in a list, you put commas before but not after *like* and *such as*, and commas both before and after *for example* and *for instance*:

In Costa Rica some things are expensive, like clothing.

In Costa Rica some things are expensive, such as clothing.

In Costa Rica some things are expensive, for example, clothing.

In Costa Rica some things are expensive, for instance, clothing.

A final caution: after *like, such as, for example, for instance*, and similar expressions, followed by an example or examples, never put *etc.* or its equivalent. *Etc.* is not an example! (See that the list of medical examples given earlier does *not* end with "open-heart surgery, etc." It ends simply with "and open-heart surgery.")

We have taken a good deal of time here to make clear what an example is— and is not. Now let's return to the idea that one definition of *detail* is "short example." As you may have realized already, not all details are examples. The *details* of a rotary gasoline engine are the fuel-and-air intake opening and area, the compression area, the ignition area, and the exhaust outlet and area, as well as the curved triangular rotor that is moved by the explosion and the oval chamber that contains the rotor and all the areas. Obviously, these details are *parts* of the engine, not examples of it. Yet some details might be called examples: Grandfather's using deodorant and keeping his saws hung up may be thought of as *examples* of his neatness.

We often speak of details as examples because whenever we can't give all the details or don't know all of them, we give just a few—in other words, we give examples (meaning "samples") of the details. Thus, for instance, the details I gave about Grandfather's neatness are enough, but they're not all I could give. I could tell how he opens letters, how he files his nails, how he folds his money, how he always leaves his pencils sharpened, and so on, indefinitely. The details I do give are examples, or samples, of his neatness.

Let me issue a special warning, however: in giving examples of this kind, always give a generous number; don't stop with one or even two. If hard work and honesty are the virtues required for Steps 2 and 3, then hard work and generosity are the virtues required for Step 4—hard work because you cannot allow laziness to keep you from thinking of several examples, and generosity because you cannot allow stinginess to hold you to a bare minimum, like the miser who gives only a nickel to the child who has swept his walk.

Allow me to spend some time on this point, because I suspect that it is more basic than mere rules. You have to be generous in writing, as in life. You have to cast aside your defenses and give yourself wholeheartedly to a writing task. I know that many people refuse to give themselves wholeheartedly to anything.

And having given little, they will receive little. Their refusal to give themselves is a kind of selfishness, and few things are more self-defeating than selfishness. Think it over. Strangely but truly, we are never the worse off for being generous. Give yourself wholeheartedly to my writing method, and be particularly generous with examples.

Use not one example, but two, five, or ten. "Large stationery stores carry a wide range of items, from paper clips and thumbtacks and pens to reams of paper, ledgers, files, perhaps even briefcases, typewriters, and cash registers." This list by no means exhausts the inventory of a stationery store; neither does it stop at one example. "People should eat lots of fruit, like apples, peaches, and pears." These examples hardly begin to list all the healthful fruits; neither do they stop with apples!

Bringing a matter vividly before the mind's eye of a reader is the reason for generous use of examples. People don't think with facts alone; they accompany their thinking with images, with pictures; your examples supply pictures readily, so that readers can think vividly about the explanation you are giving them. Here is the first draft of a report:

> After examining the site at Fleurburg as a possible location for our new facility, I must report some negative factors. The land is not very good. The climate there is not the most desirable. There are too many insects. Shipping facilities are the poorest.

Those in the company who are going to make the decision about the location of the new facility may have learned to trust the writer's judgment, but they still may be unpleasantly puzzled when they read the memorandum. In what way is the land not good? Is it subject to mudslides? In what way is the climate poor? Are there sandstorms? What are some of the insects? Mosquitos? Moths? What is poor about the shipping facilities? Is there danger of hijacking?

This is the second version:

> After examining the site of Fleurburg as a possible location for our new facility, I must report some negative factors. The land has, among other things, some chemical dump sites. Besides seasonal extremes, the climate is said to include frequent icing-over in the winter. Every household is plagued by ants and other insects, including earwigs. There is no longer any railroad line near, and I wonder how the roads would stand up under heavy traffic.

With such a report before them, wouldn't the officers of the company feel more confident in making their decision? Ask yourself, too, which passage gives *you* a clearer picture of the land around Fleurburg. Notice at the same time that simply including a few examples creates the apparent magic of a better picture. In your own writing, achieving this simple magic involves asking yourself at what point a reader would ask, "What, specifically, are you talking about? Can you give me an example?" There you insert one or more examples. You will find that anticipating your reader by including examples makes all the difference in the world.

Have you noticed how, in order to make the use of examples clear, I must give examples, and give them generously? You'd like another? Very well, here is the first draft of a theme written by a young woman.

X   A student can benefit from spending a year in a foreign country.
1.   She can learn many practical skills.
2.   She can discover the customs and conditions of the new country.
3.   She can benefit personally from the experience.

- -

X   A student can benefit from spending a year in a foreign country.
1.   She can learn many practical skills. Without the help of parents or friends she must take care of the details involved in traveling from one country to another. Once she arrives, she has to learn how to use the public transportation system to get around. She must learn to manage her own money and possessions. With hard work she can even master a foreign language.
2.   She can discover the customs and conditions of the new country. The climate is not like ours. Holiday celebrations seem unusual by our standards. Strange new sights are everywhere, and people's behavior seems embarrassing at times. Even prejudice is different, because it is based on social class, not color or race.
3.   She can benefit personally from the experience. Living with another family can teach her to compromise. Accepting other people's differences and difficulties will make her tolerant. She can mature a great deal as a result of making her own decisions and handling her own life. The year abroad can be invaluable to her in later life.

Notice first that the freshman who wrote this paper has used Steps 1, 2, and 3 well. She does stick to her sentence X. What is lacking in the theme? What do you still want to know about the experience in the foreign country? Remember the questions you need to ask to improve the examples in your writing—"What, specifically, are you talking about? Can you give me an example?" Possibly you're most curious about the foreign country. Which one is she talking about? What language do they speak there? What possessions does a student have to manage? What is the climate like? What behavior would seem embarrassing to us?

    Taking these questions and Step 4 seriously, the author of the first version rewrote her three short paragraphs, inserting examples whenever she could. The revised version is twice as long as the first—there's length without mere repetition!—and it contains a good deal more specific information. Notice that often the change is accomplished simply by replacing an abstraction with a concrete picture.

X   A student can benefit from spending a year in Brazil.
1.   She can learn many practical skills.
2.   She can discover the customs and conditions of the new country.
3.   She will also benefit personally.

X   A student can benefit from spending a year in Brazil.

1.   She can learn many practical skills. Without the help of parents or friends she must deal with customs agents, handle a passport, enroll at a new school, and conquer the public bus system. Managing her money and possessions might be new for her, but with effort she can learn to do her own laundry, organize her books and papers, and balance her checkbook. If she is efficient and thrifty, she can learn to make $75.00 last a month. With hard work she can even master Portuguese.

2.   She can discover the customs and conditions of the new country. Since the seasons are the opposite of ours, the temperature is over 110° on Christmas Day. The holiday seems strange anyway, because instead of a big dinner at home, everyone visits friends and goes from house to house drinking wine and eating. Poverty is a fact of life in Brazil, so it is common to see children begging on the streets. Some customs are so different they seem embarrassing to an American; for example, teenage girls hold hands when they walk down the street, the way small children do in this country. Even prejudice is different: racially mixed couples are common, but a person from the upper class cannot marry a person from the lower class without being disowned by his family.

3.   She will also benefit personally. By living with a new family, she will have to learn to compromise when she wants to study or shop and the mother is sick and needs help. A student who sees begging children daily develops not only compassion, but also judgment, since she has to decide which one is trying to sell her a ribbon and which one is going to grab her money and run away. Being accepted by the Brazilians can in itself give the student a better feeling about herself than being accepted by her own kind. The maturity and strength she gains, the knowledge of how to fill out applications and pack suitcases, the experience of living with a whole new family—all of these will change her and prepare her for going to college or working with others.

When some writers of composition textbooks speak of examples, they seem to have in mind a single long example. We'll consider that now.

I've specified examples in the statement of Step 4 because they are extremely

useful, extremely important. They are as important to a writer as a pocket calculator to an engineer, a drill to a dentist, a large knife to a chef. As a matter
of fact, if you took a book (such as is often used in freshman college English)
of well-written essays and went from paragraph to paragraph, keeping count,
you'd probably find that in many paragraphs—perhaps over half—the second
sentence (or sometimes the first) contains the connective *for example*, or some
equivalent like *for instance*.

An example is a wonderful way to make something clear and real and convinc-
ing. An example by its nature is nearly always concrete and fairly specific, and
thus it gives the reader a kind of picture to look at instead of an invisible idea
that must be juggled in the brain. Remember how back in the earlier part of the
book I introduced Step 2 and said that its three sentences were to be about the
whole of the sentence in Step 1, not just part of it? At that point my statement
was very vague, very unclear in your mind. As a matter of fact, I often used to
present that step to my classes and then deliberately stop and wait. Sure
enough, after a moment some brave student would always ask apologetically,
"Could you give us an example?"

It is the most typical and soundest of human instincts to want an example.
When I gladly give my class the example I gave you, they understand, just as
you understood. Ponder that as an instance of the remarkable power of an
example. It is like a flashlight focused suddenly on a page that you have been
trying unsuccessfully to read in a room lit only by moonlight.

Remember, your ideas are clear to you, so you may assume that they're
equally clear to the reader (after all, you've stated them in clear words, and the
reader is presumably as intelligent as you are). But your ideas are clear to you
not only because you have thought them out, but especially because you have
accompanied them with pictures—examples—in your mind, and may in fact
have derived them from concrete, specific realities (such as examples are).
Those ideas, then, even though it seems to you that they *have* to be clear, are
not clear to the reader—at least not as clear as they could be. So you might say
writing a theme consists in filming the game for the reader, not just reporting
the final score.

Therefore, like any other successful writer, you say at once, "For example. . . ." For easier ideas ("My grandfather is neat"), a succession of little instances will suffice ("His detective novels stand in neat rows"); but for harder
ideas ("Being cannot be defined"; "A falling body increases in acceleration 32.17
feet per second per second"; "Friction produces heat"), longer, more elaborate
examples are necessary ("Rubbing your hands together is an example of friction;
and if you keep rubbing them fast, you'll *feel* an example of the heat friction
produces").

ASSIGNMENT

Write a theme in which you use examples liberally. Make sure each
paragraph has at least one sentence that *begins* with "For example" and

then is followed by a sentence that is a long example. Remember to put your X, 1, 2, 3 above the line and then to write X and your three paragraphs below it.

E. ABSTRACT AND GENERAL

In this section, though I want to enlarge on one or two matters, I will in fact be insisting on the key instructions of this chapter. So first let's re-examine the all-important Step 4.

STEP 4

Make the material in the four or five sentences in Step 3 as specific and concrete as possible. Go into detail. Use examples. Don't ask, "What will I say next?" Instead, say some more about what you have just said. Your goal is to say a lot about a little, not a little about a lot.

Most students will ask, "What about sentences X, 1, 2, and 3? Are they supposed to be concrete and specific, too?" No, that's the very point. Sentences X, 1, 2, and 3 by their very nature tend to be general and sometimes abstract. They tend to be general because, after all, they summarize what is to follow; and a summary, being brief, tends to be general because specific details take up space. Sentences 1, 2, and 3 are indeed to be more specific than sentence X—but only by one degree; the sentences that complete the paragraphs (Step 3), on the other hand, are to be *as specific as possible* (Step 4).

Likewise, by their very nature sentences X, 1, 2, and 3 are sometimes abstract, because in them you are presenting your *ideas*—and as we said before, abstractions are precisely that: *ideas about things* (for example, *coldness, speed, beauty*); whereas the concrete is the realm of *things themselves* (*snow, racing car, flower*).

I say it's the very point that sentences X, 1, 2, and 3 must be general because to be understood, to make a point, you have to make brief statements ("Power corrupts: it corrupts the powerful; it corrupts the powerless; it corrupts every relationship between the two"). But those brief statements, precisely because they are brief and general, and sometimes abstract, do not register sufficiently with the reader: they are not *real*; they are not as clear as they could be; they are not deeply convincing. They need details.

This, then, is the very function, the very purpose, the reason for being of the four or five or ten sentences that follow sentences 1, 2, and 3: to bring the briefly stated abstract and general notions of sentences X, 1, 2, and 3 down to the concrete and specific, down to details.

As a child, you lived in the concrete and the specific. As you approached adolescence, you began to understand the power of the abstract and the general, which is a later and more sophisticated development of the human intellect. Many good students, at the college freshman level, have learned to look down on concrete, specific examples as juvenile. These students, mistakenly but understandably, attempt to write in nothing but abstractions and generalities, and they will thus resist Step 4 as a return to the childish writing they think they have outgrown. Their mistake is not in moving to the abstract and general—which is real progress—but in rejecting the concrete and specific. True sophistication in writing requires not just the concrete and specific, nor just the abstract and general, but a skillful combination of the two. Look at any professional writing you admire, and you'll see what I mean.

Here is a professional writer I admire, the eminent biographer Lytton Strachey. Early in this century he wrote the following description of the conditions Florence Nightingale found when she arrived at a military hospital near Constantinople in 1854. Notice Strachey's use of the concrete and specific to support the abstract and general, and his use of the abstract and general to organize the concrete and specific:

Want, neglect, confusion, misery—in every shape and in every degree of intensity—filled the endless corridors and the vast apartments of the gigantic barrack-house, which, without forethought or preparation, had been hurriedly set aside as the chief shelter for the victims of the war. The very building itself was radically defective. Huge sewers underlay it, and cesspools loaded with filth wafted their poison into the upper rooms. The floors were in so rotten a condition that many of them could not be scrubbed; the walls were thick with dirt; incredible multitudes of vermin swarmed everywhere. . . . The structural defects were equalled by the deficiencies in the commonest objects of hospital use. There were not enough bedsteads; the sheets were of canvas, and so coarse that the wounded men recoiled from them, begging to be left in their blankets; there was no bedroom furniture of any kind, and empty beer bottles were used for candlesticks. There were no basins, no towels, no soap, no brooms, no mops, no trays, no plates; there were neither slippers nor scissors, neither shoe-brushes nor blacking; there were no knives or forks or spoons. The supply of fuel was constantly deficient. The cooking arrangements were preposterously inadequate, and the laundry was a farce. As for purely medical materials, the tale was no better. Stretchers, splints, bandages—all were lacking; and so were the most ordinary drugs.

ASSIGNMENT

It's time for an assignment. This one will be connected not with the material we have just studied, but with Step 4 in general. What I want you to do is to write two pairs of sentences. The first sentence of each pair is to be in general, even abstract, terms; the second is to state the same idea in specific, concrete terms. Here are a few examples:

1. Some students are guilty of putting things off./Ted Jenkins, like other students I know, is always telling Dr. Gaetzmann, his chemistry

teacher, "I'll have it in next Monday," and then scrambling to get the chapters on the Civil War read for his history quiz the next day.

2. In her room I noticed two books./On the small table near Jessica's plaid easy chair I noticed Heller's *Catch-22* and Galsworthy's *Man of Property*.

3. If he didn't have a job, he could study more./If Joe Greenberg didn't have to work thirty hours a week as a checker at the Spend-Easy Supermarket, he would have more time to study his chemistry and calculus.

4. Because of transportation difficulties, there will be a delay in the delivery of your order./Because two of our trucks broke down, we can't get the eggs to you until tomorrow.

F. THE FUNCTION OF A PARAGRAPH

This is a good time to do what some of you have been eager to have me do: give sentences X, 1, 2, and 3 their traditional names. Sentence X is called by a number of names: thesis sentence, thesis, thesis statement, central idea, main idea, theme sentence, or simply theme (from which a composition called a theme gets its name). Sentences 1, 2, and 3 are, as far as I know, always called topic sentences. And the topic sentence together with its four, five, or more sentences (often called material, support, development, or specifics) is called a paragraph.

We've already solved the puzzling old question of when you begin a new paragraph, haven't we? It's simple: you begin a new paragraph when you are finished providing the examples and the other concrete, specific details for one topic sentence and move on to the next topic sentence. And you already have all your topic sentences; they're sentences 1, 2, and 3.

Notice that the sign to the reader that you are beginning a new paragraph is (a) dropping to the next line and (b) beginning that line with an indentation at the left. Let me caution you that, while every new paragraph begins with this indentation, not every indentation *in what you read in print* begins a new paragraph! An editor, or the writer, may within a single paragraph add one, two, or even several indentations, so that a single paragraph *looks* on the printed page like two or three paragraphs. The reason for doing this is to make the page seem more inviting to the reader, who is dismayed at the sight of a page of solid type; to give the reader more frequent breathing spaces, opportunities to swallow one mouthful before taking another bite. That breaking up of paragraphs by additional indentations has been done frequently in this book.

But let me add two more cautions. First, until you have fully mastered the six Steps, *do not add extra indentations yourself!* Make *no* indentation until you come to a new topic sentence; if you do, you will lose your grip on the important sense of paragraph structure that you have acquired. (Later on, when you write for others, you will want to modify this rule to allow at least one indentation every page or so.) Second, because what look on the printed page like paragraphs are often not whole paragraphs—as well as for other reasons—*do not rely on your reading to teach you about paragraphs*; learn about them by actually building them yourself according to the method you are studying here.

But you may ask, "Then why bother with paragraphs, if, as it seems, a writer or editor can indent just about anywhere?" The answer is that *paragraph* in printing means a block of type indented at the beginning. But *paragraph* in composition—even if it were not indented—means a unit of thought, and we can no more write, in the proper sense of the term, without strict regard to paragraphs than we can make a coat without cutting out all the pieces according to patterns.

What, then, is the function of the paragraph? If writing seemed to you, before you began to study this book, a process of putting down one thought, then thinking of another thought and putting it down, then racking your brains to think of still another; then a paragraph, for you, meant an indentation marking some greater break in thought than occurs between sentences. But now you know that a paragraph is a group of sentences whose only function is to provide specific, concrete details for the thought expressed in its topic sentence.

While you are adding details, you must be on your guard against violating Step 3 by introducing new ideas into your paragraph, for the paragraph must be kept busy expanding on the first idea (that is, the idea contained in the topic sentence). If you are properly following Step 3, any other idea must begin a paragraph of its own (or be omitted altogether). Look at this piece of writing.

> Eric Ambler never uses a professional spy as the hero of his superb spy stories. The hero is always a salesman, an engineer, a language teacher, a businessman, a writer, a young doctor, who unintentionally becomes involved in a web of intrigue where he is not at home and from which he keeps wishing he could free himself. Ambler himself, of course, is an engineering graduate. Perhaps that is why his writing has such neat construction. His use of nonprofessionals allows his readers, who are usually not professional spies, either, to imagine *themselves* rather easily as the central character—to *identify* with him, as we say. Graham Greene, another fine writer of foreign intrigue who obviously admires Ambler, may have picked up this trick from him.

Well, what do you say? Has the writer stuck to the point here? Some of the sentences fit the original statement perfectly. Others, only halfway. One, not at all. Study the paragraph to see for yourself before I comment.

All right, the second sentence fits perfectly, for in fact it simply repeats the idea of the first sentence in a more fully detailed way. The sentence beginning "His use of nonprofessionals" obviously keeps to the announced subject, fitting in as an *effect*—even though I wish that the writer of the paragraph had gone into greater detail about Ambler's nonprofessional heroes, giving specific details and even a somewhat expanded example or two of the kind of web of intrigue they fall into, then saved identification and other *effects* for another paragraph.

But, in contrast to the two sentences just mentioned, the thought that "Ambler is an engineering graduate" lends no support to the writer's point; it is a thought merely suggested by Ambler's choice of an engineer as his hero. There is a connection, of course. The writer of the paragraph does not unaccountably throw in a remark about Ambler's moving from Bel Air to Switzerland, much less a remark about an entirely unrelated subject, like car prices or rose gardening; still, Ambler's own original vocation does not fit *clearly and directly* with the original idea—that he uses nonprofessionals as heroes. Similarly, that Greene sometimes uses the same trick keeps to one part of the topic sentence, all right, but sends us off on another *idea*, for we are concerned with *Ambler's* use of nonprofessionals as heroes, not with *Greene's*.

Let's look finally, at the mention of Ambler's neat construction, in the fourth sentence of the paragraph. Though it follows in an association (hero as an engineer—Ambler as an engineer—precision as the business of an engineer), it does not fit at all into the idea of having nonprofessionals as heroes. It may be well to dwell, again, on this fault: we have associated nonprofessional spy, engineer, Ambler, neatness—all naturally enough. But the real question is not "Are those items connected among themselves?" but "Is the idea that Ambler's writing shows neat construction connected with our *original* idea, that Ambler uses nonprofessionals as heroes?" If you answer, "Well, I'm not sure whether they're connected or not," then you've made my point; for if you can't see at once, for sure, a connection between two ideas, then either they don't belong together or the connection should be spelled out (as the "clearly and directly" of Steps 2 and 3 requires).

Well, what's to be done about that paragraph about Ambler—or, rather, about the fact that Ambler uses nonprofessionals as heroes? Clearly, what at least seems to be, and probably is, the topic sentence has to do with Ambler's use of nonprofessionals. The paragraph should stick closely and clearly with that, going into detail about it, probably with the use of specific examples—like the playwright-become-special-news-correspondent to cover a political trial in a Balkan country (*Judgment on Deltchev*), or the writer of mysteries who visits Istanbul and there discovers a real crime, which in turn leads him into a real mystery.

Only after we have discovered the real focus of the topic sentence can we deal with the facts we found in the paragraph that don't—or don't quite—fit. What to do with them? What a shame to throw out such interesting material! Yet what a crime just to leave it in, as is. (Would Ambler, just praised as a neat constructionist, do that?)

The solution is to put each interesting idea into a paragraph of its own, and to give each the detailed treatment, the examples, it deserves—not to leave it in undeveloped isolation within a paragraph where it doesn't belong. Or, if one or more of those interesting facts don't really fit into the whole theme at all, use them as material for another theme or themes.

What do I mean by "really fit into the whole theme"? No more and no less than following Steps 2 and 3. Material fits into the whole theme only if it *clearly and directly* helps explain or prove the point of that theme—your sentence X. No paragraph, no matter how highly interesting in itself, fits in if it violates the rules you learned for Step 2.

In a theme on Eric Ambler's use of a certain kind of hero, there is no place for a paragraph on Graham Greene's use of the same kind of hero. If you introduce that paragraph on Graham Greene, perhaps you have simply forgotten that the grammatical *subject* of your sentence X is Eric Ambler, and what you say of a certain kind of hero is the *predicate*. Suddenly you have made the predicate the subject; and in your mind (without your realizing it) your sentence X has become "The use of a character who is not a professional agent is valuable in a novel of foreign intrigue," or "The use of a character who is not a professional agent is sometimes found in novels of foreign intrigue." You'll avoid this kind of pitfall if you carefully figure out what you really want to write about, state *that* as your sentence X, and stick to that point throughout your theme. Then a paragraph on Graham Greene won't be wandering into a theme that you announce, in your sentence X, is going to be about Eric Ambler.

But suppose you still want to say something in your theme about your notion that Greene imitates Ambler, even though you see that you can't make a paragraph out of that notion. Perhaps you think you can put it in as a detail—part of Step 4. Well, only you can settle this problem. You must *question yourself*— ask yourself *why* you want to bring in Graham Greene. Is it because what you have to say about Greene will clearly help your reader to understand what you assert about Ambler? If so, fine—include Greene in an appropriate place as part of Step 4. If, however, you find by questioning yourself that Greene's practice will not really help explain Ambler's, my cold, objective advice is: leave Greene out.

In the same way, I would advise you to leave out mention of Ambler's background as an engineer—and as a vaudeville performer, a writer of popular songs, and a film maker, for that matter. Admittedly, such interesting information provides much of the liveliness of chatty conversation about Ambler or about any other subject. It may even enliven an instructor's classroom presentation. But a theme is neither a conversation nor a classroom presentation; nor is it a "literary" essay, intended to entertain your readers and enrich their general knowledge or satisfy their general curiosity, rather than directly enlighten them on a single point. So, in writing a theme you must resist the temptation— however attractive—to be chatty.

True, I have not criticized the "superb" in the sentence "Eric Ambler never uses a professional spy as the hero of his *superb* spy stories." Is there really a connection between the "superb" quality of Ambler's stories and his choice of heroes? There may well be; but that connection is not made explicit in the paragraph. But it's implicit, you say. Yes, perhaps. Perhaps, though, the word is really irrelevant. If irrelevant, someone may point out, it is at least unobtrusive, and unlikely to set the reader off on a wrong track. So I leave it to your judgment: would you cross it out or leave it in?

(Once you decide to delete material, for whatever reason, you may find that it is a painful process. It's hard work to get words on paper, and you may not want to cross any of them out. But if some words or passages *detract* from your topic, they need to be eliminated. If you plant a vegetable garden, you may have to pull out a flower simply because it does not belong.)

G. USING ANECDOTES

Right now there seems nothing left for this chapter except to point out a particular kind of example called an *anecdote*. This is a little story, sometimes told in only one or two sentences. There is an example of an anecdote—the daring rescue of a little boy from a flaming building—in this chapter (see page 42). An anecdote is a story that provides an example, an instance, an illustration. The anecdotal method is effective and frequently used, especially in speeches and in popular magazines. Later, in Chapter 13, we will find a more extended anecdote in a popular article on science that was originally a speech ("The Method of Scientific Investigation" by T. H. Huxley).

Obviously, it would be a mistake to use an anecdote so lengthy that readers would tend to forget the point it was supposed to illustrate, or so lengthy that room would be left for little else. It would also be a mistake to use too many anecdotes, with few or no other kinds of example and detail. But if you avoid these mistakes, you will find the use of anecdotes easy and profitable. Repeated warning: don't make anecdotes your only, or even your favorite, method of completing Step 4.

SUMMARY

In the body of the paragraph (the four or five sentences of Step 3) be specific: *Joyce Carol Oates's newest novel*—not *a book*; *an African violet*—not *a flower*; *glazed doughnuts*—not *food*. Be concrete: *breaking shop windows and overturning cars* to accompany the abstract thought *violence*; *white stone spires soaring into the blue sky* to go with *beauty*; *buzzing flies settling on the fetid remains of a dead hawk* to go with *ugliness*. Sentences X, 1, 2, and 3 are the place to be the opposite—general (*flower*) and abstract (*beauty*).

Go into detail. You assert that Beulah is disorderly? Give details of her disorderliness: the single beige stocking hanging out of a drawer, the sticky glasses and cups all over the kitchen, the botany notebook pages lying among discarded sections of yesterday's *Daily News*. And *be generous* with your details. Give examples. A profession is work, the primary purpose of which is not making money? Explain a doctor's or minister's purposes as an example. These are the ways that you get decent *length* for your theme without using weak repetition and without racking your brain over what to say next.

ASSIGNMENT

Write a theme on the following sentence X: "A student must have a regular schedule of study."

And please note: First, *study* here means what we generally call homework. Second, *schedule* refers to time, not place or condition, so the quiet room, the study lamp, and so on, should be brought in only incidentally—certainly not as sentence 1, 2, or 3. Third, if you disagree with the sentence X in this assignment, pretend that you do agree with it. Imagine yourself, for this assignment at least, to be a student who does need to study regularly.

Remember the form you are to use in writing your theme down on the page (see page 33). Remember that sentences 1, 2, and 3 must be about the whole of sentence X. Remember that you must have at least four or five sentences each after sentences 1, 2, and 3.

But most important—*because this is what the assignment is for*—be specific and concrete, far beyond what you feel necessary. Go all out in this respect. Go into detail. Give examples. Don't feel ridiculous. You are not expected to produce a "good" theme here; but you can make it a good exercise.

(Some students wonder whether in being instructed to write "a student must have" they're being instructed to argue, preach, or express a mere opinion. No, you're being instructed simply to *explain* what you either found out in high school or else can plainly see, now that you're in college. So don't argue, preach, or offer opinions; simply explain what all students discover.)

Chapter 5

CORRECTING THE PAPER

We will not take up a new step in this chapter, for before we go on we must carefully go over the assignment you have just completed. The best way I can help you correct your theme at long distance is to present here a theme more or less like yours and indicate what is good and what is bad about it. Then you can say, "Oh, I made the same kind of mistake," or "Yes, I can see what's wrong with *this* theme, but I didn't do that kind of thing" (good for you). Very well, here's the theme.

    X   A student must have a regular schedule of study.
    1.   Time must be set aside for study if there is going to be any time.
    2.   Often, only time to be filled provides the necessary spur to study.
    3.   Only time set aside will make study a serious profession.

    X.   A student must have a regular schedule of study.
    1.   Time must be set aside for study if there is going to be any time. During vacation, for instance, a student finds his time filled up with a number of things. During the school year he would find many of the same or similar things filling each waking hour, except for classes, if he didn't set aside certain hours for study. So without those hours he would reach the end of each day with little or no study done, because he had been "too busy." People, too, might take up his time if he didn't have hours when no one could see him.
    2.   Often, only time to be filled provides the necessary spur to study. Sometimes a student is tired, and only the fact that he has contracted with

himself to spend an hour on the study of a certain subject will give him sufficient reason to go on. Sometimes he finds some part of the material too boring,
but if he asks "Why study this?" his answer can be that he has the hour to fill
up and he may as well spend it on that material. In both cases there is the
temptation to turn to something else, but if he has agreed with himself to devote certain hours to study, he will not do so. If a lesson is too short to fill the
hour, the extra time will give him sufficient reason to do the review, the extra
drill, or the suggested extra reading that he knows he ought to do.

    3.   Only time set aside will make study a serious profession. Though for
various reasons a person may have to be a part-time student, he will not be a
serious student at all if study is just a hobby he turns to at odd moments. The
hobbyist is satisfied with little effort and little accomplishment; only the person
who dedicates a real part of his business day to study and thus invests a real
part of his life in study gives himself seriously to his work, expects something
out of it, and can count himself a real student.

    Yes, a regular period of study is the best tutor to keep a student at his tasks.

    Well! The young man who wrote this theme (a young woman, thinking of
herself as an example, would have used "she") seems to be fairly bright. The
ideas in the theme happen to be good, I think, but more to the point here,
sentences 1, 2, and 3 are really and truly about sentence X. Similarly, the Step
3 sentences following the topic sentences (sentences 1, 2, and 3) in each paragraph stand the test—that is, they are clearly about the whole of their topic
sentences.

    Notice, though, that paragraph 3 has only *two* sentences following the topic
sentence. True, those sentences are long; but a theme does need the full com-
plement of sentences, short and long, in each paragraph. I tell my classes that
there is a foolproof way to make sure you have the number of sentences you
need in a paragraph: count them.

    But back to the writer's accomplishments. The length, then, is good for a
beginner: about 380 words. I notice also that the writer has added something
that I haven't yet mentioned: a short *rounding-off sentence* at the end that neither
just repeats sentence X on the one hand nor changes the subject or introduces
a new topic on the other, but sums up what the writer has said about sentence
X. (We'll come back to the rounding-off sentence in the next chapter.)

    Let me pause here to say that *you* may, in your paper, have written three
quite different topic sentences. Your sentences 1, 2, and 3 may have said, for
instance, something to the effect that students must pick certain hours in which
they know they are going to be free, must spend the whole time—except for a
ten-minute break each hour—studying, and must stick carefully to that schedule despite temptations and the urging of friends. Or perhaps one of your topic
sentences warned against devoting more time to easy or favorite studies and

less time to difficult or less interesting studies. Again, one of your topic sentences may have been a caution to give some time in the schedule to each and every subject, in proportion to the amount of homework ordinarily needed for each (accounting classes may require more homework than English classes, for instance). Or you may have had a sentence on flexibility, saying that if an assignment for one class is brief, the extra time can be used for part of an unusually long assignment for another.

Good. You see what scope for *originality and individuality* (*creativity*, if you want to use the word) a seemingly very rigid method affords—even when sentence X, the key sentence, is assigned and is the same for everyone. In fact, there is enough variety possible for two hundred students each to write on the same sentence X and not duplicate one another.

Of course the sentences 1, 2, and 3 you thought up are different! And the only test you need to apply to see whether your ideas are any good or not is to ask yourself whether sentences 1, 2, and 3 are actually, honestly about the whole of sentence X. Though I can't see your paper, I suspect they are.

But to return to our criticism of our anonymous theme, we have indicated that it seems well thought out, well put together, if too short in the third paragraph. But though we cannot accuse the writer of putting down on paper just vague generalities, he has clearly not caught the real spirit of Step 4, has he? He has been concentrating on his *thought* (and that's certainly praiseworthy in itself); but that is perhaps the reason he hasn't also given *full consideration* to Step 4.

To understand this thoroughly so that you can detect and correct similar weaknesses in your own paper, you must go with me from point to point of our sample paper, from beginning to end. (You understand that this will be not an analysis of the theme, but an analysis of the fact that the theme is a violation of Step 4.)

First, paragraph one: "a student"—not bad, but the writer ought to be more specific about his central character. How about giving "a student" a name? *John Swenson* or *Karen Swenson* (using "she" and "her" in her case) would make a stronger, brighter, more vivid picture in the reader's mind. I will not urge here the use of *blond, lanky, six-foot John Swenson* because, though it's more vivid still, it's likely to distract the reader from the main point and thus violate Step 3. But I do think John—the student—should be further identified. His name, for the purposes of this theme, is not the most important thing; we need to know the kind of student he is. A high school senior? A college freshman? A college math major? This, notice, is a simple process of reasoning as follows: *student* is fairly general; the rule says I am to be as specific as possible, so I'll at least change it to something like *a college math major*. Yes, what I'm saying is true for all students, not just college math majors; but I am using—and can introduce—a college math major *as an example*. As you think of specifics, however, think of real students. Do not make up facts! An imaginary student, even with a name, is likely to be just as general as "a student."

"His time filled up with a number of things"—good, as far as the idea goes. This is all the *information* the reader needs. But the information isn't alive to the reader because he doesn't *see* it—or sees it, so to speak, only dimly, in the far distance. And by the way, isn't *things* almost the most general word you can use? So let's at least say that this student's mornings were taken up with swimming, reading the sports page in the *Daily Clarion*, and shopping at the supermarket for his parents; his afternoons with chess or tennis and working on his car or riding his motorcycle; his evenings with going to the ball game, watching television, reading, or visiting his friends.

"Well! Isn't this getting a little long?" you ask. It is. And not just with more words, but with more *things*—things that give the reader a concrete picture of what is said abstractly and generally in sentences X, 1, 2, and 3. This is legitimate length; this is how you get length. Does this objection come, perhaps, from the student who after writing a couple of dozen lines said, "I can't think of anything more to say"?

But you have another objection. "All our practice in Steps 1, 2, and 3 amounted to sticking to the point. And I can see how you *should* stick to the point. But all this stuff is not sticking to the point. The *point* is that the student found his time filled during vacation. What filled it is beside the point."

An excellent objection that deserves not only one answer but four! First, it is true to say "During vacation a student finds his time filled" satisfies readers' *logical* needs; but it does not satisfy their *psychological* needs. They can say "I understand it," but they can't say "I see it" or "I feel it."

Second, by specifying, writers can imply something beyond what they say, yet to the point. In this case, by specifying swimming, tennis, chess, television, and so on, the writer has implied that the student's time in summer vacation was not wholly taken up with essentials like eating and sleeping, but with occupations that could be eliminated or cut down.

Third, I think it's important to see that the details, though not essential to the writer's point, aren't really off the subject. Things one does during vacation are part of the writer's point, and *chess, tennis,* and so on are just another, more specific way of saying that. Just as important to see is the fact that if the writer began to talk a lot about the student as a chess player, he would be going off the point; chess then would *become* the subject, instead of just contributing to the real subject—namely, summertime occupations.

Fourth, in a somewhat similar way the law of diminishing returns begins to operate in Step 4. For readers' logical needs, a bare statement of the idea is sufficient; but because of their psychological needs, a writer makes generous use of details, specific and concrete material, and examples. But the writer can go beyond the bounds of generosity—in fact, beyond the bounds of common sense. Common sense must guide us. We must ask: When does the number of details, the degree to which I become specific, stop being useful to readers in giving them the picture I want to give? It is time to make the point that the *as possible* in "as specific and concrete as possible" in Step 4 means not only "as far as you are able" but also "as far as you can without going beyond the bounds of common sense and hindering rather than helping you to achieve your purpose."

So to list *playing tennis with his neighbor Jim* among the student's summer activities might not be going too far, but adding the location of the courts probably would, and giving the whole roster of opponents—Jim Jackson, Mary

Rizzo, Nancy Chan, Herb O'Brien, Willa Mae Washington, Sally Yamafuji, Alicia Rodriguez, and Hank Feder—certainly would. Do not be one of those students who avoid the hard work of finding *relevant* details by listing whatever details come to mind, whether or not they are clearly connected to the point. Of course, after a while experience in writing will guide you in this matter, as well as experience in reading, if you watch to see how other writers use specific details.

Did *you* exceed the bounds of common sense in your paper? Happy fault! That's all right, because you were told to go beyond the necessary, to go all out. As you know, in learning something new we often have to exaggerate our motions. My fear is rather that you didn't do enough—like the anonymous writer to whose theme we must now return.

"He would find many of the same or similar things filling each waking hour"—why not say something like *When school reopened, tennis might give way to skiing and the sports page to football, but there would still be recreational activities to take up his time?* (I like the wording of "filling each waking hour," but I'm willing to sacrifice it—in this assignment—in order to be more specific.)

"Certain hours for study"—a schedule is what this theme is all about, isn't it? "Certain hours"—*what* hours, for example? Neither here nor elsewhere in the anonymous paper do we get a sample of this student's schedule, of his "certain hours." I wouldn't recommend—in this particular theme—a complete schedule (though if you included one in your theme, good; for you may have used it as one way to go all out). But since this is a theme on schedules, we should have at least a sample. What hours on what days did he set to study what subjects? We could say, *For instance, Tuesday and Thursday evenings from seven to ten he set aside entirely for chemistry. . . .*

"With little or no study done" could be *with his French untouched and only two of ten chemistry problems done.*

"People, too, might take up his time"—*what* people, specifically? And how would they take up his time? Again, it doesn't matter logically, but it does matter psychologically. What will be more real, more clear, more convincing to the reader is the specific statement that Joe Allen comes in without knocking and wants to spend an hour describing the neat motorcycle (make?) on sale at Clifton's.

At this point, however, it may occur to you to remark that we are asking the anonymous writer to sacrifice the dignity and formality of his original theme. To that extent, you may say, we are ruining it. It is certainly true that most pieces of writing which the writer—and you—will be called on to produce will demand a degree of dignity and formality. Such will be a letter informing an insured person that his change of beneficiary has been recorded, or explaining to a customer why this new cash register does not require oiling; a memorandum to a supervisor explaining why at this point an engineer specializing in thermal conduction should be called in; a history paper on the various causes of the Reformation. And the anonymous writer has surely produced a dignified theme with a fairly formal tone.

But here are three answers to this problem. First, to produce a theme marked by dignity and a certain formality wasn't the assignment, was it? The assignment was to write a theme marked by concrete and highly specific content. Perhaps, therefore, the writer should have momentarily put aside his customary dignity and formality, which apparently got in his way.

Second, as I mentioned toward the end of the last chapter, do not confuse dignity and formality with abstraction and generality. True, we progress from the concrete and specific, as young children, to abstract and general ideas, in our teens; but the most elevated stage is the *combination* of abstract, general ideas with concrete, specific embodiments of those ideas. To exclude Step 4 is not to gain in formality but to lose touch with reality, and with your reader.

Third, couldn't the writer have kept his dignity and formality by a different choice of example? Visitors *his* sort of student might expect would perhaps stop by with a chess board or ask him to spend some time explaining grammatical cases in Russian. Our anonymous writer, if he is careful in his choice of examples, can keep his tone elevated and give concrete, specific details at the same time.

The rest of the analysis—which I can now leave to you—goes in the same way. "Tired"—from what? "A certain subject"—what, for instance? "Some part of the material"—what part of the material? "Turn to something else"—*what* something else? "Review"—of what? "Drill"—on what? But especially I would ask what some of the reasons are that a person "may have to be a part-time student." Does the student have a job? Where? Doing what? Does the student have young children? How many? Of what age?

When the writer mentions "a hobby," I would give a trivial hobby or two as instances; but I'd leave the last two sentences of the student's theme alone. I would, however, fulfill the requirements of Steps 3 and 4 by adding two sentences to the end of paragraph 3, perhaps using the new sentences for an extended example or an anecdote.

ASSIGNMENT

Take your theme and go through it in the same way. If you are fortunate enough to have an instructor correct it for you, the corrections may take the simple form of *What? Who? For example? Be specific!* in the margins. (Correcting papers for this assignment is unusually long and tedious work.) Guided by such suggestions, but not limiting yourself to them, go through every sentence of your paper, changing every term—if you can—to something more specific and adding examples where you can.

Unless your instructor wants you to rewrite your paper, do not try to make your corrections look beautiful; write over what you have written, or even scribble down the changes and additions on a fresh piece of paper. It is the process of correcting we are interested in here, not the preparation of a neat-looking paper.

Remember the purpose of what you are doing—have you spoken simply of "homework" in your original paper? Isn't *homework* the most *general* term you could use and still be understood? (Just *work* would be misunderstood for the student's job as a checker at the Spend-Easy Supermarket.) What if your instructor announced, "For your assignment for

Wednesday, do homework"? *What* homework? Beware of words like *way*, *thing*, *something*, *somebody*, *a certain*, and especially *etc*. in your writing; they are the least specific of all.

CONSISTENT GRAMMATICAL SUBJECTS

Here is another matter. It's not one of our steps. But it's a rule that, if kept, will improve your themes surprisingly, and experience shows me that this is just the point at which I should introduce it to you. So don't be annoyed at the interruption. Like everything else in this book, it's intended to be of practical use to you.

The rule I'm talking about might be approached something like this: look over the theme you've just written for the special purpose of seeing whether, as you went along from sentence to sentence, you didn't say "students" in one or two sentences, then perhaps "student" in the next, and then, in another, "you" or "we." If you did, then study this rule: *as far as possible, keep the same grammatical subject throughout your theme*.

Let me explain. The grammatical subject is the person or thing that does something in a sentence—does something or is something, did something or was something. For instance, in "Einstein persuaded Roosevelt to undertake the production of the atomic bomb," *Einstein* is the subject; it was he who persuaded. In "He was afraid that Germany might produce the bomb first and thus win the war," *he* is the subject; *he* is the person who was afraid. And the same sentence leads on to a subordinate subject, *Germany*; for Germany is also doing (might do) something: "Germany might produce."

Keep to the same grammatical subject. That means start out talking *either* about a student *or* about students—or about you, we, I, or anybody or anything else. But then in every sentence you can, keep talking about either a student, or students, or you—in other words, don't jump back and forth from one to another. Of course, you can and should often call a student *he*, *she*, *he or she* (to avoid sex bias), or students *they*. (Do not, however, call the *same* student first *he*, then *she*. One student has one gender! Give the sexes equal attention by changing pronouns, not in the middle of one example, but when you come to your *next* example. And notice that you can avoid the problem of sex bias altogether by choosing the plural *students* to begin with, so that the pronoun reference is always the plural *they*.)

Let me give you an obvious example of *not keeping* to the same grammatical subject—the wrong thing to do.

A student who is not wealthy ought to find a college with low costs. In fact, if students sat down and figured all the expenses before they enrolled in college, he or she might avoid serious trouble. An expensive school is not necessarily a good school. Actually, what college gives you depends mostly on how seriously you do your work there, whether attending it is expensive or not. If we loaf through school, no amount of money paid is going to make much out of us.

Now there are five different grammatical subjects used for the actual subject in that paragraph: *a student, students, he or she, you,* and *we.* Notice that in some sentences the change in subject was logical: you couldn't call an expensive school *a student* or college *he.* But in most of the sentences the switch in subject is quite pointless.

Let's reword the paragraph to get rid of the needless switches.

> Students who are not wealthy ought to find a college with low costs. In fact if they sat down and figured all the expenses before enrolling in college, they might avoid serious trouble. An expensive school is not necessarily a good school. Actually, what college gives students depends mostly on how they do their work there, whether attending it is expensive or not. If they loaf through school, no amount of money paid is going to make much out of them.

I hope you can see that revising the paragraph to eliminate unnecessary switching of subjects has improved it.

Here I need to say a word about *I* and *you.* At some previous stage, probably in high school, you were properly cautioned to avoid *I* in your formal writing. Now you should be sufficiently mature that we can relax that strict prohibition and say go ahead, use *I*—if the subject of your writing really is you and not the question, say, of protective tariffs. But if you are assigned to write about your own experience, you will want to have *I* as the grammatical subject throughout.

You is a less useful pronoun. Sometimes it is just camouflage for *I*—and if you mean *I,* say *I.* Or if *you* stands for students, stockbrokers, or sailors—say so, and continue not with *you* but with *they.*

Now the reason behind keeping the same grammatical subject is this: it gives readers one target to keep their sights on and thus makes their job of reading simpler and less likely to be distracting or confusing.

But before we go further, I'll tell you a story to illustrate a point to which we must come. Until about half a century ago people kept perishable foods and foods that they wanted to serve cold in ice boxes: insulated cabinets, the top sections of which contained blocks of ice. But about this time there began to appear the now familiar electric and gas refrigerators, which, being colder, preserved foods much better, and even had an upper compartment in which solids as well as liquids could be frozen. Large refrigerators were installed in food stores, and even some foods that had previously not been kept in ice boxes were stored in them. I can only guess how much food has been saved from spoilage and how many people saved from food poisoning since the introduction of electric and gas refrigerators.

But do you know what the reaction of some people was at the time? They said the new refrigerators were too cold! (I understand that some of the first *warmer-colder* dials were installed on refrigerators not because they regulated the temperature at all, but because they kept such people happy.) Some people object before they think, just as some people (perhaps the same people) form opinions before they think.

So naturally I have to deal with objections to everything I teach, including the rule that grammatical subjects should not be changed unnecessarily. "Keeping the same grammatical subject," our ice-box friends will object, "would be too monotonous; it wouldn't allow enough variety."

Let us deal with this objection. It rests on a basically sound but often misdirected instinct for variety—that is, beginners often want to change what should stay the same, while they leave the same what they should change. As I mentioned at the end of Chapter 2, it is not only all right but desirable to repeat key words. Repetition, in fact, is one of the first principles of art: in the course of a musical composition, a composer repeats a melody, a theme, or a phrase—sometimes, it seems, endlessly; in paintings an artist repeats both shapes and colors. So in writing it is quite desirable to repeat the grammatical subject. It is, after all, what you are talking about and what you must *keep* talking about.

Whatever monotony may result from repetition of the grammatical subject can be dealt with in three ways (to two of which I must add a caution). First, you can use *pronouns*. If you are writing about George Washington, you needn't call him Washington in every sentence; it will be very natural to call him *he*. Readers do not object to the frequent repetition of pronouns—*he, she, it, them,* and so forth—any more than to the repetition of prepositions—*of, for, with, by,* and so forth—or of articles—*a, an, the.*

Caution: pronouns are not always desirable. In some situations they are not as clear as a noun would be, and generally speaking they are not as emphatic. Perhaps we can compromise by saying: *use the noun unless it strikes the ear as unpleasantly repetitious; then use the pronoun.*

Second, use *synonyms*. If, for instance, you are writing a book report or a book review, you may find that you are writing *the book* an unpleasant number of times. (You the writer, however, will reach the "unpleasant" level much sooner than your *reader* will, so hold yourself back from being oversensitive to it.) Let's say that at one point you have just written, "The book also takes up briefly the phenomenon of migration." Then you start to write *it*, but you realize that, though *you* know the *it* here means "book," the reader may think it means "phenomenon" or "migration." So you cross out *it* and write instead *the book* and then realize that the repetition of *the book* is unpleasant. So you use instead *the volume* or *the work*—a word that's different but clearly refers to the same thing (book). In other words, you use a synonym.

Caution: like anything else, the use of synonyms can be overdone. While you are at the library, look for *The King's English* by H. W. and F. G. Fowler (3rd ed. [New York: Oxford University Press, 1958], 184–89), a work in which overfondness for synonyms is ridiculed under the name of elegant variation.

Now at least if we do not have time (and in real life we usually do not) for a complete rewriting of what we have written, synonyms are usually the best way out of an unwanted repetition in a place where a pronoun would be confusing. But read the Fowlers' book and be warned against synonyms that are unnecessary, ridiculous, or fantastic. Again, the repetition of a key word does not have to be a sin.

Third, try a *change of sentence length and form*. As I said a few moments ago, beginners want to change what should stay the same, while leaving unchanged what should be changed. Specifically, they are likely to keep switching the *subjects* of sentences, but to leave the sentences about the same *length* and have every sentence *begin* with the subject (with the result, by the way, that far too many of their sentences begin with *the*).

What those writers should do is see to it that *on the average every third sentence or so is notably longer than the others*. Are you ready with your objection? "Can't sentences be too long?" you say. Yes indeed, and a person can have too many teeth; but I've yet to meet a person with too many teeth—or a student with sentences too long.

The way to get longer sentences is not, of course, just to put in more words; that's always bad. The way to do it is instead of putting every idea in a little sentence of its own, to combine related ideas into longer sentences. We will talk more about this in the final chapter, but for the time being, perhaps one simple example will be enough. You might write: "I have a cat. Her name is Tiny. I got her when she was a kitten. Now she is old enough to be a nuisance." But you could (and no doubt should) combine all this into one sentence: "I got my cat, Tiny, when she was a kitten, but now she's old enough to be a nuisance."

Notice that when sentences are combined this way, it is easy to tell which idea predominates: in this example, the conclusion that Tiny is now a nuisance. When sentences are separate, however, each idea seems equally important, whether it is or not. So a writer can gain control and emphasis, and often eliminate wordiness, by regularly combining short sentences.

But what if you reduce the number of sentences required in Step 3 by combining your sentences in this way? (That was probably what happened to the anonymous author of our sample theme when he wrote his three-sentence third paragraph.) Then you have an especially good reason to apply Step 4 more vigorously. Add relevant information to your paragraph, like further examples or a fuller explanation of your point.

Can you go back to your old themes and here and there combine two short sentences into one long one? It will be excellent practice for you. Perhaps your instructor will ask the class to do this as an additional assignment and to bring the results to class for reading aloud.

When you combine sentences in this way you will often automatically do what you should also do—namely, vary the form of the sentences. Now regarding the form of sentences, your instructor may wish to explain to you about simple, compound, and complex sentences, and loose, periodic, and balanced sentences. But even without such a technical explanation, you will learn to vary the form of your sentences if you follow this one guideline: *be sure every third sentence or so begins with something other than the subject*.

For instance, take the sentence "I usually avoid Fifth Street because it has so many stop signs." That begins with the subject, *I*. But you could take *usually* out of its place and begin with it instead: "Usually I avoid Fifth Street because it has so many stop signs." You could also put the *because* part at the beginning: "Because Fifth Street has so many stop signs, I usually avoid it."

Doing this is a simple, natural way to get variety. You will find that it makes your themes much more pleasant to read and that it actually helps you make your meaning clear. In fact, it is an *excellent* practice—be sure to remember to do it! True, placement of parts of a sentence ought to have some reason besides mere variety. We will discuss some of the reasons when we get to Step 6. But you will eventually learn the application of such reasons more easily if you first break out of the rigid subject-first pattern.

You should watch out for something else in your theme (and I wish I knew how to stress it as it should be stressed): when you are writing the theme proper, *do not use sentences 1, 2, and 3 as headings or subtitles!* Sometimes I find students writing paragraphs that begin like this:

> 1. Railroads nowadays use diesel power. The engines that pull railroad trains at the present time all get their energy from diesel fuel.

You are *not* to follow this example. The writer has simply repeated the first statement in the second sentence, the only change being the greater length of the second. Obviously, this writer thought of sentence 1 as some kind of title for the paragraph and thought of the paragraph itself as beginning only with the Step 3 sentences. No! Your sentence 1, or 2, or 3 is the first sentence of your paragraph. Then the second sentence should immediately begin to explain it or illustrate it: it should read something like "Southern Pacific, for example. . . ."

You will have to watch out for this pointless repetition, since I notice students doing it even after they have been corrected. Remember that sentence X and sentences 1, 2, and 3 are not titles! They are as much sentences within the theme as any other sentence.

To make sure you avoid this error, your instructor may even assign you a theme in which the second sentence of each paragraph must start with *For example,* and then be followed by the statement of an example. But I will not insist on going that far in the assignment that follows.

ASSIGNMENT

Write a theme on a subject of your own choice, incorporating all the steps you have learned so far (you should be fairly familiar with them now). But in addition—and this is the point of this assignment—try to have in each sentence of the theme—in sentences X, 1, 2, 3 as well as in the sentences that fill your paragraphs with details—the same grammatical subject. (Remember that a pronoun used as a subject is considered the same grammatical subject as the noun it refers to.)

But also be sure (and you may have to do a little rewriting to achieve this) that one out of every three or four sentences is notably longer than the others, and that one of every three or four sentences begins with something other than the subject, even though it uses the same grammatical subject as the others: "*Hoping* it would rain . . .," "*To* prevent inflation . . .," "*Sometimes* . . .," "*In* the prison . . .," "*Though* the treaty was sometimes disregarded. . . ."

Naturally, your theme may be a little stiff and clumsy. No matter—it's excellent practice. After you have finished, read a paragraph or two out of any book to see how the author varies sentence length and sentence beginnings.

Chapter 6

A
BREATHING
SPACE

If you consider yourself an average student writer and if you have no objections to the method of this book so far, we probably can excuse you from understanding and remembering this chapter. Frankly, it is somewhat abstract and general—though you will find lots of concrete examples—and it demands a rather tiring attention to the line of thought. You will have to do the assignments, though; and I urge you to pay attention to what I will say in the next section about introductions and conclusions and to pay strict attention to what I will say later about reading and about being "interesting."

But if you have a special interest in writing or if you have objections to the method, brave the difficulties of this chapter; pore over it as you would over a difficult chapter in mathematics; study it until you make it your own. For it will answer your most serious objections. Moreover, it will give you a sophisticated insight into the process of writing and improve your skills.

A. A NATURAL ARRANGEMENT

I hope you've gathered that Steps 1, 2, 3, and 4 have not been just good advice. No, as I intend to show you now, what you have learned so far is how any theme *must* be written, in some way or another (and what you have learned here is the basic way).

First, I intend to show that Steps 1, 2, and 3 arise from the very nature of things. For consider that before anything else, your theme has to have a *point*.

If it doesn't have a point, obviously it's pointless. The following account will illustrate what I mean.

Suppose I told you that yesterday I left the library by the east door, went over to the Applied Arts building and entered it by the west door, then took the center staircase to the second floor. There I looked into Mrs. Bradley's office and noticed a French textbook on her desk. Finally I left by the south door, descended the outside staircase, returned to the library, and entered it by the south door.

Then suppose I took up the subject of composition again. "Why," you'd say, "what was that story for? Of course, I understood every word, but I didn't understand what it was all about. What was all that about going out the east door and coming in the west door? And what did the French textbook on the desk have to do with it? Was all that to show us something about composition? I don't get the point at all."

Exactly. By being pointless (I purposely made it so), my recital about going out the east door and coming in the west door illustrates what we mean—or rather don't mean—by *point*. And the fact that you were instinctively looking for some point in my recital illustrates that *point* is what every reader or listener is looking for and that every composition must have one. The writer of mystery stories appeals to this instinct by presenting seemingly pointless information and challenging the reader to discover the point before the detective does.

In connection with themes, some books call point *purpose*; you may call it *meaning*; but I believe you may understand it best as *point*.

Very well. You should now be able to see more clearly two things about the importance of sentence X. First, writing sentence X forces you at the very beginning of your theme to decide what your point is. That's of the greatest importance, because if *you* haven't decided what it is, certainly the reader will have difficulty in knowing what it is. Furthermore, if you haven't decided what your point is, how are you going to know what to write? (Conversely, deciding at the very beginning what your point is makes your course immediately clear—you know with certainty which way you have to go or which ways are open to you.)

Second, putting your sentence X—your point—at the very beginning lets the reader know at once what everything that follows is intended to add up to. That's what the reader has got to know in order to *read* in any real sense.

After all, the sentence 1 "Industry finds many uses for coal" does not necessarily go with the sentence X "Coal is useful" unless we *know* that is the idea it's supposed to be going with. For it could just as easily be used to support another assertion: "Industry uses many raw materials," or "Coal is not just a fuel."

Similarly, the statement "Every thinker had a theory worked out" could be about the assertion "In the Middle Ages controversy was rife," or—a very different assertion—"Each of the Founding Fathers contributed something to the Constitution," or still another, "The early nineteenth century was an age of widespread idealism."

You had better read the last paragraph again, slowly and thoughtfully.

"But surely," you say, "in those cases there could be no confusion; the writer would have made it plain." Exactly. And *you* must make plain, from the outset, what your point is. The way to do that is to begin with sentence X.

Let me deepen your understanding of the simple-seeming Step 1 by dealing with some other objections. To take one, even after hearing an explanation like the one given above, someone will ask, "But do I have to put it at the beginning? Can't I put it somewhere else?" The correct answer is another question: "Why should you want to put it somewhere else?"

The last reply I received to this was "To be creative." Well, if being different *for the sake of being different* is your idea of being creative, I can see your point. Wearing one brown shoe and one black shoe would make you different, too. Why don't you do that? If I appeared in class wearing my pajamas, I'd be different, certainly. Only I don't think my students would call me creative. They'd have another word to describe me.

But to come back to my question "Why should you want to do that?" The correct answer is, "To serve my purpose." Very well. Since purpose must govern everything, if you cannot achieve your purpose by putting sentence X at the beginning—or even by putting it into words at all—well, you must do something different. What might your purpose be in such a case? Usually, to avoid presenting your readers at once with a statement they won't accept, a statement they'll reject so firmly that they will simply close their minds to all your arguments. (On the other hand, there is a school of writers called iconoclasts who love to confront their readers thus, deliberately.)

All right. But remember three things. First, your *purpose* cannot be just to be different, which is simply eccentricity, or sometimes a mask for laziness. Second, your need to have sentence X somewhere else must be very great indeed if it makes you sacrifice the marvelous advantage of letting your readers know at once what your point is.

Third, if you don't state your point at once, you must still guide your readers toward that point through a mass of material in such a way as to convince them that they *are* moving clearly toward a point, without their ever being wholly puzzled and without their getting the idea along the way that they see your point when actually they are mistaken. To do that takes great skill. Do you have that skill? I certainly could not undertake to teach it to you here. You may develop it; but if you are going to develop it, certainly the beginning of the development will be getting the idea of *point* deeply and clearly fixed in your mind. And the best way I know to do that is to get lots of practice in writing themes based on the method in this book.

You know, it may be good to point out to both students and instructors that many objections are raised by students not out of any real doubt, but simply as a way of expressing something that stands between them and a clear understanding of what is being taught. But other objections seem to arise out of some students' unconscious feeling that they have a wealth of writing experience behind them, that they have well-developed talents, or that they are too superior to have to follow the rules given to the common herd.

No, the young girl taking her first violin lesson and concert violinists have to hold the violin bow in the same way (and incidentally, it is not the way that "common sense would tell anybody" it ought to be held; it is the way that centuries of experience have shown to be most effective). The only difference is that concert violinists will hold it in the correct way *better* than the young beginner; they will not attempt to be *different* or feel freed from the rules given to the young girl.

Of course an instructor should not take such objectors at their own evaluation. If they prove their competency in their first theme (meaning that, one way or another, they follow the six Steps), well and good. Personally, in my experience with students—excellent, fair, and indifferent—at the colleges and universities where I have taught, I have yet to meet a student whose first theme is at once well-unified (Steps 1, 2, and 3), thoroughly coherent (Steps 5 and 6), and in its content satisfactorily specific, concrete, and detailed (Step 4). Vigorous, graceful expression, embodying fine intelligence and sensitivity, sometimes yes; striking ideas firmly grasped and set before me with talent, yes; but not unity, coherence, and detail.

Introductions and Conclusions

Let's consider a somewhat humbler objection. "Well," asks someone, "shouldn't every theme have an introduction, a body, and a conclusion?" I don't know where this idea arose. It may come from a statement by Aristotle, one of the most brilliant men who ever lived, who in his *Poetics* explained that every tragedy—*not* theme, notice—has to have a beginning, a middle, and an end—*not*, notice, an introduction, a body, and a conclusion. (Aristotle elsewhere says that orators often insist on having an introduction; but he indicates that they ought not to have one.)

Perhaps, though, this idea of introduction, body, and conclusion came from observation of professional writers who in their first paragraph indicate how what they are reporting or conjecturing fits into the general body of knowledge or theory in their field. Or it may come from observation of writers in popular magazines, who, to help sell their articles, attract fickle readers with some startling or provocative idea at the beginning in hopes that they will read on into an article about coal mining or oyster fishing—subjects in which those readers are not at first likely to be interested.

In any case, the general answer is *no*: a theme need not, and ordinarily should not, have an introduction and a conclusion. Why not? The correct answer is, "Why should it?" If an introduction is necessary, then of course have one. But do not have an introduction just for the sake of having an introduction, any more than you would flap your arms up and down three times before putting on your coat—it's pointless. Of course, if you must give your qualifications ("I worked one summer in a gold mine") if the reader is to accept you as knowledgeable and your material as authentic, or if there is some term or concept you must explain before you begin—if, in a word, you have some real need for an introduction, have one, of course. But be sure it is a need and not just "a good idea" or "a way to have a clever beginning." And make it just as brief as you can.

In fact, I find one of the main troubles with themes consisting of an introduction, a body, and a conclusion is that the introduction and conclusion are often far out of proportion to the body of the theme. A not overlong essay or article—say 2,500 words—that you have read and admired in a book of essays or in a magazine may have up to 50 words of introduction and 50 words of conclusion; that is not disproportionate. But if you keep the same proportion, your theme of 500 words can have only 10 words of introduction and 10 of conclusion (since 500 is one-fifth of 2500, and one-fifth of 50 is 10). So, if you must have an introduction, the nearer it is kept to, say, a sentence of 10 words, the better.

I personally have a special objection to introductions. Too often they lead me to believe that I am going to read about Point A; only later do they reveal that Point A has been only introductory (I'd call it by a different name—*confusing*) and that I'm really to read for Point B. At the very least, I believe, I should be *warned* that what I'm reading first is only introductory. Better yet, let the writer work any introductory material (if it really belongs) into its proper subordinate place within an article, so that the article can begin with its real point.

Short Rounding-Off Sentence

Your theme, if it is under a thousand words, does not need a conclusion, certainly not a summary of what you've just said. Look at it this way: your theme is perhaps as long as a page in a book. Now would you expect to find a summary at the bottom of every page in a book?

Yet at the same time I must emphasize that your theme does need a short rounding-off sentence. This is a real need, because without such a sentence the last thing a reader reads is a mere detail of the last paragraph. The reader is therefore bound at least to feel, perhaps in fact think, that you left off before you came to the end. At least psychologically, then, a theme needs a last sentence, which can be an echo of sentence X, or some short sentence in which you manage to drive the point of the theme home. I'm sorry that I can't give you a better recipe than that; but I can point again to the rounding-off sentence at the end of the anonymous theme on "A student must have a regular schedule of study" (see page 63).

Very well, then. Do have a *short* rounding-off sentence. And do have an introduction, as brief as possible, if you can't avoid having one. At the same time realize that, in general, the very best introduction you can have is to tell the reader precisely what your theme is about—in other words, sentence X. Sentence X will lead the reader right into the theme with no foot scraping, pushing, registering, ticket punching, or price of admission.

Step 1 Yet Again

Another question that arises in connection with Step 1 is, "Does what we call sentence X have to be a sentence?"

Yes, it does. Early in your education, perhaps as early as first grade, you were taught that a sentence expresses a complete thought. What does that mean? It means that a sentence *makes a point*—that it has not only a topic (the subject), but something to say about that topic (the predicate). Turn that rule around and you get a truth you may never have thought of before. For if a sentence expresses a complete thought (makes a point), anything less than a sentence is something less than a complete thought—it is pointless. And it presents your reader with the same problem as my pointless visit to the Applied Arts building at the start of this chapter.

Thus "Coal is useful," since it is a sentence, makes a clear point. But *coal* by itself, which is not a sentence, leaves the reader baffled. That is, *coal* by itself (apart from designating the substance coal) gives no indication to the reader of what you mean by using it. In other words, it doesn't make a point.

If you're inclined to doubt this, just imagine that someone sends you a letter containing the single word *coal* ("Dear Harriet: Coal. Sincerely yours, Jennifer Harvey.") All right. What does your friend Jennifer mean? What is her *point*? There *is* no meaning or point to her letter. (You might guess that she means "Send coal," but you'd have no way of knowing whether you'd guessed correctly.) Even if she adds words (short of writing a sentence) and says "Black coal in Colorado mines," she still has not reached the place where she has made a definite point. In contrast, if she writes and tells you "Coal is useful," you may wonder why she has sent you the message, but at least it *is* a message; you *understand* what she has written; she has conveyed her meaning; she has made a point—mystifying though that point may be.

Very well. We have already discussed the idea that every theme must have a point. We express our point in sentence X. And, as we have just seen, nothing short of a sentence can express a point. Sentence X, therefore, *must* be a sentence. And, of course, if it is to supply our whole theme with a point, we must use it *as a sentence*. If sentences 1, 2, or 3 could be about just something *in* sentence X—about just coal, for example—then there would have been no need for us to make sentence X a *sentence*. *Coal* would have been enough.

But that is not all. Since sentence X makes a point, it determines a way, or certain ways, that the rest of the theme has to go. We can therefore say of a *sentence* that it has a marvelous organizing power that nothing else but a single short sentence has.

Furthermore, you will find that the single short sentence has remarkable *generating* power. If I propose as a sentence X "High school prepares a student for college," you are forced to think of three or more ways in which high school prepares for college for your sentences 1, 2, and 3. Then when you have those—the topic sentences—you are forced to think of details, of specific, concrete material, of examples, to make your point real and convincing. Thus the original short sentence *generates* your whole theme.

You will find that with a little effort you will think of sentences 1, 2, and 3— your topic sentences—rather naturally; and moreover, you will recognize them as right for your purpose when you think of them. In contrast, if you tried to write just about high school, a number of random, perhaps vague and incomplete thoughts would come to your mind, none seeming better to you than any other, none particularly demanding either to be written down or to be left out. That is because a mere term, like *high school*, gives the mind no direction, whereas a sentence points it almost at once in one or another very definite direction. In view of all this, I think we can honestly say that a theme that begins with—and sticks to—a sentence X practically writes itself.

The "Should" Sentence X

In addition to proposing all this theory, and before giving you your next assignment, I have another practical point to give you—and argue for—regarding your sentence X. It is this: sentence X not only must be a declarative sentence (not a question or a command), but for your purposes here it must also tell us what *is*, not what should be. For instance, it must be "Coal is useful" or "High school prepares a student for college" or "Each ingredient of an alloy contributes a necessary quality," not "High school attendance rules should be less strict" or "Newspapers should be made more attractive to teen-agers."

Why do I say that? True, the *should* variety of sentence X, which produces what we might call secular sermons, has resulted in some celebrated essays. If you want to, you may as well try to write some—on your own time. But writing that kind of thing is not the training you need at this stage in your career. For it is too often based on *theory*; and you must come to see that the most valuable thing you will have to offer is not the theories you can think up, but your own experiences, limited though they may be, and the facts that you have observed, few though they too may be. On those grounds, a professor I know once said, "If students want to write on juvenile delinquency, have them write instead on a juvenile delinquent they know." So I suppose that if a student wants to write on American newspapers, we might suggest something like the reporting of crimes on the first page of yesterday's *People's Tribune*—something obviously within that student's experience.

You are right if you say that theories have value. But theories that are proved valid by experiments nearly always come from those best acquainted with the facts; for instance, valuable inventions in electronics can be expected only from those who work daily with electronics—and the theories on which they are based are always then subject, of course, to verification.

It is not young people alone who are thoughtlessly enamored of theories. I'll tell you an illustrative story. In the days when I was registered as a private investigator, I used to conduct what are called insurance inspections for the large American life and casualty insurance companies. Often the people I called on as an inspector would tell me at once, "This is not the way the insurance company ought to do this at all; they ought to—" and then they would give me a theory, manufactured on the spur of the moment, and clearly seen by them as right. They never stopped to think that the insurance companies had developed their method of inspection through a fifty-year process of trial and error and knew very well what kind of inspection would produce the results they had practical need of in their business.

Do you want an example of that practical knowledge, just for fun? What facts do you think an insurance inspector should be most interested in when inspecting the premises of a small business that is applying for fire insurance? Things like heat conduits too near the wall, exposed wiring, employees who dump ashtrays into wastebaskets, or inflammables stored too near the heat? No. The first question in the fire insurance inspection of a small business is, "Did this business follow another?" And the second is, "If so, why did the other go out of business?" Only at the end of the inspection is there the blanket question, "Are there any obvious fire hazards?"

Think it over carefully and you will see the point. Think about it at length and you will come to a good understanding of the value of theories contrasted with the value of experience.

Before concluding this section, let me give you a related warning: do not write themes that attempt to describe the bad state our society is in, what with catastrophic drug addiction, widespread alcoholism, rebellion of youth, decay of morals, inflation, pollution of the environment, and the threat of fascism or communism. Many uninformed books and articles have been written about all this; do not add to them. Moreover, that kind of subject is too vast to allow you to get down to cases, to really specific details. And of course, such a theme really rests too much on theory. (If, say, you live on Lake Erie and have personally observed its deterioration, go ahead, of course, and write on that deterioration; or if you know one rebellious youth, go ahead and write what you know about that youth's rebellion.)

Perhaps, to put the matter in a nutshell, I might say: do not write sermons. Now sermons, as I have already said, are a quite respectable form of composition, and some quite respectable people have written them. But writing sermons is not the kind of practice you need at this point. And what I have mostly in mind are what may be called secular sermons: "People should drive carefully" or "We ought to keep our yards clean"—the sort of thing, in a word, that you often see in the Letters to the Editor column in the newspapers you read.

Finally, regarding the *should* form of sentence X, "It's a lot easier," as a student once remarked to me, "to tell what should be than to tell what actually is." It is in the latter—telling what is—therefore, that you need training. And that training is training, mind you, for the kind of writing that your career in school and after school will demand of you.

Before giving you your assignment, let me give you the solution to what may still be a puzzle in your mind—the method of inspection of small businesses for fire insurance. Here is the way the insurance companies' thinking goes. If the business (say a coffee shop) followed another, and if the former proprietor went out of business because he wasn't making a go of it, there is a question whether the new proprietor will make a go of it. If she doesn't make a go of it either, she may not care very much whether she has a fire or not—in fact, a fire may be the most profitable way to liquidate her bad business investment.

But if the former proprietor was doing well and sold his coffee shop only to go into a larger one elsewhere, then the new proprietor may well succeed too. And if she is successful, she won't want a fire. A fire would keep her from her daily profits until she could rebuild, and it would lose her customers, who would meanwhile form the habit of going elsewhere. Moreover, though her insurance would pay for some of the fire damage, it would not pay for all of it.

So since a fire would hurt the proprietor severely in the pocketbook (and she knows it), she would have a sharper eye for fire hazards than most insurance inspectors could have. In the person of this proprietor, the insurance company would have a representative (so to speak) on the premises every day, a person who would be as much interested as the insurance company in preventing a fire. All of this is not an opinion that insurance people dreamed up; it is the fruit of long experience.

I give this explanation at length because I deem it worthwhile to emphasize to young people that "what you'd think" an insurance inspector would ask and do is often very different from what long experience shows the inspector *must* ask and do. "What you'd think," even though common sense seems to be on its side, is what we call an opinion, and it's worthless without experience or experiment to back it up. Young people, because they haven't had much experience, sometimes fall back on opinions or theories. All right, that's natural. But don't take your opinions too seriously. Instead, take what *experience* you have and what *facts* you know and use them as the basis for your writing. The result may not be as important-sounding as you'd like it to be, but it will win you the respect of mature readers.

ASSIGNMENT

Carefully make up a sentence X for yourself, and keeping in mind the requirements of Steps 2, 3, and 4, write a theme on it. Choose as a subject something you might have to write about in one of your other classes. Don't forget to add a short rounding-off sentence at the end of your theme.

When you finish, you will find the checklist in Appendix II useful in making sure your theme does everything it should. (Of course, skip over the references to Steps 5 and 6 in that checklist; we will come to them later.)

B. THE READING YOU DO

The reading you do in your daily life can be of help in your writing. In fact, reading is obviously your contact with the *written* language. In contrast, what you hear—the *spoken* language—is different in several ways. It uses contractions (*isn't, wouldn't*), whereas in fairly formal writing—such as you are encouraged to imitate—you find the longer forms (*is not, would not*). It uses *can* for *may* ("You can sit down now"). It uses *going to* instead of *will* ("The mayor is going to hold a press conference"), *get* for *be* in the passive ("Lars got stung by a wasp and got taken to the emergency room" instead of "*was* stung" and "*was* taken"). It connects *everyone* with *they* ("Everyone on the football team did their best"), while formal written English prefers the singular *he* or *she* ("did *his* best"). And spoken English prefers "Who are you going with?" to "With whom are you going?"

Note that this book, to serve its particular purpose, is written largely in the *spoken*, not the written, language. For instance, it contains many contractions, and its vocabulary is fairly simple. But let me remind you not to take this book as a model. In fact, it is—as I told you at the beginning—not so much a book as it is a conversation.

Written language of the sort that you, as an educated person, will encounter in later life has a much wider vocabulary. If you haven't read much, you'll have to face the fact that you'll need to use the dictionary frequently. (And obviously, when you write, you can't use words you don't know.)

What is most important in connection with our work here is that something written—something printed—has an *orderliness* that you will usually not find in conversation. It has paragraphs, as conversation often has not; it has details and examples that conversation often lacks; and it has a far higher degree of connectedness than conversation.

Yet at the same time, there the difficulty begins. Not everything you read is a theme, even a long theme; so of course not everything you read follows all the rules that govern themes. For example, in novels, stories, plays, and most poems, you will look in vain for a sentence X. It's there all right, but it is seldom *expressed*. A friend of mine wrote a whole novel on the sentence X "Power corrupts"; but nowhere in the novel did he actually *say* "Power corrupts."

Moreover, in the paragraphs—often not so much paragraphs as convenient divisions—of a novel, a story, or a play, you will usually *not* find topic sentences followed by specific development. In the description of a place, in a short summary of happenings that took place over a long period of time, yes, sometimes; but in paragraphs detailing action as it takes place, hardly ever.

I want to emphasize this because I find that students entering college from high school have often read a good many novels, short stories, and plays, but they have read and studied little if any nonfiction—that is, the kind of writing that they themselves have to do in themes. As a result, they are almost alienated from the complex logical structure required in themes—a familiarity with which is also required, it is important to note, in the successful *reading* of much nonfiction. (Some students are alienated from almost any reading that does not have an immediate entertainment value; with that attitude, the kind of attention span required to follow a line of reasoning does not seem possible.)

Articles of Information

If students *have* read nonfiction, it has most likely been books and articles of *information*. And here I must point out the difference between an article of information and a theme by going back to Steps 1 and 2, where I indicated that a theme cannot be based on a topic, but must be based on a sentence, the whole of which the rest of the theme is about. If the topic of our original example is coal, the sentence about the topic perhaps is "Coal is useful."

Obviously, though, somebody has to be able to write *some* kind of composition on the bare topic of coal. Suppose, for instance, that a group of editors are preparing an encyclopedia for a publisher. Now naturally, one of the articles will have to be "Coal," because some users of the encyclopedia will want to look that up. So the editors search for someone who knows enough about coal to write an article about it.

Notice that you and I don't know enough about coal to write an article about it. And it's not only that we don't know enough facts; we are also ignorant of what aspects of coal can and ought to be treated. Nor do we know how much space, proportionately, will be most usefully devoted to each different aspect.

So perhaps the editors find a mining engineer (who may in turn consult a chemist, a sales manager, and other people in a mining company) who is able to write an article about coal. Then, depending on the size of the encyclopedia (which will govern, in turn, the size of the article), this writer may, I should guess (I am not going to peek, but you can), tell us how coal got its name and then give us the physical and chemical constitution of coal. This will naturally require her (suppose it's *her*, in this case) to distinguish among the kinds of coal broadly speaking; and since the kinds—as well as the coal itself—must have been produced by certain causes, she may then describe the forces and activities that led to the formation of coal.

Since, as the engineer will have explained, the forces that shaped the coal did not operate everywhere, she may move next to the distribution of coal and of its various kinds throughout the world (slate in one area, peat in another), with more particular information on its distribution in the country or countries the encyclopedia is written to serve; as well as the distribution of coal in the principal coal-producing countries.

I can see that after that she might have a choice of directions in which to go. Her choice might be to say, in effect, "Here you have different kinds of coal at various depths in various soils in all these different places. Now the question is, How do you get it out?" So she tells us about coal mining, perhaps giving us a history of it with concentration on the present time, and describing the kinds of mining, the techniques used, and so on.

Next the writer may ask herself, "But why go to the trouble of getting it out?" So what she might write next is a short history of the use of coal, with concentration again on the present time. (This would include chemical use of coal tar in producing, among other things, dyes, medicines, and perfumes.) At this point in her article you might find, as part of her account, a sentence X like "Coal may be used more and more," instancing, for example, California's rejection of the projected Sun Desert nuclear power plant as unsafe and the proposal of coal fuel instead to generate electric power needed by Southern California; planned pipelines to transship slurry (powdered coal mixed with water); suggested exploitation of vast coal fields discovered in the mountain states; and certain industrial reconversions from oil and gas to coal. In fact, you might find several short themes, based on several X sentences, along the way.

But my point—a very important point—is that for the most part the writer's selection and arrangement of material was *not* dictated by a simple sentence X and its sentences 1, 2, and 3, each extended with illustrative details. It was dictated by the nature of the thing itself—the topic she was writing about—coal. For if we turned to the article on tuberculosis in the same encyclopedia, we would find different kinds of aspects selected for discussion and a different method of arrangement.

True, in most articles of information we would find some or all of the following, in some form or other: definition; description; cause; effect; distribution; parts; operation; use; history; current status; opposing theories; and economic, legal, political, and social significance.

If this were a book that undertook to teach you how to write an article of information, it might develop the following recipe: use one sentence X or more in your article *if you can*; use topic sentences for paragraphs wherever possible;

always *go into detail* where space permits, especially where your readers will wonder about the details ("Coal is required in the manufacture of steel"—why? how?). For the rest, try to answer questions that will occur to most readers regarding the topic.

Try to be logical in your development, putting like things together, putting first things first, and connecting things where you can. Do not leave out essential steps in a process. In description, go from left to right, from top to bottom, from foreground to background—use some order that your readers can follow easily. If a time order is involved, go from the beginning straight through to the end; do not jump unnecessarily from 1914 back to 1900, then forward to 1920. Throughout, keep your readers in mind and be sure they can follow what you are doing. Always keep them *aware* of what you are doing; for instance, if you have to skip back to 1900, tell them "here we must skip back to 1900."

But this book does not really undertake to teach you how to write an article of information. My underlying purpose here is mainly to warn you that in articles of information you may very well *not* find a sentence X, and that in by no means every paragraph will you find a topic sentence.

Before we go on, let's make this a convenient stopping place and have an assignment—this time a reading, or rather an *investigative* assignment instead of a writing one.

ASSIGNMENT

Go to an encyclopedia—or two or three encyclopedias for comparison— and see how it treats the subjects "Coal," "Tuberculosis," "Platinum," and your choice of one of the following: "Magnetism," "Gypsies," "Jefferson, Thomas," "Furniture," "Dolls," "Mysticism." See what aspects the articles take up, note the use of details, and try to find a topic sentence or two.

C. FINDING THE POINT

You have learned that in an article of information you cannot expect to find a central idea—a sentence X—nor can you expect to find a topic sentence in every paragraph. But when you read articles in which the writer's intention is to make some *point*—articles written the way you write your themes—then an ability to pick out the writer's sentence X and topic sentences is useful and perhaps even necessary.

Why do I say that? Sentence X—in reading usually called the central idea— is, as we have learned, the point of the whole article. But if you can't put your pencil on a sentence in the article and say "This is sentence X—this is the central idea," then you can't show yourself that you really get the point of the article. You may know the meaning of every word; you may have picked up several pieces of information; but if you can't say what the point of the article is, you haven't really read it successfully, have you?

Similarly, you must be able to tell what is the topic sentence of each paragraph (if it *is* a paragraph, not just a piece of writing broken off by indentation from another paragraph). Occasionally, I'm afraid, some writers of even the kind of article we are talking about try to get by without topic sentences—something you must never do! In that case, you must make up the topic sentence you would have written had you written the paragraph. It is always the point that the rest of the paragraph is adding up to. For instance:

> A pair of trousers, half inside-out, lay across the unmade bed, at the head of which one of the rain-soaked window draperies was tied back with a purple necktie. Paperback books were scattered in profusion on the dusty carpet beside the bed, some of them open and face down on the floor. The closet door, half closed. . . .

Can you state as briefly and simply as possible what point is being made in the paragraph you've just read—what all the details are adding up to? It's "The room was disorderly," isn't it? (Or the same idea in whatever words you want to put it.)

If you're deeply interested in writing, read some articles, pick out the topic sentence of each paragraph, and show how each topic sentence is connected somehow to the sentence X—the central idea—of each article. Be very patient with yourself as you do this. First of all, it takes practice—practice that will repay you as much as, or more than, any other single experience in your whole education. Second, it's not always easy; even highly experienced people have difficulty with it at times. Yet those people—and you—succeed with it not so much by having superior intelligence, but by taking pains—by rereading, re-reading again, and testing and weighing each decision. Third, it's sometimes not easy because the *writer* did a poor job of making sure you would see the central idea of the article and the point of each paragraph.

Because of these difficulties, it will be useful for you to have an instructor help you. As you read an essay, for example, the instructor's guidance may go something like this:

> You say you think the central idea of this essay is in the sentence "Most people seem convinced that we will always have war"; you think that the point of the essay is that we will never get rid of war. But if that's so, what about the writer's statements that in the twentieth century, for the first time, some people became convinced that there could be permanent peace; for the first time we witnessed cooperation among nations in humanitarian efforts; for the first time there was a League of Nations that, if it did not prevent war, settled some disputes and therefore prevented some wars, and later a United Nations with the same purpose; for the first time there were some agreements, though impermanent, to reduce armaments; for the first time there was such a thing as a "hot line." You know, one test of a choice of central idea is this: does it cover all the points in the essay?
>
> You may say that what the writer is saying is that the League, the United Nations, disarmament, and international cooperation have all proved too weak, and that thus, despite awakened hopes, we will always have war. Is the writer saying that, or is he saying the reverse: despite the conviction of many people that war is inevitable, despite the failure of hopeful beginnings (they weren't total failures), it is significant that after so many thousands of years of human history we have finally had, in our century, at

least some *idea* that lasting peace is possible, that not just idealists but governments have for the first time made beginnings in the direction of peace?

What is the relationship of the two ideas in the essay—despite hope, failure; or despite failure, hope? Reread the essay and see what you think. Perhaps you will find that in the first part of the essay the writer presented the side of the argument opposite his in its strongest form, so that the reader would think there's no disputing it; then only in the second part did he attempt to show the weakness of that side and present his own side. That is a familiar way of arranging an argumentative essay, but it is sometimes confusing to inexperienced readers. (An experienced reader, seeing "*Most people* seemed convinced," would correctly suspect that later the writer was going to give reasons why *he* is convinced of the opposite, or of something different.) See whether this isn't one of the cases in which a writer, to serve a definite purpose, delayed sentence X until later in the theme.

ASSIGNMENT

In a library, find a collection of modern articles intended for students. (Your instructor may put some on reserve.) Choose a fairly short article that seems simple and in which you feel you can find the sentence X—the central idea—and the topic sentences of the paragraphs. Reread the article as many times as necessary for you to convince yourself that you *have* found a sentence that you can point to (not just an idea or a summary in your mind) that contains the central idea. You will usually—though not always, as we have seen—find the right one either at or near the beginning of the article.

Find also some other sentences that a hasty reader might mistake for the central idea, and prove to yourself that none of them is the central idea.

Next, reread all we have said in this chapter about topic sentences, and then try to identify the topic sentence of each paragraph in the article you've chosen. Do you have to supply any that the writer didn't supply? Are you sure you have to supply one everywhere you think you do? The topic sentence may contain more information than is needed in a sentence 1, 2, or 3. But it *will* contain the general idea that the rest of the sentences in the paragraph are meant to illustrate, define, explain, give the causes or effects or parts of, prove, perhaps even dispute, or supply facts or arguments or statistics for.

Perhaps you are in a class that is using a book of essays or articles for reading practice along with this book. In that case, perhaps the instructor will select one article for the whole class to use for this assignment. Then students can compare findings in the following class session.

D. BEING INTERESTING AND IMPRESSIVE

In this section I will take up a matter that is related to the whole writing process and is the subject, I find, of vast misunderstanding among students. It is a matter to which, experience shows, a good deal of time and space should be devoted—namely, the obligation most students feel to be interesting and impressive in their themes.

As you gather from what has gone before, someone writes a theme in order to *explain* something to somebody. I may write an article of information to give somebody information, with perhaps some explanation along the way. For example, I tell readers that coal has uses other than fuel and then proceed to show them that—or why or how—coal has uses other than fuel. Or I say that power corrupts, and backing up my assertion with facts from past and current history, I explain why that is so and what the consequences are. Or in an article of information about coal, I give readers information about all the important aspects of that subject. Along the way I assert, for instance, that coal was produced when buried plants were subject, away from air, to the hot and heavy pressure of the earth above them, and I might then treat that assertion as a kind of sentence X and proceed with a more detailed explanation.

So it is in your own experience. Your history teacher wants to know whether you understand the causes of the Reformation; you show that you do by explaining them in your own words. Or your supervisor wants to know what you think of putting a different amount of tin in a certain alloy; you tell the supervisor what you think and explain why you think so. Or you try in a bulletin to make crystal clear to a group of employees what effect a change in the tax rate will have on the amount of their take-home pay, and why.

These examples bring us to my point about being interesting and impressive. For if we agree that to explain or inform, or both, is the purpose of our composition, then we must agree that it is not our purpose to be interesting or impressive.

Being Interesting

Let's take interest first and spend a good deal of time on it. What I have just said shocks some students. They—evidently like many other students—have it in the back of their heads that they are writing "to be interesting," or to entertain.

In such cases I sometimes wonder whether those students' former teachers have not had it in the back of their heads that their students were all going to be writing for professional publication. So, assuming that an editor looks for material that will interest the greatest possible number of readers, those teachers felt it their duty to teach their students to be interesting—by which they sometimes meant, I'm sure, entertaining.

In fact, some instructors unconsciously assume that all their students are going to be writing *fiction*! For instance, some time ago I became acquainted with an English composition textbook that was advertised as practical. It did indeed have much valuable material, not available elsewhere so far as I know, especially for helping students to acquire a more adult style. But the more I advanced in it, the more I found by the author's selection of examples and choice of technique that he assumed that students using his book—and it was in widespread use—were going to be short-story writers!

Now a little conscious reflection will show that not one person in a thousand (by my calculations) becomes a published writer. And most of even that tenth of a percent are under no compulsion to be entertaining in the work they do; they write explanatory and informative material, whose readers would regard any substantial effort to be entertaining as ridiculous. Still fewer people publish fiction.

In short, students should be prepared for the kind of writing they are going to have to do. Because that is not fiction, nor entertainment of any kind, it has a purpose other than to be interesting. Students, therefore, should realize that they are practicing to present explanations and information to the history professor who is examining them for their understanding of the causes of the Reformation, to the supervisor who wants an opinion about a new alloy, or to the employees who want to understand a change in payroll deductions. None of these people wants "to be interested"—rather, *they are interested* in getting from the writer a clear understanding of something. You will be writing for readers who *have* to, or already *want* to, get your explanation.

Sometimes instructors, who have to spend a lot of time reading themes, complain that they want interesting ideas from their students, instead of theme after theme on pets, sports, cars, bicycles, and pollution. Now I think we will all agree that students, when given a free choice of theme subjects, should move progressively away from topics that would interest only junior high school students. "My Cat," "My Dog," or "Our Trip to Yellowstone" will usually provide little preparation for the kind of writing students will have to do later. Students who choose such subjects do not have the future in mind; they are concerned only with turning in an assignment.

At the same time, however, we cannot expect most students to be Barbara Tuchmans, Loren Eiseleys, Jacques Barzuns, or Joan Didions. Students can write only about what they know and understand. Instructors cannot expect them to write with the experience of someone who has been a newspaper columnist or a distinguished professor for twenty or thirty years. A decently unified, detailed, coherent, and clear My Cat theme is (though quite modest) a definite accomplishment—a far more promising performance than an incoherent, unsupported, poorly informed theme on communism or democracy.

Students ought to be encouraged—and ought to encourage themselves—to write, for example, on some lesson they have mastered in some other subject they are taking or have taken, or if they are employed, on some serious aspect of the work they do (so long as they do not write a process theme). Instructors must be prepared to read themes on plant taxonomy, carburetors, business cycles, tire trade-ins, abnormal brain waves, crop rotation, electrical circuits, and tariffs, whether they are interested in those subjects or not. For it is not their purpose, in reading themes, to be entertained. Rather, they must be interested in whether or not students are correctly applying the principles of composition to their subject matter, whatever it is, and in whether students are progressing in applying those principles. Of course, instructors may need to point out to students that they have chosen a subject which will not work well in a theme—either because it is already obvious ("Basketball is a team sport") or because it is beyond the present ability of the writers to find facts to develop it. But those instructors who can see only subject matter in themes are in the wrong business—and they usually know it.

But students will probably still want to write on something "interesting." Once, when I assigned "College is different from high school" as a sentence X, one of the ablest writers I have ever taught complained, "Must we write on something so dull?" Well, what is *dull*? A high school teacher who wants to teach in college is asked by a college administrator in an interview, "How do you see the difference between college and high school?" Then the "dull" subject becomes intensely interesting (not entertaining, mind you), for whether or not the applicant is hired just may depend on the answer. In fact, students who have entered college or plan to go to college after finishing high school should be thoroughly interested in (not entertained by) that same subject, because their success will depend partly on their understanding of it.

Some of this section is directed to your instructor as much as to you. You can guess that from the language used, can't you? That's true of the following paragraph. But you read it too, because it's no harder reading than much of what you have to study in your other classes.

No, we make a mistake in being interested in the interesting. On the one hand, we can get students so highly excited about something that they will be eager to write about it. But their eagerness will not automatically—or miraculously—teach them unity, coherence, and the habit of adequate support, for those things must be taught slowly, patiently, and systematically; and students will not be burning with desire to learn them. So while students may be eager to write on what they are excited about, I am interested in seeing what they do when they write not on some subject of intense interest to them, but on one with which, simply by being orderly and detailed, they generate moderate interest—for themselves and others—in what may seem to them ordinary or dull. For since most of the writing they will have to do in life will be on quite unexciting, in fact unpromising subjects, it is that kind of writing they must show themselves willing and able to succeed at.

Your job of writing about a subject you aren't passionately interested in will be easier if you remember that interest is in the eye of the beholder. There are really no "boring" subjects. When you say something is boring, you refer to *your* lack of interest in it, not to its lack of interesting qualities. You may know nothing about orchids, Brahms' Quintet No. 2, or glassblowing, and may therefore be tempted to say you are bored by them. Actually most people are not bored by what they understand. Understanding is a result of observing and assimilating details. The details and examples you learned to add in Step 4 will help you become interested in your subject; likewise your placement of them in a theme will generate interest in your reader. Have you ever observed a baby exploring his environment? Everything fascinates him. As a writer, you would do well to recapture this natural curiosity. I'm not suggesting that every subject you'll have to write about will fascinate you, but rather that you approach these topics with an open mind. Every subject is intrinsically interesting if you think about it intelligently, observe details about it, and connect it to the rest of your world. As long as you're going to work on the topic, you might as well use the opportunity to expand your interests.

But back to *being* interesting in your themes. If you the student were born to have an interesting way of putting things, good! If you were born to be charming, then charm will flow into everything you write. But we teachers cannot teach you those personal qualities. If we were to try, what we would produce is a phoniness that you yourself—not to mention others—would soon grow tired of.

What then? If you don't possess those personal qualities—any more, perhaps, than you possess naturally curly hair or perfect teeth—are you doomed? No! Such qualities as charm and wit should be highly valued, but they must not be overvalued. In fact, other qualities, like honesty, earnestness, diligence, and patience, can be acquired by anybody; when you practice them, they too will flow into everything you write. And to you personally, I'm willing to bet, those other qualities will in the long run prove more important than inborn charm and wit.

Now before I move on to other things, I want to tell you an anecdote from my own experience, one that has to do with interest and that will leave you with another puzzle to work on.

Once I taught a graduate class in advertising. And though that was years ago, I still remember some of the well-known principles of advertising that made up my course. One of those principles we might approach in the following way. Say you're leafing through the pages of a magazine in a barbershop or beauty parlor or in your dentist's waiting room. Suddenly you stop because a particular advertisement catches your attention. Whether it's the picture in the ad or some caption or sentence in large type, it has captured your interest. Hoping that you will not be called for your turn in the chair just this minute, you read on down the page until you discover that it is an advertisement for lawn mowers. You may not be in the market for a lawn mower, either because the one at home is giving good service or because you live in an apartment and aren't responsible for cutting grass. So naturally, after a final glance at whatever it was about the advertisement that drew your attention, you turn the page, reflecting, perhaps, that the advertisement was a good, attention-getting ad that would stop anybody leafing quickly through the magazine.

Now advertising is—or should be—a very practical thing. An advertisement of the kind that stopped you should exist, and be paid for, for just one purpose: to sell merchandise (in this case, lawn mowers). So well do shrewd people concerned with advertising realize this that they have devised ways of measuring the actual selling power of any advertisement. One way they do it is to run a certain advertisement (say the one you looked at) in an edition of a magazine sold in New England but not in the Midwest, or vice versa. Then, making allowances for several variables like weather, they find out how much higher (if at all) their sales were during the following week in the region where the advertisement was run, as compared to sales in the region where it was not run. Then they try another advertisement and see how much more or less effective it proves in selling their lawn mowers.

Mind you, it is not in people's reading their advertisement that they are ultimately interested. Does the reader then buy a lawn mower? is the question they're concerned with. In your case, they simply provided reading matter—at considerable expense to themselves—while you waited for the dentist, and they got no return, except perhaps your unvoiced thanks.

Now here is the curious fact: advertisers who have measured the selling power of their advertisements have discovered that those advertisements that will "stop anybody"—as the lawn mower advertisement did you—sell *less* merchandise than advertisements that attract and are read by only those people who are in the market for the product advertised. Now why should that be? There's a puzzle for you to work on.

Meanwhile, however, learn a lesson from the advertising people: when you write a theme, assume that the person or persons for whom you are writing are already interested in the subject. Ignore other people—there's not much chance of your interesting them for more than a minute or two. And what's the point? If people are not interested in coal, why bother them with coal? About all you'll end up doing is annoying them; they don't want to know what you have to say about coal and are impatient with your bright beginning and the gimmicks you have dragged in to make your paper "interesting."

Remember the encyclopedia articles? Did they employ cheap devices to get readers to read about subjects in which they had no interest—coal, tuberculosis, or whatever? No, the writers of the articles assumed that a reader who would look up a subject would want or need to read about it, and they got down to the business of making it as clear as they could. Not "When you see a freight train passing and notice among the cars those open ones loaded with coal, do you ever stop to think. . . ."

I suspect the notion that in writing a theme you have to be interesting at all costs may be partly the result of students' having to read—or listen to their instructors read—their themes to their classmates. This public reading of themes has great advantages, but after many years I have decided (though I may be wrong) that it has, in the long run, greater disadvantages. Among the immediate disadvantages of public reading is that it may popularize the notion that how a writer's classmates react to a theme is the measure of its worth. That notion naturally makes attention-getting gimmicks and sophomoric humor seem desirable, with the result that many young writers neglect their proper purpose—explaining something—and seek instead to be entertaining. Of course, if class discussion of a paper centers on clarity of point, clarity of connection, and clarity through the use of concrete detail, then that may be another matter.

Practically, therefore, what do you as a student do? Seek to amuse the other students? That might be good practice if you plan a career as a gag writer for television comedians. Living as you do in a world whose heroes and heroines are entertainers—"stars," as they are called—maybe without really thinking about it you have it in the back of your mind that you too are called on to be an entertainer. No—no more than you are called on to pull your schoolmates' teeth, ticket them for overtime parking, wash their shirts, or repair their shoes. Lay down this unnecessary burden of being their—or anybody's—entertainer, of being "interesting."

Instead, in writing a theme seek to do a solid, sober, serious piece of work. That will gain you the quiet respect of your real friends in place of the noisy applause of those who would like your free services as a clown.

ASSIGNMENT

Choose some subject that interests *you*, but that does not seem to have much interest for most people you know. It may be a hobby, a school subject, a form of recreation—anything. You may even, for this particular assignment, choose a topic that would interest only a junior high school student. Write a sentence X about it (decide carefully what that sentence should be), then sentences 1, 2, and 3 as usual, and then finally a theme.

Pretend that your reader *is* interested in your explanation. Do not be apologetic. Do not *try* to be interesting. Above all, *avoid all humor*. Do a serious piece of work. Do not suppress, of course, aspects of the subject that seem interesting to you; but do not try to coax imaginary readers to be interested in them.

E. YOUR READERS

This is a convenient place to take up the idea of *the reader*. After all, the reader is the person whom you might be tempted to interest or to impress. Let's bring this reader out of the shadows and get acquainted with him—or her. The reader appeared several pages back when I remarked that a theme is intended to explain something *to somebody*. That somebody is your reader. If your reader is actually your history professor, a supervisor in your office, or your employee, then, of course, you can write accordingly.

But since you are now writing practice papers with no actual reader but your instructor, you are going to have to *imagine* some particular reader or readers. Of course, you can choose your instructor as the person for whom you are writing the theme. That's what most students do, and it isn't a bad idea, because the instructor is pretty much like most people for whom you'll be writing something outside your English class or outside college.

Still, that may not be enough. What I suggest that you do, therefore, is select some real person whom you know, then imagine that you're writing your theme to make something clear to that person. This real person may be a boy or girl younger than yourself, or a relative who is older than you are, or some other adult. This person should *not*, however, be a classmate—too much temptation to be "interesting" or overfamiliar there!—unless the classmate is someone you're used to doing serious study with and explaining things to. Keep this person in mind in every line you write. Do not get so intent on your subject matter that you forget who your reader is.

Now the purpose of your doing this is twofold: first, it keeps before you the general purpose of all themes—namely, to explain something clearly to *somebody*. Let me illustrate that point. If I want to discuss with a linguist why in English we say "he *was*" but "they *were*," I might simply talk to him of rhotacism, the change from an intervocalic *s* (Proto-Germanic *z*) to *r* as a result of the Germanic stress assimilation known as Verner's Law (or, more accurately, Verner's phenomenon).

If I were explaining the change in verb form to a beginning linguistics student, however, I'd do it somewhat differently. I might say, "Sometime in the history of the forerunners of the English language, people began to pronounce the *s*'s that came between two vowels (including the vowel that is now silent final *e*) as *r*'s. The *s* in *was* had a vowel before it but not after it; so it stayed *s*. But the matching *s* that once was in *were*, since it had a vowel before and after it, became *r*. You get the same thing in 'he *is*' (which still has an *s*) and 'they *are*' (in which the original *s* became an *r*). Why did *were* and *are* have a vowel after them? The vowel was part of a stressed ending which, earlier in history, showed that *were* and *are* were plural."

That is to say, you learn to keep in mind that how you explain something depends on whom you're explaining it to.

Second, keeping a certain reader or readers in mind tends to keep your *tone* constant. You won't speak of an altercation in one line and call it a rumble in the next, or speak of juvenile delinquency in one line and call it "mixed-up kids fouling up" in the next—the kind of change of tone that gives the same unpleasant effect as the sudden jump from bass to soprano we sometimes hear from a boy whose voice is changing.

So to repeat: keep a certain reader in mind as you write.

Being Impressive

While we're talking about readers, the way you explain something to them, and the tone you use with them, perhaps you can see certain difficulties in the simple rule I'm about to give—namely, *do not try to impress the reader*.

Let's take up the difficulties first, then come back to the rule. There are three difficulties: first, I said a short while ago that in talking with a linguist, I'd explain something differently than I'd explain it to a beginning linguistics student; and you noticed that in speaking with the linguist, I used a different vocabulary, including the technical terms *rhotacism*, *intervocalic*, *Germanic stress assimilation*, and *Verner's Law*. But while those words may have impressed you, I did not use them to impress *the linguist*. It's simply as natural for two specialists in linguistics to use the technical terms they're used to calling things by as it is for two carpenters talking together to use words like *joist* and *strut*. The carpenters are not trying to impress each other! That's just the way carpenters talk.

The trouble is, you'll naturally think: "That's the way so-and-so, for whom I'm writing, talks—and, I suppose, writes. He presents difficult ideas and uses big words. So I suppose that's what he wants me to do. Probably nothing else will satisfy him."

No. The sort of person you have in mind (perhaps your instructor) will certainly want you to do your best and to be dignified in your writing. So don't use contractions (like *don't* for *do not*) as I do here. Especially, don't use *any* words that you feel are slang. In other words, doing what your reader expects you to do will probably come down to this rule: *do not offend the reader*. This rule puts to use the general rule of life "Try not to offend anyone on whom your success depends." "Of course—common sense," you say. But how often overlooked!

Otherwise, concentrate on explaining things clearly and forget about big ideas and big words (unless the *assignment* is to use them, of course). Deal only with ideas that are clear to you, and use only words that are natural to you. Otherwise, you won't be impressive. You'll be comic, in a way that you didn't intend. And the person you've tried to impress will be out of patience with you and will reject your work. You will come nearest to satisfying your reader if you do your *honest* best—that is, your very best can only be your attempt to be as clear as possible in language familiar to you. If you try to do *better* than your best, you'll land in the soup.

You do not write a theme in order to use fancy talk. While most students realize this, some of them have still *got* to get it into their heads!

I hope you will not read this as an argument for going through life with a limited vocabulary. Quite the opposite. As your thoughts grow (I hope) in number, kind, and complexity, your vocabulary must grow to match them. Pay close attention to the new words you meet in your reading—but master them before you put them to use in your own writing. And make sure that your reader will understand and appreciate your big new words.

The second difficulty, though, is exactly this: some of what you read, some of the great works of literature that have been admired by generations of readers, are in a sense fancy talk. Or they may seem so to you. Lincoln wrote "fourscore and seven" when he could have written *eighty-seven*, the way he normally would have said it. Now we haven't time here to go into the theory behind this. Put practically, your question is this: "Shouldn't I be imitating those writers?" The answer is: probably not now.

Why? The explanation is that though the language in Lincoln's Gettysburg Address was unusual, *it was not unnatural to him*. Is it natural to you? Because it was natural to him, he knew how far to go without seeming to strain. He knew what *not* to do. And if he correctly chose the solemn *fourscore and seven* instead of *eighty-seven*, he also correctly chose the short and common *met* instead of the fancier words *gathered*, *assembled*, or *congregated*. Can you do that?

Maybe someday you can. The language that is *natural* to you will grow and develop and be enriched as you read more, write more, live more, and grow older. When fancier language becomes *natural* to you, then go ahead and use it (if the readers you have in mind will understand it, of course—otherwise, what's the point?).

But—reaching the third difficulty—you may argue that this development of yours, this growth, must take place, and how is it going to take place if you don't stretch yourself, if you don't strain? Very well. Some people reach a stage at which they become fascinated with words. Good! And just as when a boy reaches an age at which he becomes fascinated with cars, he will not be satisfied until he drives one, whether he has learned to drive or not, so people at this stage with words will not be satisfied until they use them, whether they have a clear idea of what they mean (or any place to go with them) or not.

If you are one of those people, this is a passing stage you are in, and it has good reasons for being ("It has its *raison d'être*," you might say). But it should be quickly followed by a stage in which you're willing to look the words up to see whether they're really the words you want.

Finally, I think we can sum up all we have said about being interesting and being impressive with this rule: *if what you write is a genuine effort to give a clear explanation by being orderly and detailed, it will be both interesting and impressive in just the right way.*

SUMMARY

1. Steps 1, 2, 3, and 4 are not rules that someone has decided on, like the rules of a game. They can't be changed, as in the case of the elimination some years ago of the center jump in basketball. No, they arise out of the very nature of writing, and are as necessary for writing as heat is for cooking, cloth for clothing, fuel for an engine.
2. A short theme should not have an introduction and a conclusion. They would be as much out of proportion as an introduction and a conclusion someone might write for "The Star Spangled Banner."
3. But a short rounding-off sentence is needed at the end of a theme.
4. No one can write a theme on a topic. You must write a *sentence* about a topic, then write the theme strictly on that sentence. Once that sentence is well written, the theme nearly writes itself, because that sentence dictates what must be said.
5. We do not practice writing articles of information in this class, because they require only common sense—and information—not, like themes, instruction in thinking.
6. But an article of information—which is not a theme—can be and often is written on a *topic*. Then the nature of the topic, what must be said about it, and the needs of the reader dictate both the choice and the arrangement of the material. The article must be as complete as necessary; it must also be orderly and clear.
7. Do not hope to find either a sentence X or any topic sentences in all that you read. You will rarely find a sentence X or topic sentences in stories, of course. But when you read, always try to follow any writer's *explanation*.
8. Students' themes should be written on what *is*, not on what should be.
9. Students' themes should not be written on their unsupported opinions, nor on vague notions they have picked up from their reading on "Pollution," "Communism," "The Energy Shortage," "Inflation," or "Capital Punishment." Students should write on what they have observed firsthand, or on what they are learning in an orderly and detailed way in their other classes. Complementarily, students should be encouraged to be gaining knowledge and understanding, not just forming opinions.
10. Always keep in mind your purpose of explaining something to somebody. Make that somebody one real or imagined person. Fit your tone to that person and try not to vary it.
11. Do not attempt to be interesting. (Remember, that is not your *purpose*.) You will not be called on to write for a reader who is not already interested. And what your reader is interested in is a good, clear explanation of something, backed up by real, clear, convincing details and examples.

12. Do not attempt to be impressive. (Again, remember that's not your *purpose*.) You will end up being unintentionally funny. Good, clear explanations with well-chosen details and examples are, themselves, always truly impressive.

13. Do not let your thought be "I must make this artistic," "I must make this beautiful," "I must make this clever or amusing," or "I must make this important-sounding," but "I must make this real, clear, and convincing to a certain reader; and to do that I must follow Steps 1, 2, 3, and 4."

Chapter 7

STEP 4 AGAIN

I'm afraid some of my own students refer to this chapter as "Son of Step 4," or "The Return of Step 4," or "Step 4 Strikes Again." But they're not really surprised that the question should be reopened.

For, on the one hand, you have the author of a fine old textbook saying, "Three-fourths of all good writing consists of details and plenty of them." On the other hand, you have students' mysterious resistance to Step 4, their persistence in being abstract and general, their reluctance to get down to real cases, their hesitation to use examples, their failure to use the most specific term.

My students came face to face with this resistance when their own themes on students' need for regularity in homework came back to them covered with red-inked indications that they had not used Step 4 at all. Then, both they and their instructor were delightedly surprised to find that in their *next* theme they had indeed used Step 4, so well that some of them found it was the first piece of real writing they had ever done in their lives, a theme in which they took amazed pride.

Still, their mysterious *tendency* to be abstract and general remains; it has not been permanently corrected by one lesson, any more than Cindy, forced by her mother to straighten up her room because Aunt Joan is flying in this evening from Atlanta for a visit, becomes forever thereafter an orderly person. So if this chapter could only serve as an effective reminder (oh, how I wish it could!) that for the rest of their lives, in all the themes, class papers, essay examinations, letters, reports, and interoffice memoranda that they write, students must resist their tendency to be abstract and general, and that they must stop, consciously, and force themselves to be concrete and specific—then the reintroduction of Step 4 would serve a wonderfully useful purpose.

While I hope this chapter will serve that purpose, its immediate concern is to cast some light on the mystery of why, when everything they read and admire is concrete and specific, students tend to be abstract and general. You may, if you wish, call it "The Mystery of the Locked Door," and I wonder whether Nancy Drew or the Hardy Boys might not find the key in something I've just said: *they read.*

We all read along at a rapid pace (too rapid, I fear), with no stopping to supply details that the writer has left out. That has been our habit in reading—the habit we have formed of *getting on with it*. We are not aware that the *writer* may have stopped to find the specific, concrete instance ("Steve's green biology notebook"), the example ("for instance, if Professor Ucla says 'media is' instead of 'media are' "), the analogy ("like a clock face if it rotated"), or the details ("the Representative's own aides, the lobbyists, the man with the pleasant little freebies, the constituents hungry for profitable contracts"). Thus, as we read, so we think we can write—*getting on with it*. Carrying our reading habits over into our writing, perhaps even unconsciously thinking that the writer is writing as fast as we are reading, we tend to want to get on with it when we write; we assume that concrete instances and details are automatically going to come to our readers' minds as fast as they are presented to our minds when we are reading. We forget that our own readers read as fast as we do, not stopping to figure out details that we should have figured out and supplied them with. Perhaps we even had such details in our own heads, wrongly assuming that if they were in our heads they would appear automatically in our readers' heads, too, without our putting them down on paper. But, in the case of most of us, who are really nonwriters forced to write—as American government students, later as functionaries in an insurance office or as doctors—our concrete instances, details, and analogies involve deliberate, tedious work that *we*, when we are writing, must do.

Perhaps then the unconscious rejection of Step 4 springs from a suspicion that the rule is going to involve some patient work that human nature would rather shirk. In fact, when a young woman said to me, "Are we to assume that our readers are too stupid to think up their own specific examples?" my answer was "No, but they're too lazy."

Too lazy or too impatient, readers are reading too fast to stop and think up examples for themselves. For instance, if I say "One quality you see in professional workmanship is patterning" and then go on to my connected point "so you, as a writer, should use patterning too," my readers are going right on to my connected point with me. They aren't going to stop to think of the windows in their English classroom all made alike; the buttons on a new cardigan sweater all the same size and the same distance apart; the matching headlights, fenders, and doors on each side of a Stutz Bearcat; and the equal planes on the yellow pencil lying in plain sight on the desk (a desk that has four legs just alike).

No, my readers haven't been trained to read that way. And the unfortunate result is that my point—that patterning is a sign of professional workmanship—makes little impression on them; they aren't struck by it enough to be convinced; in fact, I'm not sure they really understand it. So since *they* are not going to think up the examples, it's up to me, the writer, to do it. It's the writer's business, not the reader's, to be specific, concrete, and detailed and to show connections. In fact, if you ask me, that *is* the writer's business: what the writer's work consists of—and it is work—is showing connections and going into detail.

If you're a doubting Thomas, look into what you read to see whether the rule in Step 4 isn't one that all writers seem to be following. I'm going to refer to some specific examples here; you can look them up—or any others, since in one way or another all writers use Step 4. I'll leave the poets alone; since images of the specific and the concrete are their very bread and butter, you'd just say "Well, of course, poetry. . . ." (It's remarkable, though, how many students in creative writing courses think they are writing poetry when they are writing down *thoughts* instead of things: *sadness* instead of a bent head, a slowly twisted ring, a knotted brow, a sigh, or tears.)

But to go back to prose. Striking examples of the concrete and specific are to be found in Ian Fleming's James Bond novels. They've sold by the million, so perhaps you've read one. Why, by the way, *have* they sold by the million? I can think of a few reasons, but the one that concerns us here is that they contain outstandingly specific material. When Bond lights a cigarette, we are likely to get the brand name of the lighter; if he stops to eat, we get the menu, including the year and name of the wine; when he gets up, we may learn exactly what clothes he puts on, beginning with underwear. If Bond is near a woman (as he sometimes is), we often learn the brand of perfume she uses. Bond opens a bathroom cabinet and we get a catalogue of the toiletries contained—nearly all by brand name.

Now a successful and highly conscientious writer recently remarked to me that he detested the use of brand names as a way of being specific. I can well understand that. But he went on to agree that practice in being very specific may save students, when they write papers for their classes, from the tendency to write what are called generalities, generalizations, or unsupported generalizations. (And by the way, in rereading this friend's autobiography, published a few years ago, I find a number of brand names—Studebaker, Mennen, and Lucky Strike among them.)

But to get back to Mr. Bond and the details, including brand names, that the author gives us about him, the point to notice is that such details have nothing to do with the story line. Sometimes they help to show what kind of person some character is, but usually not. Well then, you may say, why use them? To help sell your books by the million is one quick answer. But the real answer is that Ian Fleming's scenes are above all remarkably *clear*, and that capturing the reader's imagination with exact details contributes to their clarity. With no effort at all, then, the reader can have the exciting vicarious experience of life in the fast lane—and is happy to pay for that privilege.

Since nothing is better than an example, go to a library and take out one of Fleming's books and look for examples. And while you're there—if you're inclined to dismiss Fleming as "a popular writer" — go to the works of some of the outstanding makers of today's literature, writers like Flannery O'Connor, Graham Greene, Evelyn Waugh, Eudora Welty, and see whether you don't find the same thing.

"Well!" you may say, "you've picked out writers of fiction. A constant, generous use of the concrete and specific is their stock in trade. We're writing *themes*, remember." Yes, you are. But the first and constant duty of a writer of fiction is to enable readers to pretend that instead of reading a story, they are really experiencing the events of the story—and this the writer does not only by making every event seem the result of a cause, but also by constantly feeding the readers' imaginations with convincing details. As a writer of themes, you say, you have no such duty.

True enough. But are you going to let your readers' imaginations go to sleep while, you hope, their minds continue to plow right ahead through your generalities and abstractions? No, readers are not made that way. Their constant experience as human beings is one of quite specific, concrete sights, sounds, smells, tastes, sensations of temperature, and so on. *These* are the basis of their daily thoughts. And even when they try to shut off the outside world and to work in their minds with abstractions—like justice, peace, prosperity, progress—their imaginations will *automatically* try to summon up pictures to go with those abstractions, often producing vague pictures, sometimes just the look or the sound of the abstract word.

It is into this fundamental psychology of readers that you must fit what you write. You must help—not ignore—the effort made by their imaginations to produce good accompanying pictures. So do not hesitate to borrow from the stock in trade of the writer of fiction. (That writer does not hesitate to borrow from yours; an astonishing number of short articles of information form parts of the James Bond novels, and a number of even longer ones occur in the novels of Eric Ambler, the master of the spy genre.)

Still, you would naturally remain suspicious if I could not come up with some outstanding *example* of the use of detail from nonfiction as well. So I will. At the same time I want, though, to approach my example—helpfully, I hope—from a distance. So let me begin with a very intelligent question that students ask quite frequently: "About the specific and concrete—what if the nature of what you're writing about is general and abstract, as it is in philosophy?"

Well, here is an example. (I think it's safe to admit by this time that on many an occasion the specific material in the four, five, or more sentences after the topic sentence will consist of specific *explanations* or even be combined to present one specific explanation.)

> *Being* cannot be defined. Yes, we all know what it is. In fact, that things exist was obviously our very first thought, our first realization, when our minds came to life (whenever that was). But knowing something and defining it are two different things. Defining means *limiting*—that is, cutting off the thing we define from everything else that is not *it*. So if we defined a vacuum cleaner simply as "a machine," people would say, "Why, a car is a machine too, and so is a lawn mower. What *is* a vacuum cleaner?" We go on, then, to say that a vacuum cleaner is a machine that uses an electric fan to produce suction at an opening that is passed over rugs and furniture to remove dust and dirt.
>
> In this way we have cut the vacuum cleaner off from every other machine, like a car or a lawn mower, with which it might otherwise be confused, and have *defined* it. But *being*—existence—cannot be cut off from *anything*. For one fact about *everything* is that it *exists*, has being: a vacuum cleaner, a car, a lawn mower, steel, wood, air, an atom, an electron—they all exist, all have being. So we cannot say that being is different from anything else, because the anything else will also have being. Or, if you say that we define by describing something in terms of its parts or its origin,

why, pure being *has* no parts, has no origin (obviously, its origin would have to exist—have being—too). True, you could say "Being is existence" or "Being is the quality by which something *is*." But *existence* and *is* are just different ways of saying *being*; they are synonyms; and synonyms do not really define, they just translate. Being, it is said, cannot be defined because it must enter into and transcend every definition.

Now admittedly that kind of explanation is very far from "If Joe Greenberg didn't have to work thirty hours a week as a checker at the Spend-Easy Supermarket, he would have more time to study his chemistry and calculus. As it is, all day Sunday. . . ." The essential details of the paragraphs on being—I mean the details we couldn't really leave out—are specific *explanations*, or arguments; and admittedly, though they are specific in their way, they still tend to be made up of abstract and general terms.

But at the same time, you must have noticed that the passage does contain *examples*. And they are not there, you understand, just to make the paragraphs more lively. For exactly where the vacuum cleaner is introduced as an example, the ordinary reader would have stopped being able to follow the line of argument. Thus the examples of the vacuum cleaner and the lawn mower and the car are used to help make the explanation clear. Other concrete things are also introduced, you notice, and serve the same purpose. In fact, further examples both near the beginning and near the end of the passage would have been useful.

I did not intend to bring the following matter to your attention, but as long as it's right here in front of us we may as well deal with it. It's this: the passage we've just been talking about has also been made easier for the reader to read, follow, and understand because, despite talking about things, it also keeps mentioning *people*. The rule is that the more often you mention *people*—man, woman, child, letter carrier, neighbor, student—and use pronouns referring to people (*I, my, me; we, our, us; you, your; he, his, him; she, her; they, their, them*)—the easier it is for readers to grasp the meaning of what you write.

Very well. Now our explanation was in the highly general and abstract field of philosophy. And you see how we introduced concrete and fairly specific material into it. So to answer your question "What if the nature of what you're writing about is general and abstract?" I'd say that then you may have to use many general and abstract terms, but that precisely because you're doing so, it's especially important to add specific, concrete examples or at least comparisons.

To illustrate what happens if you don't add concrete, specific examples, let me present the following paragraph, which, like the others, is in the field of philosophy.

What is general does not exist formally outside our minds, where it is not independent of the particulars that it includes. But individuals that make up a genus or a species must have some common trait or traits actually in them to allow us reasonably to place them in their genus or species. Thus we can assert that though the general exists formally only in the mind, it exists fundamentally outside the mind. True, the mind can know only the general, and the senses only the particular, so that it might be argued that there is a permanent gap between the two. But the answer is that, in fact, it is neither the mind nor the senses that know, but the person, who knows by using both.

Well, how do you like it? Do you understand it? Or do you feel that you may understand the beginning, but begin to get lost as you go along and finally give up on it? Why? It's perfectly clear—in itself. *But it's not clear to you.* However, let me assure you that I could make it perfectly clear to you if you let me put in abundant examples.

But some of you won't let me, of course. You wanted an abstract and general paragraph on an abstract and general subject. Well, there it is; I hope you like it. Go ahead and write like that if you want to, without concrete examples. Most modern philosophers do. (They apparently write for one another; the greatest part of even the educated public can—or will—no more read what they write than they could read Aristotle in Greek.) So let those who reject Step 4 consider that last example. When they do succeed in reading it, they will find that its point furnishes a proof from philosophy for Step 4.

I said "most modern philosophers," and that brings me at long last to the outstanding example of the use of Step 4 in nonfiction that you wanted. To make the example a particularly striking one, I'll take you to a book from the field of philosophy (which, as you have gathered, is the most general and abstract). The book I have chosen as an example is, in fact, the work of a modern philosopher: *Language in Thought and Action,* 4th ed. (New York: Harcourt Brace Jovanovich, 1978). The author is S. I. Hayakawa (yes, the former president of San Francisco State University and U.S. Senator). Hayakawa's book actually deals with *semantics,* which today is considered to be in the field of philosophy. Now during the past half century (his first edition was in 1939!) quite a number of books have been written in that field. Some have sold well, some fairly well, some poorly—I'm sure unsold copies are yellowing in some basement to this day—but they all have been more or less forgotten. Young people, of course, have never heard of them. There is one exception: Hayakawa's book has gone on selling steadily for decades, has gone through I don't know how many printings, and is being used as a textbook today.

What is the reason? Why has Hayakawa's book in its field achieved a success comparable to that of Ian Fleming's James Bond books in the field of the spy novel? Could it be that Hayakawa and Fleming have something in common? Apparently. For if there is any one thing that characterizes Hayakawa's *Language in Thought and Action,* it is the abundance of specific, concrete examples, the generous use of details. And I mean generous! Where another author would be content with one example, Hayakawa uses three, four, or five. Where another author would offer us a couple of details, Hayakawa sometimes gives us half a dozen or even a dozen. Never, that I recall, does he state an abstract or general proposition without turning at once to an example—or two, three, or five.

"But," you object (if you are anything like the students I know—and the objection is, again, an interesting one), "doesn't he use maybe *too many* examples? Too many specific, concrete details?"

Well—if I may be crass—I suspect Hayakawa's bank account would provide the answer to that objection. Few writers write books that sell (though the books may be highly meritorious and may be, for example, simply ahead of their time); Hayakawa did write one that sold and that continues to sell. It's pretty hard to argue with success, isn't it? Not that the sales by themselves prove anything about the worth of Hayakawa's book (that rests on other grounds), for many worthless books have sold very well while excellent ones have languished on the bookstore shelves. But the point is that certainly Hayakawa, writing on a *technical* subject, could not have had that many readers, year after year, if he hadn't some way of making difficult subject matter readable.

I think you'll be inclined to agree that his way is, or includes, the extraordinarily generous use of details and examples. If you'll go to the library, find Hayakawa's book, and open to almost any page, you'll find him doing exactly what I've been describing him as doing. (Or your instructor may choose to bring the book to class and read a number of short passages aloud.) But since the details and anecdotes are so interesting, you'll have to remember not to get lost in the material, but to concentrate on what we are using the passages as examples of: generous use of specific, concrete details and abundant examples.

Remember the unsuccessful attempt at a paragraph on Ambler that we read earlier? (See pages 57–59.) It was one example of writing that is *not* specific enough. Let's look at some other brief examples.

> Charlemagne was a great king. He is celebrated in history and legend. He was of great aid to Christianity and to education during the Dark Ages.

Admittedly, this kind of writing may be partly a matter of scale and partly also a matter of your understanding of the material. If a student has only a minute or two to cover Charlemagne on a long test and can recall him only fairly well after a whole semester of history, a few of the highlights of his reign are about all we can expect.

But if the student has more time and is expected to know more about Charlemagne, we must criticize this student's statements as generalizations. Why? First, "Charlemagne was a great king." So was Otto I; so was Louis IX; so was Frederick of Prussia. Were they all great in the same way? What does *great* mean in the student's statement? How was Charlemagne great? Next, "celebrated in history." May not this be said of a good many people? If *celebrated* means "praised by historians," what do they praise him for? If it means that they devote a good deal of space to him, how much? A whole chapter in a college textbook covering the history of Europe? Next, "and legend": What legend, or legends? Any of importance? How about "of great aid to Christianity"? That might be said of hundreds of people. *How* did Charlemagne aid Christianity? Take "and to education." Alcuin, Thomas Aquinas, Noah Webster, Maria Montessori, and Charlemagne's contemporary Harun al-Rashid all aided education; did Charlemagne do so in any of the same ways as they? Or would it be better to draw a parallel with King Alfred? Did Charlemagne's aid to education have anything to do with his aid to Christianity?

From this criticism you can gather that the generalities we condemn are statements so broad that though they are perhaps true, they are almost meaningless until we add some details; they are so broad that they describe not *this* case, but a thousand cases. It's as if someone (a native of the Brazilian jungles, I suppose) were to ask you, "What's television?" and you were to tell him, "Oh, it's a thing people have in their houses." That's true! But it's so general it's meaningless. For it's also true of a stove, a bed, a chair, a clock—the list is endless.

What we probably have to bring ourselves to see is that "My grandfather is neat," an assertion discussed earlier, is really not much better than "Television is a thing people have in their houses," because, standing alone, it's too general: I'm neat, you're neat; so is the next person—we tie our shoes, comb our hair, and do not carry unwrapped roast beef sandwiches in our pockets. What is *neat*?

True, we are allowed *in passing* to make fairly general remarks about people or things without going into details, like "Brummel was a fastidious dresser," "Lincoln was homely," "My brother is a quiet fellow," "Ms. Bauwens keeps records neatly." But the thing to note is that in these cases our listeners or readers find us specific enough; they get the picture; questions do not come to their minds. If even in passing, though, we said, "The speaker, who had an impairment, needed someone standing at his side on the platform," a listener or reader would immediately wonder "What was the impairment? Was he hard of hearing? Likely to fall? Terrified of crowds? What?"

From all this you can probably extract a rule. It calls, of course, for the exercise of good judgment, for it is this: you are to ask yourself, "Have I explained what I have said? Or will questions immediately come to my reader's mind?" Decide what such questions would be if they did come to the reader's mind and supply sufficient details to answer them. And as you consider each detail, ask yourself further, does this detail follow Step 3 and relate to my point? Does it, in short, help make the point—or distract the reader from it?

ASSIGNMENT

Write a theme on a subject of your own choice. As you write, be very critical of your use of sufficient detail. When you have finished your draft, refer to the checklist in Appendix II, focusing on items 3 and 4, details and specific examples. (Again skip Steps 5 and 6 for now; we'll get to them very soon.) Impress on your mind as you write that in all the writing you do for the rest of your life you must remember the need for specific detail. It is all too easy to forget.

Chapter 8

STEP 5

Up to this point all our work—Steps 1, 2, 3, and 4—could be summed up this way: from Step to Step we have simply kept increasing specificity and at the same time have maintained strict relevance and faithfulness to a single idea. As a result, our themes have been *thoroughly connected*—in themselves. So far, however, we have been given no directions for *showing* those connections to the reader. In other words, our themes have had what we may call *interior* unity and coherence; now we must deal with *exterior* unity and coherence—signs that will *show* our readers that our themes are connected, and furthermore that will show *how* they are connected—so as to lead the readers smoothly and unfalteringly from paragraph to paragraph, from statement to statement. This will be the work of Steps 5 and 6.

At the outset let me say that Step 5 sometimes causes students special difficulty when they first begin to use it. I don't know why this is so. In just about everything they have read, students have witnessed Step 5 at work, paragraph after paragraph—but they've often never been conscious of it. In much the same way, students have met but may never have noticed Step 4 regularly at work. So it is with Step 5.

Let me tell you, also, that Step 5 is going to cast new light on Step 2. More work? That's one way to look at it. Better themes? I think *that's* the way to look at it. Still another kind of thinking involved? Well, if it's a kind of thinking that other people are doing and we're not doing, hadn't we better find out about it? In fact, if we're not among the "fellows whom it hurts to think" that A. E. Housman writes of, we ought to welcome the challenge of new problems of thinking. But the reconsideration of Step 2 will come up only in a later chapter, so at this point let's just consider Step 5 itself. It's simple.

STEP 5

In the first sentence of each new paragraph, starting with Paragraph 2, insert a clear reference to the idea of the preceding paragraph.

ASSIGNMENT

Memorize Step 5. Be prepared to recite it—as well as Steps 1, 2, 3, and 4—in class.

Experience shows that both the meaning of some of the words in Step 5 and my use of them need explaining. So let's get that out of the way at once. First, the words: *preceding* means "which goes before"; *insert* means "put in"; *reference* means "mention," and here *reference to* means "mention and inclusion of." My use of *clear* may take some more explanation, but the time given to it will be worth it, because it's a key idea in both Step 5 and Step 6.

Clear as I've used it here is a synonym for *explicit*. *Explicit* means "spelled out, actually put into *a word or words that a person can point to on the page*." And what does that mean in terms of Step 5? It means that in the first sentence of each new paragraph, starting with Paragraph 2, you will be able to point to a word or words you have added. It means, for example, the words added here to the theme on the next page, the simple little theme that served as our first example of Step 3 (page 33).

As I said back then, this is *not* the kind of theme you should imitate; it is much too simple in its ideas and in the Dick-and-Jane sentences of its paragraphs. But precisely because it is simple, it clearly illustrates what happens in Step 5. You look for the beginning of a new paragraph, starting of course with Paragraph 2; and you *add* to the first sentence of that paragraph something that reminds the reader of what was said before. In this example, the words added by Step 5 are *italicized*. Do you see that the added words in Paragraph 2 refer to the cold weather which is the subject of Paragraph 1? And the added words in Paragraph 3 refer to the clothing ("dressing") which is the subject of Paragraph 2? Look at the example until you can clearly see the connections.

Now that we have seen our first example, let's return to our discussion of the wording of Step 5. *Explicit* is the opposite of *implicit* (or *implied*), which means "suggested, hinted at, or understood, but not actually put into words." An example will help you understand this. Suppose someone says to you, "Here it's 7 p.m. and I haven't had anything to eat all day." She's probably implying that she's hungry and would like something to eat, but she hasn't actually said so. She makes the fact that she's hungry or wants something to eat *explicit* only if she actually puts it into words: "Here it's 7 p.m., I haven't had anything to eat all day, and *I'm hungry*." Likewise, in the sample theme on winter, we have not just thought of a reference to the preceding paragraph but have *added words* to the first sentences of Paragraphs 2 and 3 to make the references explicit.

Personally, I think some of the ills in our society would be remedied if people were willing to say just what they mean—when there's no reason not to, of course. If "I always have trouble moving this heavy table" means "Will you please move this table for me?" or "Will you help me move this table?" why doesn't the speaker say so? It's not an indecent suggestion, after all, nor is it likely to make the speaker lose a friend. And it will save the speaker the customary grievance or anger over the fact that someone didn't take the hint—

X I dislike winter.

1. I dislike the winter cold.

2. I dislike having to wear heavy winter clothing.

3. I dislike the colds that I always get in the winter.

- -

X I dislike winter.

1. I dislike the winter cold. It makes me shiver. It chaps my lips. It gives me chilblains. It can even freeze my ears.

2. I dislike having to wear the heavy winter clothing *that cold weather requires.* I hate to wear earmuffs. I hate to wear galoshes. I hate to wear a heavy coat. I hate to wear long underwear.

3. I dislike the colds that, *despite dressing for the cold weather,* I always get in the winter. The colds stop up my nose. They give me a cough. They give me a fever. They make me miss school.

which in many cases this someone simply isn't alert enough at the moment to catch. I say this in the belief that many people resist Steps 1, 2, and 4—not to mention Step 5—out of the feeling that for some reason it's not nice to come right out and say exactly what you mean. Admittedly, there are occasions when it would be very wrong to be blunt. But when there's no need for tact, why hesitate to express your point—definitely, specifically, explicitly? You want to be understood, don't you?

But to get back to the wording of Step 5. "In the first sentence of each new paragraph, starting with Paragraph 2," means, obviously, in your sentences 2 and 3 (and others, if you have them) *in the theme proper—below* the broken line, not in the X, 1, 2, 3 that you write above it. Now I get a puzzling objection here; students say, "But you said earlier that below the broken line, sentences 1, 2, and 3 are to be copied down exactly as they are above the broken line." Yes, of course I did. But having reached a new step, we are now going to go further with what we have done; we are going to improve on it.

Another Example

Now though Step 5, besides being simple, seems clear as day to me, I know it still may not seem so to you. So what would I use to make it clear? Yes, that thing that *you* must always remember in order to make what *you* write clear— another example. Let's go back for this example to the anonymous theme on the need for a regular schedule of study. In that theme, above the broken line, we find sentences X, 1, 2, and 3 as follows:

X   A student must have a regular schedule of study.
1.   Time must be set aside for study if there is going to be any time.
2.   Often, only time to be filled provides the necessary spur to study.
3.   Only time set aside will make study a serious profession.

All right, let's see what we should insert in (add to) sentences 2 and 3 according to Step 5. (We won't do anything to sentence 1—not yet, anyway.) Well, sentence 2 is now to include a mention of the idea in paragraph 1. What *is* the idea in paragraph 1? Although there's only one main idea in the paragraph, spelled out in the topic sentence, there's more than one way to look at it. First, sentence 1 says time must be set aside or there won't be any time. But what it says—and this is the second way of looking at it—is actually a *reason* for what is said in sentence X, isn't it?

Taking the first of these approaches, we may add to our sentence 2 to make it read this way (I'll put what I add in italics so you'll see clearly what I've done): "2. Often, only time *thus set aside and then needing* to be filled provides the necessary spur to study."

See? *Thus* here means "in this way," "in that way." In what way? In the way just talked about in the preceding paragraph, obviously, and so we've made an explicit reference to the idea in the preceding paragraph. Moreover, we've inserted the word *then*. The idea is this: the writer has said in sentence 1, "if there is going to be any time"; and the *then* in our revised sentence 2 means "then, when there *is* time." In other words, in sentence 1 the writer provides the time; *then* when we've got the time, we have to fill it.

Or an easier—but weaker—way of doing the same thing is to make sentence 2 read: "Often only *that* time to be filled provides the necessary spur to study." *That time* can hardly mean anything but the time discussed in the previous paragraph, can it? So with just the word *that* we've made a clear reference to the preceding paragraph.

Here I should point out that if you examine a number of essays or articles, you'll discover that over half (I'd guess) of the paragraphs you find will have *this, that, these,* or *those* in the first sentence. (Furthermore, you will notice that, say, half of all paragraphs have or imply some equivalent of *for example* in the *second* sentence—something we've discussed already in connection with Step 4.) The reason for *this, that, these,* and *those* in the first sentence of a paragraph is that it is a common way for writers to fulfill Step 5.

Back to our discussion. I was saying that we could also look at "Time must be set aside for study if there is going to be any time" as a *reason* for sentence X. In the same way we see that sentence 2 can be thought of as a reason for sentence X. So we could revise our sentence 2 to read: "*Another reason for a regular schedule is that,* often, only time to be filled provides the necessary spur to study."

Another reason can only indicate that we've already given *one* reason; otherwise *another* wouldn't make sense. But where did we give that first reason? In the first paragraph. So just by saying *another* we've made an explicit reference to the *idea* (in this case, we're viewing the idea as a reason) in the preceding paragraph.

Then right away we see that sentence 3 can be thought of as a reason, too; and that would take care of Step 5 in sentence 3: "*Still another reason is that* only time set aside will make study a serious profession."

The method we have just described—indicating that each new paragraph provides a reason (or a cause, result, exception, objection, or qualification, as the case may be) *just as the preceding one did*—is a good, sufficient, and sometimes necessary way of observing the rule in Step 5, of linking paragraphs as it is called. But it is not the very best way. The best way, I think, is the way I showed you first.

But often there is still another way: in the first sentence of a paragraph a writer often links paragraphs explicitly by saying *therefore* or *thus* or *for this reason* or *as a consequence* or *the result is that*—meaning that what the writer said in the preceding paragraph is the cause or reason that produces the result or consequence to be discussed in the new paragraph.

Sometimes the writer just begins the first sentence of the paragraph with *and,* which is an explicit sign (though not as specific as I'd like to see for Step 5) that tells us that the new paragraph is carrying on the same line of reasoning that we saw in the old. If all of the paragraphs, after the first, could begin with *and*—that is, if each new paragraph is simply one more reason, aspect, or example, along the lines of the one before—the writer can signify this by beginning the paragraphs *First, Second, Third,* and so on. (In this case Paragraph 1 must be involved, too, as the one labeled *First.*)

Importance of And and But

I must stop to say that many of my students have told me they've heard somewhere that it's wrong to begin a sentence with *and.* They have! But they heard it, probably, for the first time at a very tender age, say in second or third grade. At that age, when they were just learning to write, they felt like connecting every sentence to every other with *and*—properly sensing the need for connections, but not having much variety of connective words to use. To prevent the childish misuse of *and*, grade-school teachers wisely prohibit it. For the same sort of reason, children are not allowed to possess handguns, drive motor vehicles, or vote.

Please do *not* learn from Step 5 that you are supposed to go back to that primary-grade style. You will earn low grades on your papers for other classes—as well as complaints for your English instructor—if you leave this course convinced that you must start every sentence with *and*. No. But now you ought to be ready for responsible adult use of the word.

Let's take a look at the writing of Irving Howe, one of the more famous literary critics of our time—and an English professor too: "*And* something more would have to be said, as I am glad the Berkeley students did, about the pressures faced by state universities from boards of regents heavily weighted toward conservative and business ideologies and almost always without faculty or student representation" (*Steady Work: Essays in the Politics of Democratic Radicalism, 1953–1966* [New York: Harcourt Brace Jovanovich, 1966], 83). And what do we find when we look into Cardinal Newman, accounted the best English stylist of all time? "*And* this is the reason why it is more correct, as well as more usual, to speak of a University as a place of education than of instruction" (*Idea of a University*, Discourse V). Or in his *Apologia* (Chapter 3): "*And* thus I left the matter."

No, *and* is a very important connective, regularly used at the beginnings of sentences by our best writers. What you should remember out of what you have learned in the past about connectives is this, which *is* a sound practice and will make your writing more fluent and professional: do *not* always put words like *also*, *however*, or *therefore* at the beginning of a sentence or a clause; move them to second place. (We will discuss placement of connectives further in Chapter 11.)

Or, instead of *and* and similar expressions like *moreover* and *furthermore*, the situation may call for *but*. *But* indicates that the writer has presented something as true, and that you therefore might think a certain other thing is also true, whereas actually it is not. Thus we say, "It's raining today. *But* I'm going swimming anyway." Or "You can bisect an angle with a compass and a ruler. *But* you can't trisect one that way." Or "Financiers expected Giannini to oppose Franklin Delano Roosevelt's election. *But* he came out in favor of it." Or, of course, the writer may use some equivalent of *but* by inserting a word like *however*, *nevertheless*, or *still* into a sentence (keeping in mind that it is better for *however* and *nevertheless* not to begin the sentence). Sadly, some of those people who Artemus Ward said "know too many things that ain't so" insist that adults, as well as children, must not begin a sentence with *but*. Some of these same people praise Lincoln's Gettysburg Address. Maybe they'd better reread it.

A Special Case

A special case is a linking or connective expression like *true, I grant, I admit, of course, naturally,* or *admittedly*. These expressions mean that in the new paragraph the writer is about to grant the truth of some facts that are, or seem to be, *against* the point the writer is making. They must eventually be followed, in the same paragraph or the next, by the word *but* (or its equivalent), followed in turn by an explanation of why they do not make the writer's point untrue.

For example, you may be arguing against the reelection of Q. T. Cicero as mayor of your town. "*True*," you admit, "without a rise in taxes, he succeeded in creating lovely new municipal parks and in adding sidewalks to all our streets." Now you can't stop there, or it will look as if you've changed your mind about Q. T. Cicero—that he's not a bad guy but a good guy! So you have to go on and say "*But*" and then something like "what good are parks if you can't sit in them without being blackjacked, or sidewalks if you can't walk on them without being mugged, as happens every day under Q. T. Cicero's administration?"

The need for a word like *true* before arguments or facts opposed to your point—always eventually followed by *but* and an explanation of why those facts or claims do not demolish your point—is sometimes overlooked. And the result is utter confusion for the reader.

More Examples of Step 5

Let's look now at a few more examples of Step 5. In Chapter 5 of *Hard Times* Charles Dickens talks about Coketown as a town of monotonous appearance, sounds, and habits, and then begins the next paragraph with "*These attributes* of Coketown"—meaning, of course, the qualities of the town he has just mentioned in the preceding paragraph.

In *The Descent of Man* Charles Darwin talks at one point about the development of his book *The Origin of Species*; he begins the following paragraph with "The main conclusion arrived at in *this work*," meaning by *this work* the book he has just been discussing in the previous paragraph.

In an article in the *Edinburgh Review* (1830) Thomas Macaulay summarizes in one paragraph Robert Southey's views of the manufacturing system, then begins the next paragraph, "Mr. Southey does not bring forward a single fact in support of *these views*."

But I'm doing your work for you. Let's get on with your assignment.

ASSIGNMENT

Find two articles in a recent publication (but not news stories in a newspaper) and examine the beginnings of the paragraphs for evidence of Step 5. Circle the word or words near the beginning of each paragraph that link it to the idea of the preceding paragraph. (To help with this assignment I allow my students to look ahead two chapters at the Seven Forms of Explicit Reference, also summarized in Appendix III.)

A Note About Style

If you are one of those better students with a serious interest in the fine art of writing, you should pay attention to this next paragraph; others may be excused to go on to the last assignment.

In the foregoing I have remarked that Cardinal Newman is considered the best stylist in English. (Style is a difficult concept. Briefly, it is the way a writer uses language.) The best stylists in *any* language have probably been Demosthenes, Cicero, and Bossuet. (All were orators. Does that fact suggest anything about the value of reading *aloud*? Does it suggest anything about keeping a certain audience—readers—in mind?) The best *modern* English stylist, in my view, has been Evelyn Waugh, and the best modern American stylist, the Pulitzer Prize-winning E. B. White—or perhaps John McPhee. The style advocated throughout this book is, in one of its aspects (frequent use of connectives), Ciceronian; the opposite style (which *omits* as many connectives as possible) is called Senecan. (Seneca was a Roman writer who lived during the time of Christ. Cicero, the greatest writer of Latin prose, was, like Seneca, a statesman and philosopher, but he lived two generations earlier.)

ASSIGNMENT

Write one of your customary themes. Take as your topic material from one of your other courses—anthropology, chemistry, business administration, or any other subject that interests you. In the first sentence of the second and following paragraphs, practice Step 5 by inserting an explicit reference to the idea of the preceding paragraph. Underline that insertion so your instructor is sure of what you are attempting.

Do not make an insertion such as "Besides having its headquarters in Akron, the company is listed on the New York Stock Exchange." That is only faking; there is no *connection* between being headquartered in Akron and being listed on the New York Stock Exchange. You might as well say "Besides being from Canada, she has red hair." There is no connection; and Step 5 helps you to see that your three or more points explaining sentence X must not only be connected to sentence X but must have some logical connection among one another. External coherence must reflect internal coherence.

So Step 5 may require modification of what you did in Step 2. That is to be expected; each step interacts with the others. The next chapter will elaborate on this interaction.

Chapter 9

STEP 5

New Insights

If we are going to hook the first sentence of each paragraph to the preceding paragraph, as explained in the last chapter, then those paragraphs must already be related in some way. To take some easy illustrations first, suppose you wrote for sentences 1, 2, and 3 (as I know you wouldn't) that a certain person always wears brown suits, plays tennis, and is a Democrat. How would you ever connect paragraphs about those three statements? You could only do so artificially by saying something like "Besides wearing brown suits, he plays tennis." But nobody would be fooled into thinking that you had really established any connection between the two ideas. Yet, a warning: some students do try to fake connections in that way. Don't you do it!

No, you must learn to connect the *ideas* of your paragraphs as closely as Step 5 requires. From now on, when you have completed Step 2 in writing a theme, pause and consider what Step 5 connections may be made between the three sentences of Step 2. Do they fit in a logical progression—infant, child, adult; family, friends, strangers; morning, afternoon, night? If rearranged, would the sentences connect more naturally, and lead to an emphatic final statement? And what if you find no natural connections among the three statements? In that case, your Step 2 sentences need more work.

Now let's take a slightly harder—but still real—example. Say someone's sentences X, 1, 2, and 3 are the following:

X   Nikola Tesla was a remarkable inventor.
1.   He could correctly visualize in his head the most complicated electrical apparatus in exact detail.
2.   It was he who successfully put Faraday's alternating current to work in the polyphase power system we all use today.
3.   He also discovered an unlimited source of electrical power, transmissible over any distance without wires and almost without loss of power.

113

Now how are you going to connect sentences 1, 2, and 3? Sentences 2 and 3 are easy: both tell us of revolutionary inventions in electronics, the one invention now universally used because of the failures and breakdowns that accompanied Edison's old direct-current system, and the other never used because of the impossibility of monopolistic control of it.

But what about connecting those two sentences to paragraph 1? Aren't we back to brown suits, tennis, and membership in the Democratic Party? True, the extraordinary ability to visualize complicated apparatus in practical detail may well have helped make Tesla a remarkable inventor. And his two great inventions, the polyphase power system and the unlimited source of electrical power, are obviously connected with "was a remarkable inventor," too.

But the trouble is that though sentence 1 as well as sentences 2 and 3 are all connected with sentence X, they are connected with it in such different ways that there is no connection between sentence 1 and the other two. It is as if you said, "This orange weighs six ounces, is soft, and contains potassium." All three statements are true of the orange, but they are such different truths that they just don't belong together. One has to do with weight, another with consistency, and still another with chemical content, which in turn have nothing to do with one another.

So in our example, sentence 1 has to do with a quality of Tesla's mind and imagination, and sentences 2 and 3 have to do with another *kind* of thing entirely—that is, two electronic systems he invented. Thus sentence 1 and the other two sentences just don't belong together.

I know that an objection has been forming in your mind. You say, "On the contrary, I can see how sentence 1 *is* connected with sentences 2 and 3. For it was Tesla's almost unique ability to visualize things (sentence 1) that enabled him to produce those revolutionary inventions (sentences 2 and 3)." That's a good objection, and you seem to have arrived at a solution to our problem. (Whether you have or not, readers will at least be more comfortable with "As a result of this almost unique power of visualization, he was able to invent. . . ." than they would be with such *obviously* false connections as "Besides wearing brown suits, he also played tennis"—where despite the word *besides* you have shown no connection in the world between brown suits and tennis.)

But I'm afraid that even with *as a result of*, we're still in trouble. For I have still another question: is the theme about Tesla's powers of visualization? Or is it about two of his inventions? It can't be about both; they're different subjects. Oh, I can see that if it were about Tesla's powers of visualization, you'd naturally *bring in* the inventions; but you'd keep it clear to the reader that the inventions were there strictly to illustrate Tesla's ability to visualize, and that the theme hadn't turned into something about *them*. That is, they would be clearly *subordinated*, as we say, to the main topic; you wouldn't make independent statements about them. (By the way, for a good treatment, complete with exercises, of keeping to the point in main clauses while enriching a paragraph with additional information, but confining that information to subordinate constructions—adjectives, adverbs, prepositional phrases, participial and gerund phrases, relative clauses and subordinate clauses—see Joseph D. Gallo and

Henry W. Rink's *Shaping College Writing: Paragraph and Essay*, 4th ed. [San Diego: Harcourt Brace Jovanovich, 1985].)

Or conversely, if the theme were about Tesla's inventions, I can see how you'd *bring in* his power to visualize, but not give it a paragraph of its own. It would be clearly subordinated to the main subject (the inventions).

Perhaps it will help you to see this point if you notice that despite all the talking I've been doing about Tesla, this chapter hasn't turned into a chapter about Tesla. For everything I've said about him has been clearly for the sake of illustrating my point: namely, that in a theme the paragraphs all have to be connected among themselves, as well as with the thesis sentence, and that to be so connected they must all be the result of taking the thesis sentence *in the same sense*: "remarkable inventor" can't mean "having remarkable mental powers" at one moment and "producing revolutionary inventions" at the next. It must mean the same thing throughout your theme.

But I think we can get to the root of all this if we ask ourselves, "How did the writer of the theme on Tesla get into this trouble in the first place?" And I believe the answer is that the writer was too hasty and careless in writing sentence X. We've got to face the fact that sentence X is not just something that pops out of our heads and that we hasten to get down on paper so we can go on to sentences 1, 2, and 3. *It is the whole theme*—reduced, of course, to one sentence. It is our whole point, our one idea. So much are we inclined to forget this that I'll take it up again in the next chapter.

Meanwhile, in our theme here the writer made the assertion that as an inventor Tesla was remarkable. Now *remarkable* is one of those words that do not convey definite information about anything, but simply praise or condemn. Other such words are *good, bad, fine, poor, wonderful, marvelous, disappointing, interesting, dull*, and of course *fantastic* and *fabulous, terrible* and *awful*.

It's easy to assert that surfing or skiing or my aunt Minnie is fantastic, that Greek is dull, or that a book is interesting. But where will you get the sentences 1, 2, and 3 that will *show* those things? How am I going to prove that chess is wonderful? Oh yes, I can make assertions of various kinds about it; but will those assertions really add up to the fact that it's wonderful—really make a reader, too, feel that it's wonderful?

A second trouble with *remarkable* and other words like those just listed is that they also often say too much. What is advertised as a remarkable new dishwashing detergent turns out to be satisfactory. It washes dishes. But it doesn't dry them and put them away! We might as well call every student who gets an A in mathematics a genius, or everyone who has a thousand dollars in the bank rich. So not only is it difficult to *show* that anything is, say, fascinating; it is also assuming too heavy a debt to promise to show most things as fascinating when they are, in sober truth, fairly commonplace after all.

Given adequate facts about Tesla—a rare genius indeed, whose inventions are found in the homes of every one of us—the reader might very well be persuaded that he's remarkable. But let that be the *reader's* reaction. Let the writer just supply information that will cause that reaction.

But the real trouble with words like *marvelous, interesting, wonderful, dull*, and *disappointing*—as I said back in Chapter 2 (p. 15)—is that they describe not the thing you seem to be talking about, but someone's (perhaps your own) *reactions* to that thing. The result is that if my sentence X is "My Aunt Minnie is fascinating," I should logically tell whom she fascinates—for example, "My aunt Minnie fascinates me." Then my sentences 1, 2, and 3 should really be not directly about Aunt Minnie, but about my reactions to her.

There is another problem with words like *good, bad,* and *remarkable* in your sentence X: they are too *general* to fit the Step 2 sentences you have chosen—unless your Step 2 sentences are also too general. Make it a rule, once you have written sentences 1, 2, and 3, to see that sentence X is *as specific as possible* while still covering the points of sentences 1, 2, and 3. Your sentence X should fit sentences 1, 2, and 3 like a hat, not like a tent.

In our sample theme, *remarkable inventor* is like *great king,* which we saw was so broad as to be almost meaningless. Isn't there a hat that will fit Tesla a little more closely, or not fit so many other people? Wouldn't it at least be more informative to say that Tesla was a *revolutionary* inventor? (His alternating-current polyphase system *revolutionized* our use of electricity, and his wireless transmission of power might have done so.)

Practically, I believe that if the writer of the sentences X, 1, 2, and 3 on Tesla had avoided the trap of *remarkable,* the result would have been a series 1, 2, and 3 that was actually connected, and that could easily have indicated the connections in the first sentences of paragraphs 2 and 3.

X, 1, 2, 3 as Introduction

Since we're speaking of *showing connections,* I'm going to deal with two related matters here. First, I'm sometimes asked whether we can't put the connective material called for in Step 5 *above the broken line.* Then sentences X, 1, 2, and 3 above the broken line could be used in the theme proper, as the introductory paragraph.

My answer is *no,* for two reasons. First, wait until you're writing the theme proper to use Step 5, because knowing how one paragraph ends will help you swing gracefully with your connective material into the new one.

Second, a combination of sentences X, 1, 2, and 3 and their connectives as an introduction would be both disproportionate and confusing; disproportionate, because roughly a whole fourth or fifth of your theme would be introduction, and confusing, because you would, as a result of it, repeat some material so soon that the reader would say: "Didn't the writer just say that? Or have I lost my place? Yes, the writer did; what's the writer repeating it for?"

As an experiment, try adding the Step 5 connective material to your X, 1, 2, and 3 on a scratch piece of paper. Do you see how the connectives put there conceal your main points? No, Step 5 belongs below the broken line, in the actual paragraphs of your theme, *not* above it in your list of topic sentences.

In a much longer theme, however, you might well add to sentence X a summary in advance of the points the paragraphs are going to cover. Thus, "The conquistadors found in Mexico an Indian civilization surpassing the European civilization in certain regards—notably in the construction of cities, the estimation of the movements of the stars, and the production of hybrid grain."

Then the writer would go on with a sentence 1 saying that the Mexicans were able to build the largest cities in the world at that time (the sixteenth century), followed by a very long paragraph (perhaps subdivided, as we will discuss in the final chapter). In sentence 2 the writer would indicate that the Mexican calendar, more accurate than the European, showed superior knowledge of astronomy, and the writer would go into considerable detail about that. Finally, the writer would say that the Indians, by hybridization, or artificial selection, had produced what is now the staple feed crop in North America—corn—and then go on to discuss that.

The second matter related to showing connections is this: you can make a similar summary in advance for a paragraph. In fact, a friend of mine, William F. Smith, advises the use of a summary of this kind *with each topic sentence.* (See William F. Smith and Raymond D. Liedlich, *From Thought to Theme*, 8th ed. [San Diego: Harcourt Brace Jovanovich, 1986], 14–17.) That is, this kind of topic sentence will first state the point of the paragraph and then indicate briefly the line of development the paragraph will take. I'll show you an example of such a topic sentence, with its paragraph, and I'll put the added material in the topic sentence in italics.

Social justice seems the only protection against communism, *for where it exists communism cannot prevail, but where it is absent many see communism as inevitable.* A certain minimal social justice, that provides the majority of workers and tillers of the soil with something definitely more to lose than "their chains," leaves most of the common people with no incentive for radical change. Such is the situation in most places in the United States, except for the inner-city ghettos, the camps of the migrant laborers, and the backwoods homes of the mountain people and the rural poor. The majority of people in America have their beer and baseball, their television and annual paid vacation, their health insurance and Social Security, a full stomach, clothes on their back, shoes on their feet, and elementary school and high school for their children; the underprivileged in the United States are the minority—albeit a large minority, too large a minority. But how different is the situation in some parts of Latin America, where hunger, bare feet, and tattered clothes are the rule, where most people live in hovels, in swarming tenements, or in the streets, where illiteracy is widespread, where illness goes untreated, and where most people live without hope. There is where communism, which at least promises something better and at the most could hardly be worse, can gain a foothold. Until the people are given something more to lose than their chains, until they can see a minimum of social justice established, there and in other countries where the people have nothing, the threat of communism is imminent. No amount of propaganda, no amount of gunfire will stop it. Social justice, in contrast, will render it powerless.

Though I could criticize that paragraph on several grounds, it does illustrate, I think, the device of adding to the topic sentence a clue to what line of development the paragraph will take. It also demonstrates what a useful device that addition to the topic sentence is: it keeps the writer thinking of what he is going to say before he says it, and it guides the reader to a quicker, surer understanding. Moreover, knowing ahead of time what the paragraph is to be like, the reader has the comfortable feeling that the paragraph is developing as it should.

While I don't insist that you use that device at this point in your career, I obviously recommend it. Remember, however, that it is more useful in *long paragraphs* than in short ones, and that while you are using it you must not forget Step 5—namely, to make in your first sentence a clear reference to the preceding paragraph.

ASSIGNMENT

On a carefully selected sentence X of your own choice write a series 1, 2, and 3 that are connected not only with sentence X but among themselves. Write a theme—incorporating, as usual, these sentences X, 1, 2, and 3—giving careful attention to Step 5. If you want, also add to the topic sentences of the paragraphs a brief indication of how they will be developed, a device we illustrated at the end of this chapter.

Chapter 10

STEP 1

A Useful Review

Sentence X and Answering Questions

Since Step 1 is of central importance in the whole matter of composition as well as of central importance in any individual theme, it may be good at this point not only to reemphasize its importance and caution you to give it your most careful consideration but to suggest by way of review that you apply to any sentence X three tests.

First, is this sentence X the *point* of your theme? Is this the point that you're really seeking to make? If you are asked to write a theme on some teacher you have had and choose as your sentence X "Miss López was my geometry teacher," you must ask yourself if that is what you want as the *point* of your whole paper. Certainly it is not. At best it is an introduction or a beginning or a title; and you should get it out of your head that sentence X is a beginning sentence or a title.

Second—getting at the same things from another point of view—is this sentence X what you really intend to write about? Suppose you choose as your sentence X "*Cinderella* is an interesting story." Do you really intend to discuss the sources of interest in the story—or something else? Most likely you mean simply "The story interests *me*"—a matter we have discussed before, in Chapters 2 and 9. The sources of interest in *Cinderella* are as different as the people who read it, but they might include a central character suffering injustice (at the hands of her stepmother and stepsisters), the reader's various fears for her (principally that she will fail to win the prince), a culminating revelation (when the slipper fits), and a reversal of the situation. Or perhaps the interest may lie in the story's treatment of sibling rivalry and jealousy—and its message of how these may be overcome, as discussed at length in *The Uses of Enchantment* by Bruno Bettelheim (New York: Knopf, 1976). Or the interest may be in the male-dominant, patriarchal attitudes implied by the story, with Cinderella meekly submitting to her oppressors and passively waiting for her rescue by the prince, as discussed in *Kiss Sleeping Beauty Goodbye* by Madonna Kolbenschlag (New

119

York: Doubleday, 1979). Cinderella is less passive in the Grimm Brothers' version of the tale, but there we have the episode of the older sisters mutilating their feet to fit the slipper, a practice reminiscent of Oriental foot-binding for women. There are significant differences between the many traditional versions of this story. Which of these points of interest do you plan to discuss? Or is your sentence X merely a way to introduce the topic *Cinderella*, whereupon you simply retell the story?

Third, getting at the same thing from still another point of view, pretend that your sentence X is an answer to a question. To what question is, for instance, "Miss López was my geometry teacher" an answer? Is it an answer to "Who was your geometry teacher?" or "What did Miss López teach you?" Is that what you are imagining your reader wants to know? No, you are probably imagining the reader wants to know "What was Miss López like?" So your answer—your sentence X—must sum up what sort of teacher she was: "Miss López made complicated things seem clear"; "Miss López made us think"; "Miss López was conscientious."

This third test becomes more important when a question has actually been asked or implied. A question, as I have said before (in Chapter 2, page 14), is an excellent way to stimulate the production of a sentence X. But to guarantee to yourself that you are answering the question asked (or implied) and not some *other* question, you must learn and apply these additional rules: first, *answer specifically the interrogative words (question words) in the question*. If the question is "Where is rich soil to be found in Iowa?" you must answer the question word *where*, and thus your answer must be a *place* (since, you know, *where* means "what place"). If the interrogative is *who*, your immediate answer must be a person; if it is *why*, your immediate answer must be a reason (and will no doubt contain the word *because*). You already know to do this in conversation, because if someone asks you "Where is the library?" and you answer "George Eliot," you will be met with raised eyebrows or a frown and a repetition of the question: "No, I asked *where*?" In writing, there is no one looking over your shoulder to make sure you directly answer the question word, so you must do it yourself.

Now when you answer a question in conversation, you often give not a complete sentence but just a word or phrase: "Yes," "No," "In the northwest," "Because she reads *The Wall Street Journal*." But a sentence X is a sentence! So to make this third test work, you must have an answer that is a complete sentence X. If the question is one that can be answered yes or no, for example, answer it immediately, yes or no—and follow with a full sentence, which will be your sentence X. "Does character development take place in *Cinderella*?" "No. Character development does not take place in *Cinderella*."

After giving your answer in a complete sentence (your sentence X), you can elaborate on it either briefly or at length, as the circumstances dictate. We are looking, of course, for questions that require elaboration—that need a whole theme's worth of explanation to satisfy the questioner. I hope you understand the difference in need for elaboration between the simple "Where is the library?" and the more complex and debatable "Where is rich soil to be found in Iowa?" The first requires the shortest answer possible, and thus is not suitable for a sentence X; the second calls for considerable explanation.

Second, as far as possible, *use in the answer the words in the question* as you make your answer into a sentence X. Thus, "Where is rich soil to be found in Iowa?" "*Rich soil in Iowa is to be found* in the northwest quarter of the state." (The answer does need some qualifications, I admit; but give the qualifications *later*, and do not use them as an introduction to your answer. Instead, answer the question immediately, using—as I just said—as far as possible the words in the question.) Similarly, "How does the glass slipper function in the story?" "*The glass slipper functions in the story* as the instrument of the central revelation," or perhaps "*The glass slipper functions in the story* as a symbol of Cinderella's sexuality." (And notice that *as*, in this case, goes naturally with the interrogative word *how*.)

I want you to give some thoughtful attention to these considerations. For instance, you might choose as a sentence X "Professor Smith had an important influence on my life," a sentence X that superficially seems good. But what question does it answer? Simply, "Did Professor Smith have an important influence on your life?" And the answer reduces to just "Yes, Professor Smith had an important influence on my life." Is that really the question that a reader would ask? What we can imagine our reader as really wanting to know, and ourselves as wanting to tell, is *what* influence did Professor Smith have—*how* did Professor Smith influence your life? So you should think over the 1, 2, and 3 that you plan to use and see whether (in accordance with "Step 5—New Insights") they aren't somehow connected—whether the three influences can't be summarized in a statement of one master influence, like "Professor Smith taught me always to *think* about my thinking" or "Professor Smith taught me to try to unify what at first might seem scattered, random thoughts," or "Professor Smith taught me always to question whether my reasoning was really conclusive." You may find that some such sentence X was really in the back of your mind, but that you rushed in to form a sentence X that would somehow cover the matter. It was actually too general—and, in fact, really the answer to the wrong question.

Question words that are especially helpful in harvesting productive sentences for Step 1 are *how* and *why*: "*How* does the Supreme Court interpret the First Amendment guarantee of free speech?" "*Why* does Canada worry about acid rain?" "*How* do children learn manners?" Such questions have many possible answers, and the answers will require further explanation. In other words, such answers will be productive Step 1 sentences.

Telling Stories

In the beginning of this chapter I asked if your intention in writing sentence X was to retell the story of a subject assigned for a theme. For students who plan to go on to other English classes, in which they will have to write papers on stories, novels, plays, or poems, it is important to learn still another rule: *in your theme, unless you are expressly instructed to do so, do not retell the story.* That is, do not give the plot; do not tell what happened.

The reasons for this rule are not difficult to understand. First, since the author has told the story once, it is utterly pointless for you to tell it again. Second, in your theme it is up to you *not* to tell the story (which has already been told), but to *write about* the story, which is a very different thing. It is your *understanding*, your *interpretation* of what you read that matters most, not mere parroting of it. Third (though actually this is the same reason as the one preceding), except in a creative writing class, you are supposed to be writing exposition, not description or narration, and a summary of what happened in a story is narration pure and simple.

No, you must use of what happened only what you *must* use. If you assert that chance intervenes at several points in *Cinderella*, you will want to specify at what points: when the prince gives a ball and when Cinderella leaves one slipper behind. You tell only enough of what happened to support your assertion.

If you cannot cure yourself of the fatal malady of summarizing the plot, do this: *pretend* that at the beginning of your theme you have written a whole page or more in which you have told all that happened in the story, novel, play, or poem. Or actually do it (it's a good exercise in its own right) but *set it aside* and do not include it in your paper. Then begin your actual writing *after that*, discussing character, theme, imagery, or whatever you have chosen or been instructed to write on.

Advice on writing about stories may seem irrelevant to the purpose of this textbook—except that being assigned to write *about* a story and then, instead, writing the *story* is certainly *not* writing to the point.

ASSIGNMENT

Make up a series of short questions followed by answers that need some further explanation, that are full sentences, and that include as far as possible the same words as the questions: "Which way does water running out of a sink turn?" "Water running out of a sink turns clockwise in the Southern Hemisphere and counterclockwise in the Northern Hemisphere." "Why do flowers have colors?" "Flowers have colors to help attract insects to pollenize them." "Who was the first modern dictator?" "Admiral Horthy was the first modern dictator."

Then make up a sentence X, followed by a series 1, 2, and 3, that is an answer to some such question; for example: "Why do we pay taxes to support education?" "We pay taxes to support education because the education of others eventually benefits us." Take care that sentences 1, 2, and 3 are connected not only with sentence X, but among themselves, as explained in the preceding chapter.

Chapter 11

Read on your own

STEP 6

Step 6 is really the logical forerunner of Step 5. But I've put it in sixth place for reasons I won't delay you by explaining; I think you'll see for yourself. Anyway, let me approach Step 6 in this way: you remember that you learned somewhere, perhaps as far back as grade school, that every sentence must—what? Every sentence must express a complete thought, wasn't that it? (By this the teacher meant that every sentence must have a subject and a predicate, for only a statement that somebody or something is or was, does or did something can be a sentence and make a point; a word or words by themselves are pointless.)

Today you are going to learn a second thing that every sentence must do.

STEP 6

Make sure every sentence in your theme is connected with, and makes a clear reference to, the preceding sentence.

That statement stuns some people. It seems to claim to be a truth—a big truth—about all writing; yet since they have never heard it before, how can it be true?

In fact, I had teaching with me once, as a practice teacher, an intelligent young woman who was doing graduate work in English at one of our state universities. She had previously been a technical editor in the aerospace industry. She enjoyed her work teaching Steps 1 through 5 and did it excellently, I am happy to say. I suspect Step 5 may have been something of an eye-opener for her; but when I proposed Step 6 to her, she looked at me as if I were out of my mind. "Why, that's simply not so," she said.

"Well," I said, "don't take my word for it. But go to any printed essay or article that you think is well written, and see whether every sentence in it doesn't connect with, and make clear reference to, the preceding sentence."

She went away shaking her head, her eyes clouded with doubt. But a couple of days later she returned, after having done some conscientious and extensive investigation, and said simply, "Now I see why I haven't been getting A's on my papers at the university."

Before making further comment, however, I must turn to Step 6 itself. So it is time for the final call on your memory.

ASSIGNMENT

Memorize Step 6.

Now that you have Step 6 precisely in mind, let us go on to a precise understanding of it. First, what does *connected with* mean? It means that the idea of any sentence must be an idea about the sentence just before it. An example (of course!) will make this clear:

> Believing that in order to buy American products workers had to have the money to pay for them, Henry Ford raised his automotive workers' wages to five dollars a day. At first, this unprecedented raise for workers shocked and angered many other manufacturers throughout the country.

There you have two sentences coming one after the other somewhere in the course of some paragraph in an article. This coming one after another, of course, is the situation Step 6 is talking about. Now the first point is that the second sentence of this pair (of *any* pair) must be about the first of the pair. Is it, in this case?

Why, yes! What shocked and angered some manufacturers in the second sentence was the decision to raise wages explained in the first sentence. This, then, is what we mean when we say that the second sentence is connected in thought with the first.

True, Step 6 is not as strict as Steps 2 and 3 in this regard. You do not need to make the second sentence about *the whole of* the first, about both its subject and its predicate—though that will often turn out to be the case when you have written a theme following Steps 2 and 3. But you do need to make sure that your second sentence is about *something*—and something major—in the first.

I hope I make myself clear when I speak of two sentences. I mean *any* two sentences coming one after another. In other words, take your pencil and put it at random on any sentence in any book; we'll call that sentence B. Now move your eyes to the sentence just before the one you have your pencil on; that sentence we'll call sentence A. Now sentence B has to be about sentence A; it's as simple as that. What you see is that any sentence anywhere has to be about the one just before it.

Let me caution you that in the kind of analysis you have just made, you should always move backwards, from sentence B to sentence A. (That is because the particular words of Step 6 are always to be found in sentence B.) If you want to, you can then go forward from sentence A to sentence B in the same pair of sentences, seeing how sentence A receives further development in sentence B.

At this point you can, if you wish, put down this book and make a brief investigation of any two sentences in an essay or article of your choice, seeing how those sentences illustrate Step 6.

So much for the first part of Step 6—the principle of connecting every sentence. For the second part, the practical application, we can start with our previous example. And the second part should be easy, because you're already acquainted, from Step 5, with the idea of a clear reference. Let's see:

> Believing that in order to buy American products workers had to have the money to pay for them, Henry Ford raised his automotive workers' wages to five dollars a day. At first, this unprecedented raise for workers shocked and angered many other manufacturers throughout the country.

Now what words can we actually point to in the second sentence that refer to words in the first sentence? Well, there is "this raise" in sentence B, which goes with "raised . . . wages" and "to five dollars a day" in sentence A; to five dollars a day is, in fact, what the raise was, and "*this* . . . raise" means the one already mentioned. What about "other manufacturers"? Well, "manufacturers" goes with "Ford," who was—and is being presented as—a manufacturer; and "other" not only implies but actually means that there is at least one manufacturer mentioned elsewhere—the one in this case being Ford. (This is the relationship of contrast, made explicit—clear—by the use of *other*, which we'll talk more about in a moment.)

And there is more, for this particular pair of sentences shows an abundance of Step 6 connections. "Workers" in sentence B refers back to the two uses of "workers" in sentence A. Finally, "the country" of sentence B echoes the "American" of sentence A.

Thus we have analyzed two sentences that occur together, and have seen that they follow Step 6, because the second is about the first and refers to it in actual words. That is the essence of the matter. But before I conclude this chapter, I must explain *clear reference* more systematically. First, you remember that *clear* here means "explicit" or "spelled out"; what is explicit you can actually point to, with your pencil, on the page. But what forms, you may ask, can explicit reference take? Well, we are about to consider the principal ones (and as you study them, all of Step 6 will become clearer to you).

Seven Forms of Explicit Reference

Before I present these seven forms, I must clear up something that confuses some students: a writer is required to use *one* or *another* of these forms in every sentence—certainly not all seven! In your reading you will notice that writers sometimes use more than one form in a single sentence, but never, I repeat, as many as all seven.

In fact, this is the place to point out a significant difference between Steps 5 and 6. Step 5 requires that you always *add* something—*insert* a word or words—in the first sentence of each new paragraph. A new paragraph is a major turning point in your theme; you must always *add* an explicit statement of the connection between the previous paragraph and the new one.

But a new sentence is not a major turning point. So Step 6 does not require that you *add* something to every sentence. Rather, it tells you to *check* every sentence to make sure a connection exists, and add something only when you do not find a connection—or when, knowing what you will know about the forms of explicit reference, you see that you can make the connection clearer.

I can tell you now that this is one reason why Step 6 comes last. The proper time to apply Step 6 is *after* you have written the draft of your theme, just before you write or type the final version to hand in. At this time put your pencil on each sentence in the theme, one sentence at a time, and see if it contains an explicit reference to the sentence that comes before it. If you have properly followed Steps 1, 2, and 3 and are sticking to the point, you will be pleasantly surprised to find that most of your sentences already meet the requirements of Step 6 by using one of the seven forms of explicit reference.

Now let's look at those forms.

First, *repeat in sentence B (the second of any two sentences) a word used in sentence A (the first of those two sentences)*. For instance, "Educated in classical culture, and a passionate admirer of antiquity, *Gerbert* gave the young Otto III a lively sense of the majesty of the Roman Empire and a desire to revive it. In 999 *Gerbert* himself became pope." Here, the *Gerbert* of sentence B repeats the *Gerbert* of sentence A.

Second, *use in sentence B a synonym of a word in sentence A*. We use *synonym* here in the broad sense of any word or words that designate in sentence B the same person or thing mentioned in sentence A. For instance, "The *abacus* was used as a calculator in the Tigris-Euphrates Valley five thousand years ago. The *device* is still used widely today." Here *device* is used as a synonym for *abacus*. (There are other forms of explicit reference in this pair of sentences, but we'll let them go for a moment.)

Third, *use in sentence B an antonym of a word in sentence A. Antonym* means a word designating the opposite of something. For our purposes, we can extend its meaning to include anything used in *contrast* to something or anything clearly used to show a *difference* between two things. For example, "Ecuador is *hot*. Antarctica is *cold*." Here *cold* in sentence B is a clear antonym of *hot*. (The more easily the reader can recognize two words as opposites, the clearer the connection between the two sentences will be.) But not only is *cold* an antonym of *hot*; we see also that Antarctica is presented as an opposite of Ecuador, or at least as something significantly different from Ecuador. Do you see that? It's important that you do. Moreover, I consider it of highest importance that when you read aloud (as I trust you often do—especially your own themes), you put distinct emphasis on words that are opposite, or contrasted, and put *no* emphasis on words that are repeated. Even when you read silently, pretend that you hear that emphasis.

Another example: "The world, of course, is approximately *round*. But the surveyor, for practical purposes, pretends that the world is *flat*." Here *flat* in sentence B is obviously an antonym for *round*. You notice that *the world* stays the same, so to speak (while *round* changes to *flat*): it is repeated in sentence B from sentence A. But a sharp student will notice that *for practical purposes* forms a kind of opposite to *of course* and that *pretends* is clearly an opposite of *is*.

Another example: "In Southern California, *wall-to-wall carpeting* is almost universal. Even in the houses of the wealthy, *Oriental rugs* are rarely seen." What is being contrasted here? Though we can't say that *Oriental rugs* and *wall-to-wall carpeting* are antonyms in the strict sense, or even that they are opposites, in this pair of sentences they are being *used* as antonyms; that is, they are clearly being contrasted. (If the particular reader or readers the writer has in mind wouldn't sufficiently understand the contrast, the writer would naturally have to explain at greater length.) *Rarely seen* is, of course, an opposite of *universal*.

Fourth, *use a pronoun in sentence B to refer to an antecedent in sentence A.* Pronouns, for our purposes here, are the words *he, his, him; she, her; it, its; they, their, them; this, that; these, those; some; any; another, others; none; all.* For instance, "*Early American settlers* did not drink tea or coffee at breakfast. *They* drank beer instead." Here *they* (a pronoun) obviously means "early American settlers" (which we therefore call the antecedent of *they*). You will notice that this form of explicit, or clear, reference, is very common indeed, and that a pronoun acts pretty much like a synonym.

Fifth, *use in sentence B a word commonly paired with a word in sentence A.* What do I mean by *commonly paired*? Well, *pen* and *ink* are examples; so are *brush* and *paint*. There are perhaps thousands of others, and sometimes the group includes more than a pair: *reader-writer; hub-spokes-rim; seeing-hearing; bacon-eggs; knife-fork-spoon; container-contents; time-clock; actor-audience-stage-theater-play.* Mind you, they must be things so commonly thought of together that the reader makes the connection automatically. By sensing such associations yourself, you can see how this form of reference works in the following examples:

The *time* seemed to drag on. She looked at her *watch* and wondered whether it had stopped.

The *actor's* silence continued, as if he had forgotten his lines. The *audience* began to stir restively.

In those two pairs of sentences, as you see, there are none of the four preceding forms of explicit reference; yet readers immediately get the connection because *time* and *watch*, and *actor* and *audience*, are so closely associated in their minds that they grasp the relationship of the sentences automatically.

Sixth, *repeat a sentence structure.* This may be the hardest form for you to understand, but you needn't worry, because it is the one used least often. Here is an example: "The air was stilled. The sky grew blacker. The leaves turned their silver side up. The thunder muttered." Here, of course, the writer is suggesting that each statement is connected with the others because each is part of the same phenomenon—the coming of a Midwestern storm. The writer signals this connection to the reader by repeating the sentence structure: each of the four sentences starts with *the*, then has a one-word subject followed by the predicate. The signal is all the stronger because the sentences are approximately the same length.

I give you this form of explicit reference not because I expect you to use it much and not even because I simply want to be complete, but because it is the real reason behind the rule (Chapter 6) that you should vary the length of your sentences and not always begin them with the subject. For if we repeat a sentence pattern—for instance, short sentences with a short subject first—our readers will at least unconsciously feel that there is also a pattern in the meaning. They will feel that our sentences are deliberately parallel, that they form some kind of series so that we could (if we wanted to) label the sentences 1, 2, 3, 4 or *a, b, c, d.*

If showing parallel meanings weren't our real intention, the reader would be misled, and our failure to vary the lengths and beginnings of sentences would interfere with clarity. (Readers of this book who are acquainted with formal rhetoric should notice that variety and euphony add grace to a composition, but that their fundamental contribution—just like that of unity, coherence, and emphasis—is *clarity.*)

But by the same token, do not make the opposite mistake: *do* express similar thoughts in the same form, so that the reader grasps their similarity at once: "He was crafty. He was self-seeking. He was dishonest." (See also the note on extended parallelism in the final chapter.)

Seventh and last, *use a connective in sentence B to refer to an idea in sentence A.* This form of explicit reference, one of great importance, is discussed at length in the next two chapters. It is enough to say now that such connectives are words and expressions like *for, therefore, as a result, for example, however, and,* and *but.*

For instance, "I cannot lend you my pen. *For* if I do, I won't have anything to take notes with in biology class." Or, "I learn that about 1050 Leo IX received the king of Scotland, Macbeth, who had come to Rome to seek pardon for his crimes. I must, *therefore,* revise my thinking about the historical background of Shakespeare's play *Macbeth.*" Or, "The postal clerk asked Sullivan for identification. *But* Sullivan declared that he had left his billfold, containing his identification cards, on his yacht."

In connection with this seventh form of explicit reference, let me emphasize that most writers do not notice it, let alone use it often enough. If you want to increase your word power, do not spend all your time memorizing words commonly given you to enrich your vocabulary, like *sciolist, lachrymose, bravura, fiduciary,* and *piscivorous;* you may never have a use for them. Spend your time instead learning the meanings of, experimenting with, and *using* the little words that show connections between and within sentences. Look them up in the dictionary: you will be surprised at the long and precise definitions they require. And pay special attention to them when you are reading. In short, concentrate on *them,* for it is those words that will give you word power—in reading, writing, and thinking.

In any case, whatever you write must stand up to this test: does every sentence not only refer to the idea of the preceding sentence, but also make an *explicit* (clear) reference to it?

Placement of References

When you are writing explicit references it's important that you control the placement of them, since your readers will understand you more quickly and easily when your linking word or words are put at or near the beginning of the new sentence. Leaving the linking word or phrase till later results in sentence pairs like this: "I *left out the minus sign* before my answer. The instructor counted my whole answer wrong because of *that one little mistake*." Here *that one little mistake* in the second sentence provides the link, for it refers to *left out the minus sign* in the first sentence. Now by bringing *that one little mistake* nearer to the beginning of the second sentence, we get the following smoother, more quickly understood transition: "I *left out the minus sign* before my answer. Because of *that one little mistake* the instructor counted my whole answer wrong."

As a quick mental exercise in placing the explicit reference as near as possible to the beginning, check back through the examples in this chapter to see whether or not you can bring the explicit reference nearer to the beginning of the second sentence (sentence B).

Please note, however, one refinement to the placement rule that applies when you are using the *seventh* form of explicit reference: words like *however* go best *not* at the very beginning of the second sentence but shortly *after* the beginning (page 110).

ASSIGNMENT

Go carefully through the themes you have written so far, checking (below the broken line, of course) to see whether every sentence does refer to—and does make an explicit reference to—the preceding sentence. You will find that in almost every case you have observed Step 6 without thinking about it. In cases where you have not, add an explicit reference to make the connection.

To show that you have followed Step 6, underline the word or words that make the connection in the second of each pair of sentences. And since every sentence except sentence X will be the second of a pair, every sentence except sentence X should have one or more words underlined.

Experience teaches that this is the place to urge you to pay special attention to Step 6 when you are writing about things that are not familiar to you. When you have to write about other people's ideas—the Constitution, the Romantic movement, psychosis, or erosion—*then* is when you run the danger of writing sentences that don't really join. "The moon revolves around the earth. Like the earth, it is a solid body and roughly spherical." Those two consecutive sentences make use of the first and fourth forms of explicit reference, a repeated word and a pronoun; but are they really connected in idea? No. That kind of connection is only skin deep. Step 6 is not a cosmetic to cover up the blemishes in your thinking; applied carelessly to a disconnected paper, it will only confuse and annoy your reader. Its proper use is to make clear the true connections that already exist because the theme sticks to the point.

Now if you want the shortest writing program possible, you can conclude the book right here (unless your instructor objects, of course). You have been properly introduced to all six steps. You have gone far beyond "take a deep breath and lie face down in the water" to mastery of some of the rudimentary strokes. Still, let me encourage you to take another deep breath and follow along a little further. The next chapter, in particular, offers practical remedies I have devised for common faults that I meet—and for years have met—from day to day in students' themes. Dry and drawn-out my material may seem, yet it is immediately practical. I can see, however, that in view of the difficulties, some of us may part company at this point.

But we're parting friends, I hope, because I know—and, more important, *you* know—that *you now can write a theme*. If you've done your reasonable best to follow my instructions so far, your papers will always have a clear point, be clearly connected throughout, and contain not thin repetition, but meaningful details and examples. As one student, when he reached this point in my book, enthusiastically exclaimed, "I can *write!* I didn't think I ever could."

Chapter 12

STEP 6

Further Insights

Those of us who are going on to the end of the book can now look more closely at certain aspects of Step 6. We are ready, in fact, to look at a couple of exceptions.

Students, by the way, seem to love exceptions. Perhaps they think that if a rule has exceptions, it can't be much of a rule, and that they therefore needn't bother their heads much about it. In any case, this is a good place to give two warnings: first, never try to base a rule on exceptions; second, become thoroughly at home with a rule before interesting yourself in the exceptions. So with Step 6.

But already in Step 5 we have met a possible exception to Step 6: the first sentence of a paragraph is to refer to the idea of the preceding paragraph, rather than to the idea of the preceding sentence (which is, of course, the last sentence in the preceding paragraph). In practice you will discover that the first sentence of the new paragraph usually does form a link with the last sentence of the old as well as with the paragraph as a whole and does make explicit reference to the last sentence. Granted this is not always so. I can think of situations in which a sentence would link not with the sentence immediately preceding, but with some earlier sentence. Yet such situations are rare.

And, too, in *conversation* our references are sometimes implicit rather than explicit. For instance, someone says: "I'm going to leave a balance in my checking account. Taxes are due next month." Here the explicit connective *because* (or *for* or *since*), showing that sentence B is a *reason* for sentence A, is omitted. True, the omission of the connective is not likely to confuse the listener—in that case. But connectives can be omitted to the point that your listeners are left mystified. In conversation, the listeners can respond with questions to a missing connection. When you write, you must anticipate the questions—"How does this statement connect with the one before it?"—and use Step 6 to provide answers.

You see, you understand the connection of your own thoughts so well that you may assume your readers must grasp it at once, too, and you therefore may even feel embarrassed about putting something so obvious as an explicit connective in your paper. The result can be an unintentional mystery:

(A) GTE's 16 phone companies, mainly located in California, Florida and the Midwest, are run much like those of AT&T. (B) They provide a captive market for GTE's equipment-making subsidiary, haggle with public-utility commissions for rate increases and, especially in California, battle with customers complaining about GTE's service.

Is the connection between these two sentences (taken from a national newspaper) clear to you? Is sentence B further information about A, an example of A, the result of A, or a restatement of it? Should the connective at the start of sentence B be *and, for example, therefore,* or *but*? I suspect, actually, that the writer meant *in other words.* The connection probably was perfectly clear to the writer. But if it stays in the writer's head and does not get down on paper, the connection will end up only in the writer's head, not the reader's.

So much for the exceptions. My father used to say that the trouble with many beginning bowlers is that right away they want to learn to bowl a curve. Don't you be like that as a writer; leave the curves—the exceptions—alone for a while, and concentrate on getting a straight ball down to the pins. Study Step 6 where it lies before you in your reading and resolve to see that it is always incorporated into your writing.

The Seventh Form: Four Ways to Connect Ideas

Remember that Step 6 has two aspects—clear (explicit) reference to the preceding sentence and making a connection with its content. Of the seven forms of explicit reference explained in the previous chapter, we can accomplish six by using the words that already exist in the two sentences. We don't have to add anything to make a connection between the two; we merely have to check to make sure that a connection does exist. With these six forms of explicit reference, the connection exists in the play between the repeated words, the synonyms, the antonyms, the pronoun and its antecedent, the word commonly paired with another, the repeated sentence patterns. But the seventh method, which is the focus of this chapter, calls for *adding* connective words (conjunctions and conjunctive adverbs, to give their traditional names).

We need to add these connective words where the connection between two sentences is not clear without them. For example, look at these two sentences: "Du Qiuniang tore his gold-threaded suit. He was laughing." What is the connection between the two sentences? Did Du Qiuniang tear his suit because he was laughing, or was he laughing because he tore his suit? We need to add a word or phrase to clarify the situation: "Du Qiuniang tore his gold-threaded suit, *so* he was laughing" or "*Because* Du Qiuniang was laughing, he tore his gold-threaded suit."

The inexperienced writer has not thought over the matter of connection and has rarely used any connective words except *and, but,* and occasionally *because.* That same writer, applying connective words thoughtlessly, will only make matters worse. The seventh method of following Step 6 does not call for pasting a randomly chosen connective word onto the front end of each sentence! No, just as you must choose the right size and shape of nail to join two pieces of wood, so you must choose, from among a number of possibilities, the right connective to join your sentences. And that depends on the ideas your sentences express.

As you've probably already realized, this book is actually a course in the connection of ideas—in *thinking*. One difference between people who simply know a lot of facts and people who are truly educated is that the latter are able to think—to analyze the facts, connect one to another, and articulate those connections in speech or writing. When educated people learn something new, they can join it to what they already know, fit it into a framework, and decide how to apply this information in their own lives. Connecting is a natural phenomenon; good thinkers, speakers, and writers make connections all the time. Let us, therefore, ask ourselves seriously how ideas can be connected.

The first and simplest kind of connection—though not the most common— is *identity*: we say that one idea is actually the same as another, and we indicate that connection with an expression like *that is, that is to say that, in other words,* or *I mean*. For instance, "Prehistory is an account of something that happened before there were written records; *that is*, it is something learned about the past from unwritten ancient remains like pottery and primitive weapons." Another example: "Voting in the United States is by secret ballot; *in other words*, no one but the voter himself knows how he voted." Or, "They called my grandfather a triple-threat man; *that is*, he was outstanding as a tackler, a runner, and a passer."

(Another way to express identity is with the punctuation mark known as the *colon*, which has two equal dots, one above the other, something like an equals sign. Notice the use of the colon in this way in the first and third sentences of the previous paragraph. And do not confuse it with the semicolon, a dot above a comma, which is another matter entirely. We are, however, discussing connective *words* here, not punctuation.)

The second kind of relationship is the *opposite*, in which we assert in the second of two sentences something contrary or contradictory to what we have asserted in the first. I don't mean that we contradict ourselves with something like "All triangles are equal in the sum of their angles. Not all triangles are equal in the sum of their angles." No; I mean that in the first sentence we assert something from which the reader might expect something else to be true, but which, in reality, is *not* true—as we go on to declare in the second sentence.

For instance, I say, "Most liquid substances contract, or shrink, when they freeze." Then in my next sentence I talk about the substance water, and it might be expected that I will say that it too contracts; in fact, it might be expected that I will use water as a specific example of most liquid substances. The truth is, though, that water is different: it is an exception. And so my second sentence is "*But* water expands when it freezes."

You will recall our discussion of the word *but* in Chapter 8. Though this word (or its equivalent) may sometimes be omitted, you ought never to omit it until you become a highly experienced writer. Equivalents of *but*, which you may use instead, are *yet, still, however,* and *nevertheless*. A special equivalent of *but* is *though*, or *although*, put at the beginning of the *first* statement; if *though* (or *although*) is used, the two statements are joined to form one sentence. You'll find an example at the beginning of my paragraph here; for another example, look at the following two versions of the same two statements: "This book has its difficulties. *But* you can understand it if you study it carefully." "*Though* this book has its difficulties, you can understand it if you study it carefully." (And see the puzzle at the end of this chapter.)

We saw a special instance of this relationship of opposition in the chapter on Step 5, when we discussed the use of *true . . . but.* Another special instance will be discussed later, in the chapter on contrast. Briefly, for now, we can say the following: In a *contrast* we express a difference that is not surprising or unexpected or contradictory in any way. For this reason, the connective *but* and its equivalents are not quite right for a contrast (even though *and* and its equivalents would be wrong). Thus it would not be quite right to say, "The American colors are red, white, and blue, but the Italian colors are red, white, and green." *But* or *however* or *nevertheless* or *although* at the beginning would suggest that we had somehow expected the two countries' colors to be the same. No, the proper connectives between contrasted assertions are *whereas* and *in contrast.* In formal writing these are to be preferred over the conversational (and less exact) *while* and *where.* Do not use *on the one hand . . . on the other hand* for this purpose, because that expression too implies a certain contradictoriness, since it means that one thing is being looked at from two opposing points of view: "*On the one hand* he is presentable in appearance, *but on the other hand* not so well dressed as to intimidate simple people."

And do not try to use for this purpose, as many students do, *on the contrary.* *Au contraire* in French is a proper connective for *in contrast,* but in English the expression *on the contrary* always introduces a statement that flatly contradicts another statement or emphatically says no to a question. For example: "Was he sober? *On the contrary,* he was so drunk he couldn't walk."

A third type of relationship—by far the most common—is of something *added.* The addition is expressed by the word *and* and its several equivalents: *too, also, besides, in addition, moreover, similarly, in the same way, again, furthermore, another, a similar, the same.* The *and* relationship is simple enough. Words like *and* join equals: *Jack and Jill, eat and drink.* And links words and statements which have the same function.

Accurately used, *and* has great powers to clarify a relationship. For example, in reading, when I meet a sentence in a paragraph, I want to know whether that sentence is a *new development* of the preceding idea or, instead, simply *another* example, cause, effect, detail, or whatever was in the preceding sentence. The presence of a properly placed *and* will tell us that the connection is that of *another,* not of a new development. Without *and,* I'm confused. Let me give an example.

Combat troops may fight well, ill, or not at all. The conduct of a few defenders in the narrow pass at Thermopylae is legend. "Into the valley of death rode the six hundred" used to be memorized by every schoolboy.

They may fight a half-hearted battle. Many American soldiers on both sides in our Civil War confessed later to having shot deliberately over the enemy's heads. Sometimes they may not fight at all. Once in the First World War the French troops laid down their arms. The Germans, had they known it, could have strolled into Paris. Recently, as it was becoming clear that we were losing Vietnam to the Vietnamese, some American troops simply refused orders to advance on enemy positions.

That paragraph is an example of confusion produced simply by omission of *and* or some equivalent. Despite other needed improvement, just use of *and* words will remove its basic confusion.

What confusion? First, though readers will conclude that the defenders at Thermopylae fought well, they may wonder whether "the six hundred" are intended as *another example* of those who fought well, or are intended to go with what follows: "They may fight a half-hearted battle." Then, though it is made clear that the conduct of those Civil War soldiers is not an example of fighting well, still, is it supposed to be an example of fighting half-heartedly, or does it go with what follows: "Sometimes they will not fight at all"? Next, though it is clear that the French troops' laying down their arms is an example of not fighting at all, is the remark about the Germans possibly an example of the same thing? Or is this, even, a new idea, that does not depend at all on the statement about the Frenchmen? But, if so, and if it goes instead with the next sentence, as it may, what has the mutiny of the American soldiers in Vietnam got to do with the Germans?

With your knowledge of history you could set me straight on all this, but wouldn't a proper way to set me straight be a simple supplying of the needed *and* words to show which statement goes with which?

Combat troops may fight well, ill, or not at all. The conduct of a few defenders in the narrow pass at Thermopylae is legend, *and* "Into the valley of death rode the six hundred" used to be memorized by every schoolboy. [So the six hundred are *another example* of fighting well.] They may fight a half-hearted battle, *and* many American soliders on both sides in our Civil War confessed later to having shot deliberately over the enemy's heads. [That *and* tells us that the Civil War is *another* statement about half-hearted fighting.] Sometimes they may not fight at all. Once in the First World War the French troops laid down their arms, *and* the Germans, had they known it, could have strolled into Paris. [Here *and* connects one example with *another* statement elaborating on it.] Recently, *too*, as it was becoming clear that we were losing Vietnam to the Vietnamese, some American troops simply refused orders to advance on enemy positions. [The *too* tells us that Vietnam provides *another* example of not fighting.]

The best use of *and* is to signal *additional examples or statements*. Thus sentences 1, 2, and 3 in a theme will usually be connected by the *and* kind of relationship: sentence 2 is *another* reason for or explanation of sentence X, and sentence 3 is yet another. *And* is so versatile, though, that it can also be used simply to show that two statements are closely linked, the second being an example or elaboration of the first. Because of its versatility (as you know from your second-grade teacher), *and* can be easily overused; in the paragraph above, adding more *ands* would produce the same confusion as leaving them all out.

Here is a shorter example.

> During the Renaissance (and later), musical composers avoided at nearly any cost certain musical intervals. For example, they avoided parallel fifths, like the chord *do-sol* immediately followed by the chord *re-ti*, both chords having five intervals. They avoided the tritone, any *ti* with an immediately neighboring *fa*.

Though the writer has made an effort to be clear, someone struggling to learn music may be puzzled by two things: one, is the tritone *another* "musical interval," or is it something else that the composers also avoided? Then, two, if it *is* a musical interval, is the tritone being given as an *additional example* of parallel fifths? (*Ti* to the *fa* up above it seems to be a *fifth*, after all.) Those confusions are cleared up with one *and*: ". . . *And* they avoided the tritone. . . ." Then it becomes clear that the tritone is *another example* of avoided intervals, but not an example of the parallel fifths.

The fourth basic connection between two ideas which connective words can express is that of *cause and effect*. Causal connections are often among those you see so clearly in your mind that you assume the reader must see them clearly, too. But no one can see the ideas in your mind—or the connections between them—until you put them down on paper. Suppose, for example, that I said: "The child eats dirt and plaster. She has a condition known as pica." Now do you know for sure whether I've said (a) that she has two ailments, a craving for nonfoods as food *and* a condition known as pica, or (b) that she eats dirt and plaster, *with the result* that she has become afflicted with pica, or (c) that *because* she has pica she has this craving for dirt and plaster? The third choice (c) happens to be what I *meant*; but I didn't succeed in *saying* it because I omitted the connective *for* or *because*.

As is probably already plain, when I have two successive sentences, and when sentence A is the result or effect and sentence B the cause or reason, I should connect them with *because, since,* or *for*—and make the two statements into one sentence: "The child eats dirt and plaster *because* she has a condition known as pica." If the reverse is true—that is, if sentence A is the cause or reason and sentence B the result or effect—I should use the connectives *therefore, so, as a result, as a consequence, thus we see,* or *it follows that*.

Indefinite Connectives

In the matter of choosing the right connective word for Step 6, I have focused on four basic relationships between ideas—those expressed by clear-cut connectives like *that is, but, and,* and *therefore*. There are other relationships between ideas which I will not elaborate on here: *for example,* for example, which you know well from Step 4; and *or*, which signals a choice. Much more could be said about them all, but the best advice I can give you now is simply to watch the way these little words are used in all the reading you do.

Before we leave the topic, however, I need to say a special word about the less definable connectives *in fact*, *indeed*, and *now*. Occasionally *in fact* is used with its basic meaning, "the fact of the matter is," or "the truth is." Thus "I thought he had given up drinking, whereas *in fact* he was drinking more than ever." More often it means "I can say even more" or "I can put the matter even more strongly or definitely." Thus: "Hla Myint's book is realistic. *In fact*, it is one of the most practical works that have appeared on Southeast Asia's economy." Or: "You will not find lobelia hard to grow. *In fact*, I'll give you some seeds right now that you can take home and plant this evening." Or: "Some days the barometer will be up, but it will rain; other days it will be down, but the weather will be fair. *In fact*, you never know just by looking at the barometer whether it will rain or not." Sometimes *in fact* is used to sum things up; then it means "in short," "in brief," or "to skip over whatever else might be said."

Indeed has the same meaning as *in fact*. But *indeed* is generally reserved for more formal use. In fact, you almost never hear it in conversation except in its meaning of "certainly," as in *yes indeed* or *indeed it is* or *no indeed*.

Five Uses of Now

Now, as well as meaning "at this time," is used as a connective whose meaning is a little hard to define. People say: "*Now* what is her name? I can't remember!" Or: "*Now* where did I put my glasses?" Or: "*Now* don't try to tell me that!" But *now* doesn't always lend a tone of vexation to a sentence, as in those examples; it may simply work like an exclamation point, as when Robert Browning, in "My Last Duchess," has the Duke say "I call that piece a wonder, *now*." *Now* is indeed, though perfectly understandable, just as hard to define as the *well* in "*Well*, goodbye, Mr. Supček" and "*Well*, I can't decide whether to marry him or not."

Yet besides being one of the distinguishing features of good idiomatic spoken English, *now* is also a connective useful to a writer. First, in a syllogism—a formal statement of a deduction—I would suggest *now* as a connective between the general statement that begins the syllogism and the specific instance that is the second part of the syllogism. Thus we would say: "All men are mortal. *Now* Socrates is a man. Socrates, therefore, is mortal."

Second, *now* is useful when you want to say, "You have the general picture; now I want you to turn your attention to the particulars." Thus a writer of a mathematics text, having indicated that there are certain general algebraic tools, might say, "*Now* the three main kinds of variation—direct, inverse, and combined—give us a 'tool' of this kind."

Or we can use *now* for the reverse purpose of introducing a general statement arrived at by the examination of a series of particulars: "*Now* the one thing we notice about all these tests is that they test not so much the student's knowledge and understanding of the subject matter as his ability to decipher the instructions."

Now is also used when for some reason a writer does not want to choose a more specific connective or wants to indicate a lack of connection. In those cases, *now* means something like this: "We have finished with that aspect of the subject and are turning to a new one." This keeps the reader from groping for a connection between two paragraphs that simply is not there. In effect, the writer is observing Step 2 here, but finds it inconvenient in this particular case to try to observe a formal Step 5.

And finally, *now* can simply mean "Here is the point I wish to make" or "This is what I want to emphasize" or "I want you to give your particular attention to this."

The reason I have given such a lengthy discussion to three little words might be explained like this: whenever I've suggested that students compare their themes with printed essays and articles they read, they laugh! They think their work and professionals' work are so far apart that there is no use drawing comparisons. But I think they're wrong. That is to say, I think some of the devices professionals use can be taken over by students with little trouble—like Step 5, which after a few trials students find very easy (if they can only remember to do it). Other professional techniques, though still possible for everyone, require more work. One device that admittedly requires more work—more attention, more thinking, more time—but that can still be used by students is *the frequent use of connectives*—all connectives, of course, but notably *in fact, indeed,* and *now*, which are familiar to us in printed work but are almost never used in student work.

One Brief Rule

Now how are we to reduce all we have said about connectives to one brief rule? I think this will do: *decide what the relationship is between a sentence and the sentence preceding it; then add a connective that indicates that relationship.* The thought comes first—then the connective! For example:

(A) Chopin knew nothing about the orchestra. (B) His concertos (compositions for piano and orchestra) were failures. (C) In performing his concertos, it is better to omit the orchestra or to fill in the orchestra part with a second piano.

Now what is the relationship between sentence B and sentence A? Stop and go back and figure it out for yourself. What is it? No, don't go on to my explanation until you've figured it out. Go back.

Well, sentence B gives us a *result* of sentence A, doesn't it? What are the connectives that signal a result? There are several: *therefore, so, consequently, as a consequence, as a result, it follows that.* So put one of those words or phrases in sentence B (at or near the beginning).

Next, what about sentence C? What is its relationship to sentence B? Again, go back and decide for yourself before you read on. Again, sentence C is a result of sentence B, isn't it? So also put into sentence C one of the words signaling a result (you probably won't want to use the same one you've just used in sentence B). So what do you have now? You have three sentences in which ideas are connected in a relationship that has been *explained* to the reader by the use of proper connectives. And mind you, that is your very business as a writer: to show connections. For your ideas may be brilliant, or they may be very ordinary; but be they brilliant or ordinary, you are not even *writing* if you don't have them all connected and show the reader what the connections are.

You should notice that in the example just given the relationships are those of cause and effect. As a result, instead of identifying the effect as an effect (*therefore*) you could have identified the cause as a cause. That is, it is the same to say "Chopin knew nothing about the orchestra. His concertos, *therefore*, are failures" as it is to say "*Because* Chopin knew nothing about the orchestra, his concertos are failures." Remember that in the latter case the two statements are combined into one sentence.

In the example above we have had to ignore the fact that sentence A, too, probably followed another sentence and therefore should also have had some connective word (we don't know which one) in it. We'll also ignore that fact in the examples that follow, in which you are to select the proper connective for each sentence B, depending on its relationship with its sentence A. Although I'll give you the correct answers later, decide now for yourself what connective you would put in sentence B in each of the following examples.

(A) Last night I couldn't sleep. (B) Today I can't stay awake.

(A) Sam got an F in American history. (B) He doesn't care.

(A) Judy got an F in American history. (B) She didn't study.

(A) Jim got an A in American history. (B) He's on the Dean's List this semester.

(A) I got a C in American history. (B) I got an A in chemistry.

(A) Charles followed Steps 1, 2, and 3. (B) He used a number of excellent details and examples.

(A) Washington is honored as the father of his country. (B) Lincoln is revered as a great leader.

Have you figured out the correct connectives? The first is "*So* (*therefore*, and so forth), today I can't stay awake." Then, "*But* he doesn't care." Next, "*For* (or *because*) she didn't study." Next, "*So* (*therefore*, and so forth), he's on the Dean's List this semester." Next, "*But* I got an A in chemistry." Next, "He *also* used a number of excellent details and examples." And finally the last: "Lincoln, *too*, is revered as a great leader."

Do you get the idea? Then you can no doubt do the assignment that follows. Before giving it, however, I must take care of three objections.

First, you will say that in the work of professional writers you surely don't find a connective word in every sentence. There are two answers: (a) Certainly, not in every sentence is a connective possible. (Of course, there will always be some other kind of Step 6 connection. The connective word, you will remember, is only one of seven possible forms of explicit reference.) For instance, in "This collection consists of three sections. The first section is devoted to Romania," no connective word is possible, but *the first section* does refer clearly and explicitly to *three sections*. (b) After years of writing, some writers become so highly skilled that they can lead the reader successfully from thought to thought without many connective words, relying mostly on the other kinds of explicit reference. If you wish to develop that skill, practice with all the connectives you can so that in future you will have a sure feeling for which are needed and which are not. Remember my earlier warning about "exceptions."

Second, you will ask, "But can't a person use *too many* connectives?" Yes indeed. But as I've said before, I've never met a person with too many teeth; nor have I met a student who used too many connectives—all used far too few. My job, then, is not to restrain your use of connectives, but to encourage it. If you overdo it in this exercise, it is a happy fault; your instructor will show you where to cut back. What will get you in trouble in other classes is not the overuse, but the misuse of connectives. Remember the rule: determine first what the relationship is between two sentences; then add the *right* connective.

Third, you will object, "You said earlier that it would be monotonous to begin every sentence with its subject. Surely it would be monotonous to begin every sentence with a connective." A good objection. Fortunately, not all connectives must come at the beginning. Connectives like *and, but, yet, so* (which we call conjunctions) do come at the place where two sentences join. For instance, you can't say "I *for* love my work"; you must say "*For* I love my work." But expressions like *therefore, however, also* (they are perhaps oftenest used), *too, consequently,* and *besides* can come later in the sentence or clause (we call these words conjunctive adverbs). Thus we can write "I, *however,* love my work" and "The two angles, *therefore,* are equal." Putting words like *also, however,* and *therefore* near but not at the beginning, then, provides variety and keeps your use of connectives from becoming monotonous.

ASSIGNMENT

Go patiently through the themes you have written, adding to each sentence, where possible, an appropriate connective word in fulfillment of Step 6. (A list of the words discussed in this chapter, with a few others, is in Appendix III.) Do not, of course, simply stick in a number of *for example's, however's,* and *therefore's,* whether they make sense or not! Remember to distinguish between connectives that must come at the beginning of the sentence (conjunctions: *and, but, so*) and connectives you can put in after—but near—the beginning (conjunctive adverbs: *also, therefore*) in order to avoid monotony.

A puzzle: As you do this assignment, keep in the back of your mind this question: What is the difference between *but* and *though*? They seem to be pretty much alike: "I decided to go, *but* it was raining." "I decided to go, *though* it was raining." Think it over for a day or even longer before turning to the answer at the end of Chapter 15.

Chapter 13

STEP 6

Analysis

You will not realize all you can learn from Step 6 if we don't analyze, in terms of that step, longer passages than any we have seen so far. So let's look at two essays and analyze them, and thus also provide a model for analyses you yourself can make of other passages. In the process you'll get a better insight not just into Step 6, but into the whole process of reading, writing, and thinking. The first essay we will examine will prepare you to read the second, more difficult one.

Before we go on to our analysis of each essay, I'd like you to read and reread it, in order to become familiar with it and to see whether you get the point. True, you may not want to take the time either to reread it or to analyze it. But I'm reminded of the time I objected to my dentist that I didn't have an opportunity to brush my teeth after lunch. "Oh, all right," he said. "After all, they're your teeth." So with you. After all, it's your education. So you consider what it's worth to you and decide how much of your time you can afford to spend on this chapter.

In the first essay, then, John Holt discusses discipline by dividing it into three types. The structure thus is one we are familiar with, and to emphasize the pattern I have added the numbers 1, 2, 3, and 4 in the appropriate places. (You will notice that, rather than standing alone, sentence X serves as the first sentence of the first paragraph, followed immediately by sentence 1 and then the rest of the sentence 1 paragraph. This is a common way of handling the X, 1, 2, 3 pattern in published writing.)

Read the essay through first for the meaning. Then go back and look closely at the way Holt has used the seven forms of explicit reference. You may want to underline in each sentence the word or words that make reference to the preceding sentence. Look especially for *connective words*, the seventh type of explicit reference, and note what kind of relationship they express—identity, opposition, addition, cause-and-effect, or something else mentioned in the previous chapter.

KINDS OF DISCIPLINE   *John Holt*

1.   A child, in growing up, may meet and learn from three different kinds of disciplines. The first and most important is what we might call the Discipline of Nature or of Reality. When he is trying to do something real, if he does the wrong thing or doesn't do the right one, he doesn't get the results he wants. If he doesn't pile one block right on top of another, or tries to build on a slanting surface, his tower falls down. If he hits the wrong key, he hears the wrong note. If he doesn't hit the nail squarely on the head, it bends, and he has to pull it out and start with another. If he doesn't measure properly what he is trying to build, it won't open, close, fit, stand up, fly, float, whistle, or do whatever he wants it to do. If he closes his eyes when he swings, he doesn't hit the ball. A child meets this kind of discipline every time he tries to do something, which is why it is so important in school to give children more chances to do things, instead of just reading or listening to someone talk (or pretending to). This discipline is a great teacher. The learner never has to wait long for his answer; it usually comes quickly, often instantly. Also it is clear, and very often points toward the needed correction; from what happened he can not only see that what he did was wrong, but also why, and what he needs to do instead. Finally, and most important, the giver of the answer, call it Nature, is impersonal, impartial, and indifferent. She does not give opinions, or make judgments; she cannot be wheedled, bullied, or fooled; she does not get angry or disappointed; she does not praise or blame; she does not remember past failures or hold grudges; with her one always gets a fresh start, this time is the one that counts.

2.   The next discipline we might call the Discipline of Culture, of Society, of What People Really Do. Man is a social, a cultural animal. Children sense around them this culture, this network of agreements, customs, habits, and rules binding the adults together. They want to understand it and be a part of it. They watch very carefully what people around them are doing and want to do the same. They want to do right, unless they become convinced they can't do right. Thus children rarely misbehave seriously in church, but sit as quietly as they can. The example of all those grownups is contagious. Some mysterious ritual is going on, and children, who like rituals, want to be part of it. In the same way, the little children that I see at concerts or operas, though they may fidget a little, or perhaps take a nap now and then, rarely make any disturbance. With all those grownups sitting there, neither moving nor talking, it is the most natural thing in the world to imitate them. Children who live among adults who are habitually courteous to each other, and to them, will soon learn to be courteous. Children who live surrounded by people who speak a certain way will

---

speak that way, however much we may try to tell them that speaking that way is bad or wrong.

3.   The third discipline is the one most people mean when they speak of discipline—the Discipline of Superior Force, of sergeant to private, of "you do what I tell you or I'll make you wish you had." There is bound to be some of this in a child's life. Living as we do surrounded by things that can hurt children, or that children can hurt, we cannot avoid it. We can't afford to let a small child find out from experience the danger of playing in a busy street, or of fooling with the pots on the top of the stove, or of eating up the pills in the medicine cabinet. So, along with other precautions, we say to him, "Don't play in the street, or touch things on the stove, or go into the medicine cabinet, or I'll punish you." Between him and the danger too great for him to imagine we put a lesser danger, but one he can imagine and maybe therefore want to avoid. He can have no idea of what it would be like to be hit by a car, but he can imagine being shouted at, or spanked, or sent to his room. He avoids these substitutes for the greater danger until he can understand it and avoid it for its own sake. But we ought to use this discipline only when it is necessary to protect the life, health, safety, or well-being of people or other living creatures, or to prevent destruction of things that people care about. We ought not to assume too long, as we usually do, that a child cannot understand the real nature of the danger from which we want to protect him. The sooner he avoids the danger, not to escape our punishment, but as a matter of good sense, the better. He can learn that faster than we think. In Mexico, for example, where people drive their cars with a good deal of spirit, I saw many children no older than five or four walking unattended on the streets. They understood about cars, they knew what to do. A child whose life is full of the threat and fear of punishment is locked into babyhood. There is no way for him to grow up, to learn to take responsibility for his life and acts. Most important of all, we should not assume that having to yield to the threat of our superior force is good for the child's character. It is never good for *anyone's* character. To bow to superior force makes us feel impotent and cowardly for not having had the strength or courage to resist. Worse, it makes us resentful and vengeful. We can hardly wait to make someone pay for our humiliation, yield to us as we were once made to yield. No, if we cannot always avoid using the Discipline of Superior Force, we should at least use it as seldom as we can.

4.   There are places where all three disciplines overlap. Any very demanding human activity combines in it the disciplines of Superior Force, of Culture, and of Nature. The novice will be told, "Do it this way, never mind asking why, just do it that way, that is the way we always do it." But it probably *is* just the way they always do it, and usually for the very good reason that it is a way that has been found to work. Think, for example, of ballet training. The student in a class is told to do this exercise, or that; to stand so; to do this or that with his head, arms, shoulders, abdomen, hips, legs, feet. He is constantly corrected. There is no argument. But behind these seemingly autocratic demands by the teacher lie many decades of custom and tradition, and behind that, the necessities of dancing itself. You cannot

make the moves of classical ballet unless over many years you have acquired, and renewed every day, the needed strength and suppleness in scores of muscles and joints. Nor can you do the difficult motions, making them look easy, unless you have learned hundreds of easier ones first. Dance teachers may not always agree on all the details of teaching these strengths and skills. But no novice could learn them all by himself. You could not go for a night or two to watch the ballet and then, without any other knowledge at all, teach yourself how to do it. In the same way, you would be unlikely to learn any complicated and difficult human activity without drawing heavily on the experience of those who know it better. But the point is that the authority of these experts or teachers stems from, grows out of their greater competence and experience, the fact that what they do works, not the fact that they happen to be the teacher and as such have the power to kick a student out of the class. And the further point is that children are always and everywhere attracted to that competence, and ready and eager to submit themselves to a discipline that grows out of it. We hear constantly that children will never do anything unless compelled to by bribes or threats. But in their private lives, or in extracurricular activities in school, in sports, music, drama, art, running a newspaper, and so on, they often submit themselves willingly and wholeheartedly to very intense disciplines, simply because they want to learn to do a given thing well. Our Little-Napoleon football coaches, of whom we have too many and hear far too much, blind us to the fact that millions of children work hard every year getting better at sports and games without coaches barking and yelling at them.

Holt: An Analysis

Notice that paragraph 1 begins with Holt's sentence X, the point of the entire essay, immediately followed by the topic sentence for that first paragraph. This is a typical practice in professional writing; it avoids the typographical slimness of a one-sentence opening paragraph.

Now to begin with the beginning: The subject of that sentence X is *a child*. After writing sentence 1 (notice the connection of *three* with *first* and the repeated *discipline*), Holt uses the pronoun *he* to refer us back to the child. The next five sentences also contain *he*, so we are held to the subject by that repetition of the pronoun. (Professionals use pronouns extensively. When you use them, check to make sure the reader can immediately identify the nouns to which the pronouns refer.)

Holt likewise repeats the construction *If he . . .* several times to begin each example he uses to illustrate his first Step 3 sentence. After we read *If he . . .* at the beginning of two sentences, we are waiting for it again because a pattern has been established. This anticipation helps us connect each sentence to the preceding one: we expect the construction, and we find it.

The explanation of the Discipline of Nature is necessarily general: "When he is trying to do something real, if he does the wrong thing or doesn't do the right one, he doesn't get the result." *Something* and *thing* are as general as you can get, so he immediately follows that statement not with one example but with four, replacing each generality with a concrete example: *the wrong thing* is replaced by *hits the wrong key* and *closes his eyes when he swings*; *doesn't do the right one* is replaced by *doesn't pile one block right on top of another* and *doesn't measure properly what he is trying to build*; *doesn't get the result he wants* becomes *his tower falls down, he hears the wrong notes,* and *he doesn't hit the ball.* Even the repetition of *wrong* and *doesn't* serves to connect the series of examples.

Following these, still in the first paragraph, Holt bridges the explanation of the Discipline of Nature to the explanation of its effects with the sentence "This discipline is a great teacher." *This discipline* refers back to the explanation, while *is a great teacher* looks ahead to the illustrations of the teaching. Holt uses the opposite of the teacher, *the learner*, to connect the next two sentences. The learner's answer comes from *Nature*, a word referred to in the following five sentences by the pronoun *she*. (Holt may be sexually stereotyping when he refers to the child as *he* and nature as *she*, but notice that the consistent distinction makes his pronoun references very clear. There is no question what he means by *he* and *she*.) And again the author uses a parallel construction over and over to make his connection; he begins four sentences with *she does*. Near the end of the paragraph the words "what he *did* was *wrong*" remind us of "*does* the *wrong* thing" at the beginning. These are not all the connections in his first paragraph, either, but I think you can understand from these how carefully Holt has glued his paragraph together with pronouns and the repetition of words and phrases.

In a similar way, he makes Step 6 connections within the second paragraph, on the Discipline of Culture, by referring to *people* with *man, adults,* and *grown-*

ups. Holt refers to *children* with the pronouns *they* and *them* in almost every sentence. The use of the plural *children* and *they* is a change from *a child* and *he* of the first paragraph. Is this an instance of failure to keep the same grammatical subject throughout? At first glance it might seem so. But notice that he is consistent *within* each paragraph, and that the change is consistent with the change of topic between paragraphs. That is, the first paragraph is about the individual child, the second about children in groups.

Paragraph 2 also uses the connective words *in the same way* to link similar situations and *thus* to show cause and effect.

Paragraph 3 explains the Discipline of Superior Force. The paragraph begins with Holt conceding that adults must use force occasionally to keep a child safe from physical harm. (The subject returns to the individual, *a child*, after one more use of the collective *children*.) The author repeats the word *hurt* and then refers to it in the next sentence with *danger*. In the following sentence the connective *so* leads into the precaution about the danger. Now Holt uses another transition sentence to take us from the explanation of the threat to what we must do for the child: "Between him and the danger too great for him to imagine we put a lesser danger, but one he can imagine and maybe therefore want to avoid." *Him* is a pronoun referring to *the child; the danger* is an abstraction referring to being killed, burned, or poisoned. From these Holt moves to the *lesser dangers,* which he connects to the next sentence by naming—*being shouted at, spanked, or sent to his room.* The following sentence refers to those dangers as *these substitutes.* In addition to *so* Holt uses other connectives: *But* indicates an opposite idea, a caution to use *this discipline* only when necessary; *for example* signals his instance about children in Mexico, to illustrate how even young children can learn self-protection; *most important of all* suggests not only that we are about to hear an important reason for avoiding the discipline, but also that we're about to hear the last reason. Read through the paragraph again, and see if you can find the flow from each sentence to the following one.

Now it is time for some questions, to see if you can follow the Step 6 connections on your own. Look back at paragraph 4. What word in the second sentence refers to *all three disciplines* overlapping? What connective words does Holt use in this paragraph? Which ones indicate added development, and which ones something opposite? Then look at the phrase "to do this or that with his head, arms, shoulders, abdomen, hips, legs, feet." Later on in the paragraph there are five sentences with words or phrases that refer to this phrase. Can you find them?

In each of the first three paragraphs, Holt discusses the effect of one kind of discipline on the child's personality. Can you find the effects of each kind on the child? His discussion of effects serves as another connection because, again, we come to expect it each time.

You will notice that Holt has used all seven forms of explicit reference in his essay. Can you find an example of each? Which ones does he use most often? Why are those appropriate for his discussion?

For our second passage to be analyzed I've chosen an essay which, though it appeared over one hundred years ago, is so well done that it has been reprinted in scores of books, a number of them on the market today. I'd like you to read and reread this essay, too, before we go on to our analysis.

I ruefully admit that some instructors tell me that T. H. Huxley puts some of their students to sleep. Perhaps you can stay awake by thinking about these two puzzles: One, why is it that *college students* today cannot follow with interest what Huxley prepared for an audience of *workingmen* a century and a quarter ago? Two, why was there such a spurt of interest during the nineteenth century in *observation* and *deduction*, reflected in the fascination people found in Conan Doyle's Sherlock Holmes stories and in detective stories by Conan Doyle's model, Edgar Allan Poe, as well as in this Huxley essay (which itself, by the way, contains a little detective story)?

Meanwhile, let me help you with the first two sentences in the essay: in them the author says *expression* where you might say *application*, and *mode* where you might say *way*. He simply means that scientists, working in science, use the same method of reasoning (for there is, in fact, no other dependable method) that you use whenever you work at anything. *Phenomena* are anything you can see and reason about, from sunspots to a spot on your shoe. Here, then, is the essay, slightly adapted.

THE METHOD OF
SCIENTIFIC INVESTIGATION   *T. H. Huxley*

1.   The method of scientific investigation is nothing but the expression of the necessary mode of working of the human mind. It is simply the mode by which all phenomena are reasoned about and rendered precise and exact. There is no more difference, though there is just the same kind of difference, between the mental operations of a man of science and those of an ordinary person, as there is between the operations and methods of a baker or of a butcher weighing out his goods in common scales, and the operations of a chemist in performing a difficult and complex analysis by means of his balance and finely graduated weights. It is not that the action of the scales in the one case, and the balance in the other, differ in the principles of their construction or manner of working; but the beam of one is set on an infinitely finer axis than the other, and of course turns by the addition of a much smaller weight.

2.   You will understand this better, perhaps, if I give you a familiar example. You have all heard it repeated, I dare say, that men of science work by means of induction and deduction, and that by the help of these operations, they, in a sort of sense, wring from Nature certain other things, which are called natural laws, and causes, and that out of these, by some cunning skill of their own, they build up hypotheses and theories. And it is imagined by many, that the operations of the common mind can be by no means compared with these processes, and that they have to be acquired by a sort of special apprenticeship to the craft. To hear all these large words, you would think that the mind of a man of science must be constituted differently from that of his fellow men; but if you will not be frightened by terms, you will discover that you are quite wrong, and that all these terrible apparatus are being used by yourselves every day and every hour of your lives.

3.   There is a well-known incident in one of Molière's plays, where the author makes the hero express unbounded delight on being told that he had been talking prose during the whole of his life. In the same way, I trust, you will take comfort, and be delighted with yourselves, on the discsovery that you have been acting on the principles of inductive and deductive philosophy during the same period. Probably there is not one here who has not in the course of the day had occasion to set in motion a complex train of reasoning, of the very same kind, thought differing of course in degree, as that which a scientific man goes through in tracing the cause of natural phenomena.

4.   A very trivial circumstance will serve to exemplify this. Suppose you go into a fruiterer's shop, wanting an apple—you take up one, and, on biting it, you find it is sour; you look at it, and see that it is

THE METHOD OF SCIENTIFIC INVESTIGATION From Thomas H. Huxley, "Phenomena of Organic Nature." *Darwiniana* (New York: D. Appleton and Company, 1904) 363–75.

hard and green. You take up another one, and that too is hard, green, and sour. The shopman offers you a third; but, before biting it, you examine it, and find that it is hard and green, and you immediately say that you will not have it, as it must be sour, like those that you have already tried.

5.   Nothing can be more simple than that, you think; but if you will take the trouble to analyze and trace out into its logical elements what has been done by the mind, you will be greatly surprised. In the first place, you have performed the operation of induction. You found that, in two experiences, hardness and greenness in apples went together with sourness. It was so in the first case, and it was confirmed by the second. True, it is a very small basis, but still it is enough to make an induction from; you generalize the facts, and you expect to find sourness in apples where you get hardness and greenness. You found upon that a general law, that all hard and green apples are sour; and that, so far as it goes, is a perfect induction. Well, having got your natural law in this way, when you are offered another apple which you find is hard and green, you say, "All hard and green apples are sour; this apple is hard and green, therefore this apple is sour." That train of reasoning is what logicians call a syllogism, and has all its various parts and terms—its major premise, its minor premise, and its conclusion. And, by the help of further reasoning, which, if drawn out, would have to be exhibited in two or three other syllogisms, you arrive at your final determination, "I will not have that apple." So that, you see, you have, in the first place, established a law by induction, and upon that you have founded a deduction, and reasoned out the special conclusion of the particular case. Well now, suppose, having got your law, that at some time afterwards, you are discussing the qualities of apples with a friend: you will say to him, "It is a very curious thing, but I find that all hard and green apples are sour!" Your friend says to you, "But how do you know that?" You at once reply, "Oh, because I have tried them over and over again, and have always found them to be so." Well, if we were talking science instead of common sense, we should call that an experimental verification. And, if still opposed, you go further, and say, "I have heard from the people in Somersetshire and Devonshire, where a large number of apples are grown, that they have observed the same thing. It is also found to be the case in Normandy, and in North America. In short, I find it to be the universal experience of mankind wherever attention has been directed to the subject." Whereupon, your friend, unless he is a very unreasonable man, agrees with you, and is convinced that you are quite right in the conclusion you have drawn. He believes, although perhaps he does not know he believes it, that the more extensive verifications are—that the more frequently experiments have been made, and results of the same kind arrived at—that the more varied the conditions under which the same results are attained, the more certain is the ultimate conclusion, and he disputes the question no further. He sees that the experiment has been tried under all sorts of conditions, as to time, place, and people, with the same result; and he says with you, therefore, that the law you have laid down must be a good one and he must believe it.

6.　　In science we do the same thing; the scientist exercises precisely the same faculties, though in a much more delicate manner. In scientific inquiry it becomes a matter of duty to expose a supposed law to every possible kind of verification, and to take care, moreover, that this is done intentionally, and not left to a mere accident, as in the case of the apples. And in science, as in common life, our confidence in a law is in exact proportion to the absence of variation in the result of our experimental verifications. For instance, if you let go your grasp of some object you may have in your hand, it will immediately fall to the ground. That is a very common verification of one of the best established laws of nature—that of gravitation. The method by which men of science establish the existence of that law is exactly the same as that by which we have established the trivial proposition about the sourness of hard and green apples. But we believe it in such an extensive, thorough, and unhesitating manner because the universal experience of mankind verifies it, and we can verify it ourselves at any time; and that is the strongest possible foundation on which any natural law can rest.

7.　　So much, then, by way of proof that the method of establishing laws in science is exactly the same as that pursued in common life. Let us now turn to another matter (though really it is but another phase of the same question), and that is, the method by which, from the relations of certain phenomena, we prove that some stand in the position of causes towards the others.

8.　　I want to put the case clearly before you, and I will therefore show you what I mean by another familiar example. I will suppose that one of you, on coming down in the morning to the parlor of your house, finds that a silver teapot and some spoons which had been left in the room on the previous evening are gone—the window is open, and you observe the mark of a dirty hand on the window frame, and perhaps, in addition to that, you notice the impress of a hobnailed shoe on the gravel outside. All these phenomena have struck your attention instantly, and before two seconds have passed you say, "Oh, somebody has broken open the window, entered the room, and run off with the spoons and the teapot!" That speech is out of your mouth in a moment. And you will probably add, "I know he has; I am quite sure of it!" You mean, to say exactly what you know; but in reality you are giving expression to what is, in all essential particulars, a hypothesis. You do not know it at all; it is nothing but a hypothesis rapidly framed in your own mind. And it is a hypothesis founded on a long train of inductions and deductions.

9.　　What are those inductions and deductions, and how have you got at this hypothesis? You have observed, in the first place, that the window is open; but by a train of reasoning involving many inductions and deductions you have probably arrived long before at the general law—and a very good one it is—that windows do not open of themselves; and you therefore conclude that something has opened the window. A second general law that you have arrived at in the same way is, that teapots and spoons do not go out of a window spontaneously, and you are satisfied that, as they are not now where you left them, they have been removed. In the third place, you look at the marks on the window sill, and the shoemarks outside, and you say that in all previous experience the former kind of mark has never been produced by anything else but the hand of a human being; and the same experience shows that no other animal but man at present wears shoes with hobnails in them such as would produce the marks in the gravel. I do not know, even if we could discover any of those "missing links" that are talked about, that they would help us to any other conclusion! At any rate the law which states our present experience is strong enough for my present purpose. You next reach the conclusion that, as these kinds of marks have not been left by any other animal than man, nor are liable to be formed in any other way than by a man's hand and shoe, the marks in question have been formed by a man in that way. You have, further, a general law, founded on observation and experience, and that, too, is I am sorry to say, a very universal and unimpeachable one—that some men are thieves; and you assume at once from all these premises—and that is what constitutes your hypothesis—that the man who made the marks outside and on the window sill, opened the window, got into the room, and stole your teapot and spoons. You have now arrived at a *vera causa* (a reasonable judgment); you have assumed a cause which, it is plain, is competent to produce all the phenomena you have observed. You can explain all these phenomena only by the hypothesis of a thief. But that is a hypothetical conclusion, of the justice of which you have no absolute proof at all; it is only rendered highly probable by a series of inductive and deductive reasonings.

10.   I suppose your first action, assuming that you are a man of ordinary common sense, and that you have established this hypothesis to your own satisfaction, will very likely be to go off for the police, and set them on the track of the burglar, with the view to the recovery of your property. But just as you are starting with this object, some person comes in, and on learning what you are about, says, "My good friend, you are going on a great deal too fast. How do you know that the man who really made the marks took the spoons? It might have been a monkey that took them, and the man may have merely looked in afterwards." You would probably reply, "Well, that is all very well, but you see it is contrary to all experience of the way teapots and spoons are abstracted; so that, at any rate, your hypothesis is less probable than mine." While you are talking the thing over in this way, another friend arrives, one of that good kind of people that I was talking of a little while ago. And he might say, "Oh, my dear sir, you are certainly going on a good deal too fast. You are most presumptuous. You admit that all these occurrences took place when you were fast asleep, at a time when you could not possibly have known anything about what was taking place. How do you know that the laws of Nature are not suspended during the night? It may be that there has been some kind of supernatural interference in this case." In point of fact, he declares that your hypothesis is one of which you cannot at all demonstrate the truth, and that you are by no means sure that the laws of Nature are the same when you are asleep as when you are awake.

11.   Well, now, you cannot at the moment answer that kind of reason-

ing. You feel that your worthy friend has you somewhat at a disadvan-
tage. You will feel perfectly convinced in your own mind, however,
that you are quite right, and you say to him, "My good friend, I can
only be guided by the natural probabilities of the case, and if you will
be kind enough to stand aside and permit me to pass, I will go and
fetch the police." Well, we will suppose that your journey is successful, and that by good luck you meet with a policeman; that eventually
the burglar is found with your property on his person, and the marks
correspond to his hand and to his boots. Probably any jury would
consider those facts a very good experimental verification of your hypothesis, touching the cause of the abnormal phenomena observed in
your parlor, and would act accordingly.

12.   Now, in this suppositious case, I have taken phenomena of a very
common kind, in order that you might see what are the different steps
in an ordinary process of reasoning, if you will only take the trouble
to analyze it carefully. All the operations I have described, you will
see, are involved in the mind of any man of sense in leading him to a
conclusion as to the course he should take in order to make good a
robbery and punish the offender. I say that you are led, in that case,
to your conclusion by exactly the same train of reasoning as that
which a man of science pursues when he is endeavoring to discover
the origin and laws of the most occult phenomena. The process is,
and always must be, the same; and precisely the same mode of reasoning was employed by Newton and Laplace in their endeavors to discover and define the causes of the movements of the heavenly bodies,
as you, with your own common sense, would employ to detect a burglar. The only difference is that, the nature of the inquiry being more
abstruse, every step has to be most carefully watched, so that there
may not be a single crack or flaw in your hypothesis. A flaw or crack
in many of the hypotheses of daily life may be of little or no moment
as affecting the general correctness of the conclusions at which we
may arrive; but, in a scientific inquiry, a fallacy, great or small, is
always of importance, and is sure to be in the long run constantly
productive of mischievous, if not fatal results.

13.   Do not allow yourselves to be misled by the common notion that a
hypothesis is untrustworthy simply because it is a hypothesis. It is
often urged, in respect to some scientific conclusion, that, after all, it
is only a hypothesis. But what more have we to guide us in nine-
tenths of the most important affairs of daily life than hypotheses, and
often very ill-based ones? So that in science, where the evidence of a
hypothesis is subjected to the most rigid examination, we may rightly
pursue the same course. You may have hypotheses, and hypotheses. A
man may say, if he likes, that the moon is made of green cheese: that
is a hypothesis. But another man, who has devoted a great deal of
time and attention to the subject, and availed himself of the most
powerful telescopes and the results of the observations of others, declares that in his opinion it is probably composed of materials very
similar to those of which our own earth is made up: and that is also
only a hypothesis. But I need not tell you that there is an enormous
difference in the value of the two hypotheses. That one which is based
on sound scientific knowledge is sure to have a corresponding value;

and that which is a mere hasty random guess is likely to have but little value. Every great step in our progress in discovering causes has been made in exactly the same way as that which I have detailed to you. A person observing the occurrence of certain facts and phenomena asks, naturally enough, what process, what kind of operation known to occur in Nature applied to the particular case, will unravel and explain the mystery? Hence you have the scientific hypothesis; and its value will be proportionate to the care and completeness with which its basis has been tested and verified. It is in these matters as in the commonest affairs of practical life; the guess of the fool will be folly, while the guess of the wise man will contain wisdom. In all cases, you see that the value of the result depends on the patience and faithfulness with which the investigator applies to his hypothesis every possible kind of verification.

Huxley: An Analysis

First, of course, let's see how, in paragraph 1, the second sentence is related to the first according to Step 6. I'm sorry that you'll have to keep turning back to the essay (as you'd have to keep turning back to the microscope if you were drawing a picture of a paramecium in biology lab), but you'll find doing so worth the effort. So let's proceed: *it*, a pronoun in sentence B (the second sentence), means *the method of scientific investigation* in sentence A (the first). *Is* in sentence B is synonymous with *is nothing but* in sentence A. *The mode by which all phenomena* in sentence B repeats the word *mode* in sentence A, and *by which all phenomena* in sentence B means the same as *necessary* in sentence A—just as, for instance, since all routes to San Marino pass through Italy, travel through (or over) Italy is the *necessary* mode of reaching San Marino. *Reasoned about and rendered precise and exact* is synonymous with *working of the human mind*.

But we have just shown, haven't we, that the second sentence means the same as the first—matches it term for term? In a moment we'll show that the third sentence does the same thing. Meanwhile, it would be useful for you to reread the essay to see how, as Huxley goes on, in sentence after sentence, in paragraph after paragraph, he keeps repeating the same idea, changing only the details and the comparisons. Just for example (and it is not the first you can find), when he says in paragraph 2 that "all these terrible apparatus" (used in the scientific method) are used by you every hour of your lives, what he is saying boils down to the fact that scientists think like you—scientific thinking is only ordinary human thinking—which is what the first sentence of the essay boils down to.

But I want you yourself to go through every sentence up to paragraph 7, to see how many times Huxley, in one way or another, whatever details he adds or comparisons he uses, is simply making again and again the point that scientists think like everybody else—that the method of scientific investigation is nothing but the method of thinking that you have been using all day, every day, since infancy. *Did you notice on your first reading or readings how he keeps repeating that point?* The point that scientists think in essentially the same way you do is, in effect, Huxley's sentence X (his first sentence); and this will become totally obvious to you as you go through the first seven paragraphs.

In fact, it is important to a successful reading of this famous essay for you to grasp that that *is* Huxley's point, because most students (and, I fear, some instructors) read it exactly backwards. They think Huxley is saying, "You too can think like a scientist." Precisely not; Huxley says that since you already do think, and have always thought, like a scientist, scientists think like you and must do so, for there is no other dependable way of thinking.

Why he chooses to make this point to his audience is something we'll come to shortly. Meanwhile, simply realize that he does *not* begin his essay with a sentence X like "The ordinary man in the street can learn, and can apply in his daily life, the method of scientific investigation used by scientists in reaching their hypotheses and forming their conclusions." No! To repeat, his very point is that since the ordinary man in the street (when he is acting rationally, as the essay later implies) *already* uses, has always used, and can do nothing else but use the method of scientific investigation, then scientists studying fossils are doing exactly what you are doing when you are figuring out how a spot got on your shoe.

Now that you've reread the article to paragraph 7, as I asked you to, let's continue our analysis where we left off. In sentence C, the third sentence of the first paragraph, *there is no more difference* is the same as *is simply* in sentence B (and, of course, the same as *nothing but* in sentence A). In sentence C, *mental operations of a man of science* is equivalent to *it* in sentence B, which, as we saw, means *the method of scientific investigation* in sentence A. *Those of the ordinary person* in sentence C is equivalent to *all phenomena are reasoned about* (that is, including those that the ordinary person reasons about) in sentence B.

"Yes," you say. "Now what about 'though there is just the same kind of difference' in sentence C? Huxley seems to be saying that the two *are* different." No. Do not forget that from the very first sentence Huxley has asserted that the two are the same. And remember that he begins his third sentence with "there is no more difference," which implies that any difference is outweighed by the similarity. Furthermore, he is telling us that the similarity is essential and the difference only incidental. What does that mean?

Huxley explains it in the next sentence in terms of two weighing devices, when he says that they do not differ in construction or in manner of working (*that* is the essential), but only in fineness of measurement (which is incidental). Similarly, if I show you a tray of gems and tell you they're all diamonds, you don't disagree with me because some of the stones are *larger* than some of the others. *That* difference has nothing to do with whether the stones are diamonds—it is incidental. To put it another way, a scientist's thinking and your thinking are the same qualitatively—that is, in kind; they differ only quantitatively—that is, in degree (here, in degree of carefulness).

Now at this point it is important to understand why Huxley confuses the issue by introducing this incidental difference. Thereby hangs a tale. A moment ago I said that we'd look into the reason *why* Huxley chose to make the point that scientists think like us. The reason is that he wanted to defend Darwin's hypothesis of evolution through natural selection, first published in *The Origin of Species* in 1859, just three years before this lecture was given. Huxley's concern to defend Darwin affected his lecture in several ways. First of all, as we have said, his argument is that scientists do not arrive at their conclusions (read "Darwin did not arrive at his hypothesis") by some kind of mumbo-jumbo or by some process too highly complicated for the ordinary person to judge, but by the same mental processes ordinary people use in their daily lives. "Since you trust yourself," Huxley says in effect, "when you reason about, say, the disappearance of a teapot, then you should trust scientists (read 'Darwin') when, using the same processes you do, they reach conclusions in their field (read 'the origin of species through natural selection')."

Second, Huxley takes pains to defend hypotheses; for that is what Darwin's conclusion was—a hypothesis. "You trust your hypotheses in your daily life," he says in effect. "Why not, then, trust scientists' hypotheses (Darwin's hypothesis)?"

Third, if we answer that some of our reasonable hypotheses prove false in the end, Huxley tells us that scientists reason far more carefully about science than we (or they, for that matter) do about the ordinary problems of daily life. And *that* is why he introduces, even in his first paragraph, the for-some-readers confusing quantitative difference noted above. He is saying, in effect, "You can put a double faith in scientists: first, they use your own trustworthy methods of thinking, and second, they use them even more carefully than you do."

By the way, it is because Huxley is somewhat defensive about hypotheses that he says near the end of his talk, a little sharply, that the guess of a fool will be folly while the guess of a wise man will contain wisdom and that the value of a hypothesis depends on verification—which, because he puts it last, some readers have taken to be his sentence X. But I do not intend to argue here either against or for the hypothesis of natural selection. And Huxley's lecture will be just as illustrative if you apply it to the Bohr theory or to Planck's quantum theory instead of to Darwinism; in fact, Huxley himself applies it to Newton and Laplace.

Now before asking you to do, on your own, some of this analysis of Huxley's essay in accordance with Step 6, I want to take up a few particular matters with you myself. The first thing I want to take up with you is the interesting paragraph 2. Look at the sentence "You have all heard it repeated, I dare say, that men of science work by means of induction and deduction, and that . . . *by some cunning skill of their own*, they build up hypotheses and theories." Now, most of that sentence is equivalent to *the method of scientific investigation* in the first sentence of the essay, for the method of scientific investigation is exactly what Huxley is describing. We should therefore expect the remainder of the sentence—*by some cunning skill of their own*—to match the latter part of the first sentence of the essay: *nothing but the expression of the necessary mode of working of the human mind*. But *by some cunning skill of their own* means the very opposite! It means that scientists operate not like ordinary men, but by some different, specially acquired mode of reasoning.

Is Huxley contradicting himself? Or is the hasty reader right when he says Huxley's essay means "You too can think like a scientist if you work hard at it"? Look at the expression "you have all heard it repeated, I dare say." Then look at "and it is imagined by many," in the next sentence—which goes on to say, in reverse order, the very clear opposite of the first sentence of the essay by saying that "the operations of the common mind can be *by no means* compared with these processes," and that "they *have to be acquired* by a sort of *special apprenticeship* to the craft." Look as carefully at "to hear all these large words, you would think" in the next sentence, and note that it is followed by an even firmer contradiction—an outright denial—of what Huxley said in the first sentence of his essay: "The mind of a man of science must be constituted differently from that of his fellow men."

What *is* Huxley doing here? Contradicting himself? No. The expressions "you have all heard it repeated, I dare say," "it is imagined by many," and "to hear all these large words, you would think" are *connectives*—connectives that indicate that Huxley is presenting actual or possible *objections* to *his* assertion that scientists think just like the rest of us. And then remember, above all, that connectives like this—connectives that present the opposing side of the argument—introduce statements that must eventually be followed by a statement that begins with *but* (or some equivalent). Is that the case in Huxley's paragraph 2? Look back at the essay and see.

Yes. And after *but* Huxley not only returns to an assertion of his own argument—"all these terrible apparatus are being used by *yourselves*"—but refutes the opposing argument. (Huxley's method of refutation is to prove *his* point by giving the examples that follow.)

Note as well that Huxley does not introduce the objections with a connective like *true* or *I grant*. He might have used such connectives in his *first* paragraph—"true, scientists are more painstaking" or "I grant, there is a difference of degree." But here the objections, or arguments contrary to his own, are *not* true (in fact he says "you are quite wrong"). So Huxley uses equivalents of *some people say*, which lead us at least to suspect that eventually he is going to say, "but they are wrong, because. . . ."

Perhaps you think this analysis is tedious. But I honestly believe that many people cannot read successfully because they have never been taught to understand and pay attention to *connectives*, not the least important of which is the *true . . . but*, or *some people say . . . but* variety, which appears very often in sophisticated writing. And in students' writing? Called on to use the connectives just described, *some* students get them exactly backward, and thus utterly confuse their readers.

Before we leave paragraph 2, let me point out that Huxley makes his essay more interesting by introducing a *conflict*, which he sets up by bringing in imaginary objections. In doing so, he must use the *connectives* that are proper to objections. We'll apply both conflict and its connectives to your own writing later, in the chapter on the argumentative paper. Meanwhile, we must get on with our analysis.

In his third paragraph, Huxley actually invites us to match sentence with sentence. In the second sentence, sentence B, he does so first of all with the logical connective *in the same way*. Then *you*, in sentence B, matches *hero* in sentence A. Next, *take comfort, and be delighted with yourselves* in sentence B matches *express unbounded delight* in sentence A. *On the discovery that* in sentence B matches *on being told that* in sentence A. *You have been acting on the principles of inductive and deductive philosophy* in sentence B matches *had been talking prose* in sentence A, and *during the same period* in sentence B matches *during the whole of his life* in sentence A. (I will leave you to analyze the connection of the third sentence of paragraph 3 with the second sentence. That's a little harder!) The last thing I want to take up with you is paragraph 7. It's extremely interesting. First, notice that though it appears in type as a paragraph, it is hardly a paragraph properly speaking, for it has only two sentences and a little development. This kind of paragraph is often called a transitional paragraph. Its only function (*transition* means "a going across") is to lead us from one section of an essay to the next section *without confusion*: it explains, in effect, *both* that we should be ready for a change in thought (so we won't say: "Weren't we talking about such and such? What are we doing now?") *and* that the new thought is connected with the old.

Moreover, Huxley's transitional paragraph does what transitional paragraphs often do: it begins by *summarizing* what has been said so far: "the method of establishing laws in science is exactly the same as that pursued in common life." And in this case we see that what has been said so far is, of course, what has been said in sentence X. (By the way, the word *exactly* ought to remove from your mind any doubts raised by the merely quantitative difference spoken of in paragraph 1. In other words, scientists do think just like you.)

I said this transitional paragraph is extremely interesting. For it is a little lesson in composition all by itself (except that, naturally, it lacks detail). It is so because it takes the time and trouble to tell the reader where he has been, where he is now, and where he is going; because it succinctly puts the *point* into words and lets the reader know that it *is* the point; and because its very purpose is to show the connection of ideas—*which is what writing is all about.*

Transitions in Your Writing

True, the papers you are writing now are too short to need transitional paragraphs—they would be as much out of proportion in your theme as a paragraph of introduction or of conclusion would be. But not only will you someday be writing long papers, in which you may be using paragraphs of transition, you are, right now, making brief transitional devices out of every topic sentence except the first. For your topic sentences now make a reference to the old paragraph, besides introducing the new; show how the two paragraphs are connected; and thus indicate to the reader the direction you are taking—all part of Step 5.

In fact—and this is Step 6—in a way *every* sentence is a little transitional sentence, for as we've seen, besides introducing its own new material, *every* sentence must make an explicit reference to the preceding sentence and indicate how it is connected to the preceding sentence, thus allowing the reader to follow your train of thought with ease.

Combining all we have said now about transitions, we can formulate the following rules. First, in *long* themes, introduce each new section with a paragraph that summarizes both the old and the new sections and indicates the connection between the two. Second, in *every* section and in *every* theme, introduce each paragraph with a sentence that refers to the preceding paragraph, introduces the idea of the new paragraph, and indicates the connection between the two (Step 5). Third, in every paragraph make each sentence briefly refer to the preceding sentence, present its own material, and indicate the connection between the two (Step 6). That—and nothing but that—is *writing*, in the true sense of the word.

ASSIGNMENT

Analyze paragraphs 5 and 12 of Huxley's essay, looking for all examples of Step 6. Once again, I suggest that you underline in every sentence the word or words that connect it to the preceding sentence. Find every connection you can; by no means be satisfied with one if you can find more.

In paragraph 5, do not miss the connection between *your friend* and *you*, and between *says* and *reply*; they are, broadly speaking, antonyms (that is, they *contrast*, and contrast is an important form of connection). And do not miss the *true . . . but* construction in that paragraph. In paragraph 12, do not miss the fact that Huxley is *still* saying what he was saying in paragraph 1. In both, do not miss the opportunity of seeing how Step 5 is also involved.

And Step 4? Do you find that in these paragraphs, as in the others, Huxley is being specific and concrete in the explanation of his general and abstract assertions? Does he go into detail? Does he give examples? Does he not actually say a lot about *one thing*?

Your instructor will need to give you more than one day for this assignment. It is a long one. At the same time, you may wish to analyze more of the essay than has been assigned. That's good, because this may be the most important assignment of your writing (and reading) career.

Above all, I want you to learn from this assignment that writing is *not* just putting down one sentence after another, as bricks are laid. It is more like knitting than bricklaying, in that each new sentence—like each new row of stitches—is created by hooking the new thread *into* the old. *That* is the way *writing* is done (anything else is mere amateur scribbling). And that is the way *reading* is done: we see where each new sentence has got us precisely by seeing exactly how it has departed from the old; we see the real point the writer is making with each new sentence only when we see the connection between it and the sentence before it. All this may be painfully slow for you at first; when it becomes a habit, you will hardly have to think about it.

Logic and Intuition

I imagine that from time to time your instructor brings up, in connection with your themes, points of *grammar*. In fact, from time to time, this *rhetoric* (composition textbook) has necessarily brought up points of grammar. That leaves, out of the three traditional liberal arts (grammar, logic, and rhetoric), *logic*. True, as I've repeatedly asserted, this textbook of rhetoric is a course in thinking and thus has presented aspects of logic *informally*. But now you have studied Huxley's essay, which more than touches on *formal* logic—inductions, deductions, conclusions. At this time, therefore, it would be perfectly appropriate for your instructor to introduce you to formal logic more fully, with, for example, the *rules of the syllogism* and the chief *logical fallacies*.

Now, having just read my suggestion that you might study formal logic, you may be astonished to learn that I do not fully agree with Huxley about the way the mind works—that is, about the value of induction and deduction. Granted, plodding induction has its place; and, as the medieval schoolmen insisted, nothing is in the mind that did not get there through the senses (except the powers of the mind itself, of course); and we all know the tireless experimenter Thomas Edison's dictum that genius is one percent inspiration and ninety-nine percent perspiration. But that one percent leaves a gap in Huxley's theory. Great scientific discoveries come, not without general experience, to be sure, but not by scientific induction, either; they come by flashes of intuition. It was not by induction but by intuition that Newton discovered (or rather, grasped the certainty of) gravitation (not *gravity*, as the anecdote of the apple has probably led you to believe). Moreover, none but purely analytic induction (ascertaining, for instance, that of three persons, all three are wearing glasses) ever produces scientific certainty; no measuring instrument is, or could be, fine enough to demonstrate that the internal angles of every triangle add up to *exactly* 180 degrees. You may be further astonished that my position is supported by no less a thinker than Albert Einstein; he called the modern enthusiasm for induction a fad. (For more on this subject, see *The Logic of Scientific Discovery* by Karl R. Popper [New York: Harper & Row, 1959].) I use Huxley's essay as a fine, and famous, example of good clear writing that nevertheless requires careful analytical reading; I do not use it to teach you the scientific method—nor yet to mislead you about it.

Chapter 14

CONTRAST

Up to this point I have cautioned you to *avoid contrast* in your themes—specifically, to avoid contrast in your sentence X (and thus, because all other sentences follow the lead of sentence X, in the entire theme). Of all the restrictions I placed on your X, 1, 2, 3 in Chapter 2 (avoid *description*, avoid *narration*, avoid *process*), the warning against contrast has been probably the hardest to live with. Contrast is so ingrained in our normal reading, writing, speaking, and thinking that it is almost impossible to avoid. So if you did after all use some contrast in your earlier writing for this course, I won't blame you. From now on, in fact, I will expect you to make plentiful use of it.

Why, then, did I prohibit it earlier? I did it so you could learn the all-important Steps 1 through 6 in their simplest forms. Contrast complicates a theme. As we noted in Chapter 2, it makes the sentence X of Step 1 less short and less simple. And, we will see, it allows one or more of the Step 2 sentences to be about the *opposite* of sentence X. But now that you have mastered the simple forms of Steps 1 through 6, it is time to go on and allow them the greater flexibility they can—and often must—have in real writing. We will begin by introducing the theme in which you *contrast* two people, two things, two poems, and so forth.

But you are probably half wondering why, out of all the possible kinds of composition, we are making a special bother about contrast. I must, therefore, answer that question before going on to the rules. And the first explanation is this: contrast is one of the two kinds of composition with which students have special trouble (the other is argumentation, which we will discuss in the next chapter). We must, therefore, remove that trouble.

The second reason for studying contrast is that the very process of contrast has special values, so writing themes involving it is especially useful practice. For one thing, when you seem to be unable to think of much to say about a woman, a situation, a poem, or a short musical composition, you can try contrasting it with another in the same category. Then suddenly there may be a lot to say. For instance, what can I say about Uncle Joe? Not much, it seems—

until I conceive the idea of contrasting him with Uncle Sam, and then many things spring to my mind. This is because the process of contrast gives a special focus to our vision of something, so that by using it we realize possibilities of analysis that would otherwise not occur to us.

So true is this, in fact, that we can sometimes analyze something more successfully if we contrast it with a purely imagined difference. We can, for example, better understand how the first words of Lincoln's Gettysburg Address set the tone of the speech if we *imagine* that Lincoln had begun, instead, with the words *eighty-seven years ago*.

There is a reason the process of contrast is so stimulating and productive. It is that fundamentally we perceive everything through differences (and through similarities, about which we'll say something in a few minutes). The very reason that qualities like generosity and bravery come to our attention is that they are different from stinginess and cowardice. The *tone* of any composition, like the Gettysburg Address, would never be noticed if the tone of one did not strike our attention by differing from the tone of another. (It was because *everything* in everybody's experience tended to fall earthward—even steam is relatively earthbound—that nobody paid much attention to gravitation until Isaac Newton had his curious insight into it.)

For even in the physical realm we perceive by contrast. We can read, for instance, because the black letters contrast with the white page (or the light chalk with the dark chalkboard). The reason we can't see in the dark is that everything is black, with no contrast.

Since we are coming soon to a similarly valuable process—comparison—let's take the opportunity here to say that we also perceive through similarities. As children, we see in the world around us a number of petaled, colored, fairly round, often fragrant things that typically appear amid greenery; we note how they are similar, and forming the concept that we call *flower*, we apply it to all flowers, both familiar and new. Later, when we are college students, we are able to understand *magneto* if someone tells us it is *like* a generator. (Actually, students would probably be told that a magneto is like a generator *but* has a permanent magnet. This addition of difference to similarity produces the valuable thing called a *definition*.) In fact, if I tell you I have a blue sweater, you understand me only because you have seen blue, and sweaters, before.

But we must return to the advantages of making a special study of contrast. The third reason is the very practical one that in our schoolwork and elsewhere we will often be called on to contrast two American presidents, two kinds of social welfare laws, Haggada and Halakah, a percept and a concept, a sacrament and a sacramental, a symbol and a metaphor. And experience shows that in so doing we may meet trouble if we haven't mastered a few simple rules.

Seven Rules for Contrast

First, select for treatment differences that make a difference—that is, significant, meaningful differences. Do not be like one of my students who, when asked to contrast college and high school, wrote that in high school all the buildings had been of one story, whereas in college he found that the buildings had two stories. Furthermore, if the difference you select is not obviously significant, explain its significance.

Second, contrast the *same* parts or qualities of each object or person. Make sure each comparison uses the *same* basis. Do not, for example, say, "Oranges are round, whereas bananas are yellow." There you are contrasting a shape with a color. To do so is meaningless. If shape is to be the basis of your comparison, it must be so for both of the things contrasted: oranges are round, whereas bananas are oblong. If color is the basis: oranges are orange, whereas bananas are yellow. Can you see that "Switzerland is politically neutral, whereas Finland has an arctic climate" won't work?

In the same way, neither can you say that Julia is quiet, whereas Hazel is selfish. If degree of talkativeness is the basis of the contrast, *Julia is quiet* must be matched by *whereas Hazel is talkative* if there is to be a contrast. In the same way, if degree of givingness is the basis, *whereas Hazel is selfish* must be matched by *Julia is generous*.

The *third* rule is really the same as the second, but it gets at the matter in a different way. It is this: you must say about one person or thing the *opposite* of what you have said about the other. Oh, I don't mean one has to be the complete negative of the other, like hot and cold, but they do have to be clearly opposed (and on the same basis) — a warm day versus a hot one, for example. For instance, before I started giving students instructions in the writing of contrasts, I'd call for a paper contrasting two characters in Ibsen's play *Hedda Gabler* and get themes like this:

> Thea led a closely protected life, even after she came out into the world somewhat by marrying the sheriff. But Hedda had been her father's pride and joy and had possibly been spoiled by him.

I used to puzzle over paper after paper like that, trying to find what *contrast* the writers may have had in mind, until finally I realized that my students *thought* they had a contrast because they were saying *one* thing about Thea and *another* about Hedda!

No! If I say that Thea's life was *protected*, then I must say something *opposite* about Hedda's life. I must, that is, say that Hedda's life was *not* so protected— or some equivalent: Hedda came and went as she pleased, or Hedda's father let her mix freely in society, or Hedda's father felt she must learn the ways of the world. In other words, I must say something that adds up to the fact that Hedda was unprotected (since the other part of my contrast was that Thea was *protected*). Or, if I want to keep what I said about Hedda's being her father's pride and joy and being spoiled, I have to say something *opposite* about Thea. I must, that is, indicate that Thea was *not* her father's pride and joy and was *not* spoiled.

This is a good time to recall what we said about *antonyms*—words that designate the opposite of something—in Chapter 11 when we were talking about the forms of explicit reference. For are we not saying that every contrast is built on a word and some kind of antonym for that word—*hot-cold, big-little, visible-invisible, cooperative-uncooperative*?

I must direct your attention here, however, to the fact that the antonyms I've just given are antonyms strictly speaking. They are direct opposites, or what logicians call *contradictories*. What logicians call *contraries* are simply differences *in the same line*—or, as we say, differences *having the same base*. Thus *red* and *non-red* are clear contradictories; they are direct opposites; they are in the category of antonyms. But *red* and *blue* are a somewhat different case; we think of blue as a different color from red, certainly, but we never say that it is the direct opposite of red. And the two *do* form a *contrast*, certainly.

"Well," you may say, "aren't you admitting now what you denied a moment ago? Isn't *spoiled* (which we said of Hedda) quite *different* from *protected* (which we said of Thea)?" Yes, it is. But *spoiled* and *protected* are not in the same line; they do not have the same base. We can no more make any meaningful relationship between them than we could between a frying pan and the Statue of Liberty. "Red is not blue" is meaningful; but "Spoiled is not protected" or "Protected is not spoiled" is not. And here is a final test: a thing cannot be red and blue in the same way at the same time; thus red and blue can be contrasted. But a person *can* be both spoiled and protected (or unspoiled and unprotected, as the case may be) in the same way at the same time; *spoiled* and *protected*, therefore, can hardly be contrasted.

Fourth, in contrasting two persons or things, if you mention something about one, be sure to mention the contrasting thing about the other. Do not leave loose ends! In other words, you cannot say that Hedda is selfish and then go on to something else about Hedda, ignoring Thea. You must, instead, then say the *opposite* thing about Thea. That is, when you have said that Hedda is selfish and have illustrated her selfishness by accounts of her conduct with the other characters, you must then say that Thea is unselfish, or generous or altruistic, and proceed to illustrate her selflessness. In other words, you can't say Hedda is selfish, illustrate her selfishness, and then go on to talk about her appearance and dress without first taking up Thea and *her unselfishness*.

Fifth, take up things, always, in the order in which you first present them. Don't say "Tom is different from Harry. Harry is. . . ." No, say "Tom is different from Harry. *Tom* is. . . ." because you introduced Tom first. And *keep* Tom first throughout. Otherwise you'll needlessly confuse your reader with pointless variation. Developing this habit of keeping the first element first will help you balance your information, too, so you won't end up with twice as much material on Tom as you have on Harry.

The *sixth* rule is a different kind of rule, since it has to do only with vocabulary. First, *contrast* and *comparison* (which we will come to) are names of the operations you perform; they are *not* words that you are to use for your theme as synonyms for *difference* and *likeness* (except for the expression *in contrast*). That is, do not say "There are many contrasts between Thea and Hedda" or "There is another comparison between Theodore Roosevelt and Franklin Roosevelt." Instead, use such words as *difference, dissimilarity, likeness, similarity,* and *resemblance*.

Seventh, as words to *connect* two contrasted statements, use *whereas* and *in contrast*. Thus, "Hedda is selfish, *whereas* Thea is altruistic." Or, "The Duke values things that he can possess while others cannot. The Duchess, *in contrast*, places no value whatever on ownership." (Please notice that *whereas* used to express a contrast always has only a comma before it and no comma after it.)

While is an acceptable though conversational substitute for *whereas*. Thus, "Thea is generous, *while* Hedda is selfish." But do not use the even more colloquial *where* for *whereas*, as in "John is scrupulously honest, where Andy is not above helping himself to office stationery and stamps." And the versatile connective *but* is not right for a contrast because it allows a non-contrasting second statement: "Hedda is selfish, but that's not what I want to write about here."

You will recall our discussion of these connectives back in Chapter 12. There we also cautioned against using the expressions *on the contrary* and *on the other hand*. The phrase *on the contrary* is used not for a contrast, but for a *denial*: "The common assertion is that people thought the world was flat. On the contrary, they were thoroughly convinced that it was round." Or, "Is it difficult? On the contrary, it is quite easy." *On the other hand* is used not in contrasting two persons and things, but in introducing another point of view of the same thing or situation. "He is never on time for work; on the other hand, when he does get here he sells more than our other salesmen put together."

Comparison

All that has been said of contrast can be said, *mutatis mutandis* (which you'll find in the dictionary), about *comparison*. Comparison is of likenesses, of course, whereas contrast is of differences. But both involve setting two things or people side by side and considering them on the same basis (rules 2 and 3). Thus one can compare lemons and grapefruits (both are citrus fruits), detailing their similarities; or one can compare Shelley and Keats (both Romantic poets), pianos and harpsichords (both keyboard instruments), or the government of Canada and the government of Australia.

Of course, things described as *similar* are never *identical*, else there would be no point in spending time comparing them. Nobody ever said more of the proverbial two peas in a pod than that they are virtually wholly alike! In other words, things people spend time in comparing are, while alike, also unlike. (It may interest you to know that finding similarities amid differences is the quality of a genius, according to Aristotle—himself a genius.) One of the delights of poetry rests on this quality of comparison. The reader knows there is some similarity in the metaphor or simile and enjoys the process of figuring it out: "My heart is like a singing bird. . . ."

Similarly, two things *contrasted* are always alike. Otherwise, there would be no point in contrasting them! Who would ever undertake to contrast a window and a piano, a poem and an eggbeater, a ballpoint pen and a shovel? Decidedly each is unlike the other; but they are so dissimilar that there would be no *point* in contrasting them.

X, 1, 2, and 3

Having explained that much about contrast and comparison, we can go on to the question that is probably in your mind right now: What about sentences X, 1, 2, and 3 when we are writing a contrast or a comparison?

The simplest way to incorporate a contrast is to put it in our sentence X in the form: "A and B are different." Then sentences 1, 2, and 3 can explain three important ways in which A and B are different, and the three respective paragraphs can go on to discuss and illustrate those three ways.

But that is a "promise" sentence, which we said in Chapter 2 was not the best kind of sentence X. So instead of saying simply that A and B are different, you are better off to begin by declaring *one fundamental difference* that you have in mind, of which sentences 1, 2, and 3 are aspects. For instance, I could say simply that college is different from high school and then go on to give as sentences 1, 2, and 3 the statements that in college a greater quantity of work is required, a higher quality of work is required, and less help is given by the professor. Or instead, I could see all those three statements combined under the heading of maturity. Then my sentence X could read "College demands greater maturity than high school." My sentences 1, 2, and 3 could assert that it requires an amount of work, a kind of work, and an independence in work befitting the student's greater maturity.

At the same time, the sentence X that simply promises that the writer will say something remains respectable. You may expect a good professional writer to write a sentence X like "English education and American education are different" and to follow it with a series of sentences about the principal differences, because it would be cumbersome to contain the whole essay in a sentence X like this: "English education, unlike American education, seeks selectively to provide the nation with leaders educated in depth, and hence trained to think in depth."

Remember, as I cautioned you in Chapter 2, that comparison or contrast complicates our job in following Steps 2 and 3. In fact, it doubles the demands on our sentences. For we must now make sure that every paragraph and sentence must talk about not just *one* topic and what it is or was, does or did, but *two* topics and what *each* is or was, does or did. Consider a simple, non-comparative sentence X: "My grandfather is neat." Each sentence produced by Steps 2 and 3 must then cover two things, *my grandfather* and *his neatness*. If we now add a *contrast* to sentence X, "My grandfather is neater than your grandfather," we must include in each sentence *four* things: my grandfather, your grandfather, and the neatness of each. This extra complexity, however, is balanced by the ease of finding abundant *details* and *examples* to satisfy Step 4 when we employ contrast. Thus we can write:

X   My grandfather's home is neater than your grandfather's.
1.   My grandfather's bedroom is neater than your grandfather's.
2.   My grandfather's kitchen is neater than your grandfather's.
3.   My grandfather's living room is neater than your grandfather's.

For a longer and more complex example of this type of essay, your instructor may want to read to you (or you may want to look up on your own) Bruno Bettelheim's account of the two main versions of the Cinderella story. "Perrault's Cinderella is sugar-sweet and insipidly good," writes Bettelheim; "most other Cinderellas are much more of a person." He then spells out the details (*The Uses of Enchantment: The Meaning and Importance of Fairy Tales* [New York: Knopf, 1976], 251–53).

What I have just illustrated is the most straightforward way of incorporating contrast or comparison into your sentence X and sentences 1, 2, and 3. The paragraphs that follow describe several other useful ways to do this. These, however, will be ways that require some modification of the conditions for Step 2. If after reading about it you are not sure whether you can handle that modification, stick with the first way for now. But if you now have a firm grasp of Steps 1 through 6, pay close attention to the discussion here, and you will see that Step 2 can adapt in a number of other ways to the special requirements of contrast and comparison.

Now since *like* things are also *unlike*, and vice versa, can't we *combine* comparison and contrast in one theme? Of course. And what do we do then with sentences X, 1, 2, and 3? We *alternate* them; one paragraph gives comparison, another gives contrast, rather than every paragraph referring to the whole of sentence X. This modification is permitted only in comparison and contrast themes, mind you. Do not think Step 2 is abolished. No, it is just modified in these special circumstances.

With things unlike and like, then: First of all, decide which is more important, the *unlike* or the *like*. Then give more emphasis and space to whichever is more important. If the *unlike* is more important, then in sentence X we can assert that A and B are different, *though alike*; then devote sentence 1 to the resemblance and sentences 2 and 3 to the differences. Or, if the *like* is more important, we can assert in sentence X that A and B are alike, *though different*; in the first paragraph we can discuss the difference, then in the subsequent paragraphs the likenesses. Notice that the word *though* puts the less important part of sentence X in a less important position; it is called a *subordinating* conjunction for that reason (look up *subordinate* in your dictionary).

Please reread the preceding paragraph.

Now that you have read it twice, I hope you have noticed that it means exactly what it says, and not something different. In particular, it means that the lesser statement—the one that is less important, the one you devote just one paragraph to—comes *last*, with a *though*, in sentence X and *first* in sentences 1, 2, and 3. That is so your main point—the one that takes two paragraphs—comes in the emphatic places: at the start of the entire theme (the first part of sentence X) and at the end of the theme (the last two paragraphs).

You'd like an example, wouldn't you? Let's keep to the simple example of our grandfathers:

X   My grandfather is neater than your grandfather, though both impress visitors as neat.
1.   They both have rooms that look spotless.
2.   My grandfather, however, keeps his suits neatly hung in the closet, while your grandfather piles his closet with everything he doesn't want visitors to see.
3.   My grandfather keeps the floor under his bed free of dust, while your grandfather sweeps debris under his bed.

Other types of organization are also possible for comparison and contrast themes. Some students, for example, reasonably ask whether, in a theme of, say, contrast, they can't do either of two things: make a number of individual contrasts of one kind in the first paragraph, a number of a second kind in the second paragraph, and so forth; or devote one paragraph to certain qualities of A, then another paragraph to the *contrasting* qualities of B?

The question is so reasonable that it answers itself. And the answer is *yes*. Our sole purpose is to be clear, and surely either procedure will be clear to the reader. And if the student asks "Which shall I use?" the answer is that whichever seems natural to the writer will probably seem natural to the reader, too. But I would add two precautions.

First, do not make a number of *individual* points about A in one paragraph and then give the *matching* points about B in the next. The result will be that the reader will have to keep glancing up and down from one paragraph to another to keep track of the differences. This device of contrasting the material in one paragraph with that in another serves best when there are only two opposite assertions, each developed with the details that match *it*, with no attempt to match one set of details with the opposite set of details.

For example, in one paragraph I can say that statesman Y throughout his career always acted on his dread of tyranny. Then I can illustrate what I've said by giving a few events in his career. In the next paragraph I can say that statesman Z throughout his career always acted on his dread of anarchy (an opposite of tyranny, you understand: one is too much control, and the other, none). Then I can go on to illustrate what I've asserted about Z with events from *his* career. But naturally, the *events* in Z's career won't be matched up with those in Y's. Statesman Y, in fact, may have been a cabinet minister and statesman Z a leading figure in a parliament, so that the events in their political lives will all be of somewhat different kinds. So the reader will not be called on to keep looking up from the second paragraph to see how the *details* match those in the first, for they won't match, of course.

The second precaution is that you must not end up with a two-paragraph theme. That far from the basic Step 2 you cannot go! I hope I am not sacrificing principle to expediency in saying that the only trouble with a two-paragraph theme, even a theme of good length, is that it does not look (or *feel*) like a *theme*. Well, what do you do? We can hardly demand that all twins be triplets. In fact, there *is* something *twofold* in the very nature of a comparison or contrast.

What I would do is this: to a contrast of the kind I've just described I would add a paragraph at the beginning, briefly establishing the similarity that gives the contrast its point. (Ideally, such an opening paragraph should also mention—in general terms—the contrast that is going to be made.) Both Y and Z, I can say, were nineteenth-century statesmen, both had experienced revolution followed by reaction, and so forth.

S. S. Wilson here provides an example of just such a theme.

In the first paragraph Wilson establishes the similarity between cycling and walking—the use of muscular energy. That likeness becomes the basis for a division, a contrast between mechanical and isometric work. This introductory paragraph leads naturally into two others, one on each kind of muscular action.

CYCLING AND WALKING   S. S. Wilson

1.   The reason for the high energy efficiency of cycling compared with walking appears to lie mainly in the mode of action of the muscles. Whereas a machine only performs mechanical work when a force moves through a distance, muscles consume energy when they are in tension but not moving (doing what is sometimes called "isometric" work). A man standing still maintains his upright posture by means of a complicated system of bones in compression and muscles in tension. Hence merely standing consumes energy. Similarly, in performing movements with no external forces, as in shadowboxing, muscular energy is consumed because of the alternate acceleration and deceleration of the hands and arms, although no mechanical work is done against any outside agency.

2.   In walking the leg muscles must not only support the rest of the body in an erect posture but also raise and lower the entire body as well as accelerate and decelerate the lower limbs. All these actions consume energy without doing any useful external work. Walking uphill requires that additional work be done against gravity. Apart from these ways of consuming energy, every time the foot strikes the ground some energy is lost, as evidenced by the wear of footpaths, shoes and socks. The swinging of the arms and legs also causes wear and loss of energy by chafing.

3.   Contrast this with the cyclist, who first of all saves energy by sitting, thus relieving his leg muscles of their supporting function and accompanying energy consumption. The only reciprocating parts of his body are his knees and thighs; his feet rotate smoothly at a constant speed and the rest of his body is still. Even the acceleration and deceleration of his legs are achieved efficiently, since the strongest muscles are used almost exclusively; the rising leg does not have to be lifted but is raised by the downward thrust of the other leg. The back muscles must be used to support the trunk, but the arms can also help to do this, resulting (in the normal cycling attitude) in a little residual strain on the hands and arms.

ASSIGNMENT

First, restudy this chapter, with particular attention to the seven rules of contrast. Then compare, or contrast, or compare *and* contrast one of these pairs: two characters in a story (or one in one story, one in another); two students you know (do not make up details for this comparison, much less make up imaginary students); two relatives of yours; two instructors; two kinds of manufacturing procedure; two ways of bringing up children; two periods in history; two artists; two sports (like football and touch football, for instance); or whatever other pair you feel you can do well.

Chapter 15

THE ARGUMENTATIVE THEME

Many if not most themes tend toward the argumentative. True, I suppose that a physicist who set out to explain to us the nature of the laser might involve in the explanation not even a tinge of argument. But most of us are asserting in our themes something that we can (and perhaps do) imagine could conceivably be objected to or denied. Isn't that what we just saw T. H. Huxley doing? Or at least we pretend that we may not be believed or that some readers may in effect disagree about the importance of the point we are troubling to make.

This is all to the good. For in discussing Step 4, you recall, I showed you how to steal from the fiction writer's bag of tricks; and besides the specific details you learned to adopt then, you ought now to take over *conflict*. The fiction writer uses it everywhere; besides keeping readers in doubt generally and making them wonder how things will turn out, it is the chief device for engaging their attention. When a short story opens, it may be with an argument (conflict) over who will do the dishes; or Mary Jane wants to go out, but her father expresses reluctance to let her (conflict). In any case, somebody is usually at odds with somebody over something. And conflict continues throughout the story.

Conflict—in the form of argument—gives tension to a theme and endows it with a very legitimate interest that sharpens readers' awareness of the points being made. (Even contrast, which we studied earlier, wins a share in this kind of interest because, in posing one thing against another, it at least imitates conflict. Art majors can tell us how this same principle operates in art, and music majors how it works in music.)

We are, therefore, interested in argument or conflict of some sort as a principle useful in nearly all themes. But we *call* argumentative only those themes that expressly seek to persuade or convince the reader to adopt a certain conclusion from two or more possibilities. Now I am not going to teach you the art of persuasion; that is a higher study. But I am going to stress a few fundamentals of argumentative writing that beginning writers commonly overlook.

First, of course, you have to continue to fight your natural tendency to be strong on asserting your ideas and weak on backing them up with reasons, examples, and facts. So review in your mind Step 4. You have learned it; you have had practice in it; but you must continue to apply it consciously, because your natural tendency will continue to be opposite to it.

For instance, perhaps you are arguing for capital punishment by saying that it reduces crime. Since most of your friends, it seems, agree with you, you feel you have in a sense won your argument before you have even begun. But that does not mean that your argument in itself is a good one (there was a time when most people favored witch burning). No, you must give your *reasons* for supporting the death penalty.

You start by saying that capital punishment is a deterrent to murder. Now you must say *why* you say so. "It stands to reason," you say? No; "it stands to reason" just means "anyone can see that this is so," and a statement without facts to support it is precisely *not* obviously so. It is only theory, and theory must be submitted to test. What are the facts? You say that convicted burglars and robbers now in prison assert that the death penalty was all that deterred them from shooting the liquor store proprietor they were robbing, or shooting the policeman who appeared on the scene? Now your zeal to prove that the death penalty is desirable may cause you to think that what those burglars and robbers assert also stands to reason. But to an intelligent and skeptical reader what they say may seem improbable; moreover, the reader wants not more theory—yours or the criminal's—but facts. What do the statistics show about armed crime and murder? Is there less of it (or has the increase been smaller) in states that retain the death penalty than in states that gave it up? Or the reverse? In other words, apart from what criminals *say*, what do criminals actually *do*?

If you don't know the answers to those and other relevant questions, you are hardly prepared to argue one way or the other on this issue. To have strong feelings about the death penalty and then to cast about for any plausible reasons to support your feelings is not really argument, you know. At best, it is childishness; at worst, trickery. Our feelings should be governed by the facts; we should not look only for facts that seem to justify our feelings. And, in any case, the intelligent and skeptical reader whom we must imagine as the reader of our argumentative paper is going to insist on sufficient relevant *facts*—and on logical reasoning from those facts.

The government ought simply to print more money and distribute it to the poor? States ought to require the wearing of seat belts in automobiles? You can argue until you're blue in the face, but what your intelligent and skeptical reader will want to know is whether, in fact, governments have ever tried such things and if so, what have been the results.

When you know the answers, put them in a sentence X that summarizes the facts: "Printing extra money leads to runaway inflation" or "Seat belts save lives." Leave the *ought* or the *should* for the rounding-off sentence or paragraph at the end of the paper. There you can say what we *should* do, *after* the case has been fully developed for the necessity of some change. Sentence X, in contrast, ought simply to state directly what that necessity is. Not "Firemen should have more money," but "Firemen are underpaid"; not "The police should learn to treat minorities decently," but "Minorities are treated unfairly by the police." Then, after the paper has demonstrated the truth of your sentence X, the rounding-off sentence is practically inevitable: "Firemen should have more money."

In your personal life you make choices every day that are capable of being argued intelligently. Will a certain toothpaste keep you from getting cavities or enhance your sex appeal? Will a Miser Mini car get good gas mileage? Do Earth Blast stereo speakers offer true high fidelity? You can be charmed by the advertisements, or you can look for the facts and develop what amounts to an argumentative theme. At this point in the course, an instructor I know sends his students to look at articles in *Consumer Reports* magazine before writing the argumentative theme. Look there yourself and you will see why.

Perhaps what has been said so far has convinced you that you had better not select argumentative topics that demand research unless you are prepared to do the research. Do not make up facts! Students, you imagine, should have a greater voice in governing their high schools? You realize that the intelligent and skeptical reader will want to know where, actually, students have been given such a voice and what the results have been. But do not make up a school, a plan, or a set of results! That would be dishonest, both a lie and a shirking of the assignment.

Reality

I hope you don't feel that in the paragraphs that follow I'm wandering too far off the subject of argumentative themes. Right now, the point I have in mind about the made-up theme just discussed—a point to which I will give broad application—is this: first, to *make up* a relative, a professor, a student, a school, a business deal—anything—for an argumentative or any other kind of theme is not nearly so useful as selecting a real relative, a real professor, and so forth. One reason is that pinning oneself down to a specific set of circumstances— setting oneself strict limits—is always artistically sound: the circle for Rubens, the sonnet form for Keats, and Steps 1 through 6 for our themes. Another reason is that dealing with unyielding realities is always harder and hence better practice. Still another reason is that dealing with realities is a good exercise in facing the facts of life and in keeping ourselves honest. But the main reason for choosing realities is that in your other classes and in your business or professional work you are not going to be called on for any make-believe; it is always unyielding realities that you will be dealing with, so you need to practice with them.

For, as I've said before, it cannot be too often repeated to you, nor too heavily emphasized, that *what you write in an English composition class is practice; it is what you write outside that English class that is of real importance.*

You know, my fellow English professors have sometimes remarked how often, when they are introduced as English professors, people say, "Oh, I'll have to watch my English!" Not at all; English professors are as much used to errors as doctors are to sore throats. It is other people, not English professors, in whose presence you must watch your English and be sure to express yourself clearly: clients, customers, employees, employers, supervisors, subordinates— and professors in other departments. They expect you to learn something in your English class! *Their* judgment will be harsh; and a *he don't* or a series of misspellings or a confusing memo may do you damage with them.

Similarly, I've had occasion to notice that often students who write very well in their themes for a composition class will then write letters, notes, memoranda, signs, advertisements, even papers for another class that are miserably composed and full of careless errors. Those students have the facts of life backwards! English is not something you do in English class; it is the language you speak and write hourly in your workaday life—to your credit or discredit, and with results favorable or unfavorable to you. Thus the writing you do in a composition class is only preparation; your very best writing must be in your other classes and in your business or profession.

That is why, when a young police officer I was teaching told me after class one day that for the first time a judge had praised an arrest report he had written, I felt better satisfied than if I had learned that a former student of mine had completed a novel. For as I have said before, almost no students are going to be professional writers, yet nearly all of them will have to write. And if I can really teach all those students how to do the writing they will in fact have to do and at the same time persuade them that lessons in writing are to be applied outside English class, I'll feel perfectly satisfied.

Presenting the Other Side

Let's return now to the point where I left off, when I was dealing specifically with argumentation. I was remarking, as you recall, that you should not choose such subjects as capital punishment unless you are prepared to do the research needed to test your theory. If you are not prepared to do such research, you had better choose to argue the proposition that some program at your school is—or is not—worth supporting.

You can argue that proposition if you have imagination and knowledge enough to present both sides—the side of continuing the program and the side of discontinuing it. And I say this for two reasons. The first reason is that, as some students fail to realize, there *must* be another side; otherwise you haven't got an argument, you've got an explanation (exposition) plain and simple—or, worse, a sermon. Some students mistakenly pick as an argumentative topic something like "Reckless driving is dangerous." Now is there another side to that question? Is there any sane person who would assert that reckless driving is *not* hazardous?

"Well," you may say, "at least there are many people who drive recklessly." I see. And you are going to preach them a sermon on safe driving. Well, before you put them to sleep with a sermon they too could give (they just don't happen to practice what they preach), you should recognize that for a proposition like "Reckless driving is hazardous," you don't have a real other side—those who don't drive safely do not offer facts and evidence in support of their bad habit—and hence you don't have the makings of an *argumentative* theme. So finally, unless you can present a case for both continuing and discontinuing the program (no matter which side you take), then you had better choose another topic.

The second reason an argumentative theme must present two sides is a principle that students readily understand but feel they can get by with ignoring. (So a teacher assigning argumentative themes for the first time can usually expect them to be poor; and perhaps the only thing the teacher can do is assign F's to the papers and tell the students they have one more chance to pay real attention to the principle in a second assignment.) The principle is that *the worth of your argumentative paper depends on how forcibly you present the other side of the question and how well you then deal with that other side.*

Yes, a student argues for disarmament without, sometimes, even mentioning the claims of those who oppose it. If the student does mention those claims, the student usually presents them in so poor a light that we're evidently expected to suppose that only mental defectives or madmen espouse them. But what will an intelligent and skeptical reader think if the writer neglects or slights the other side?

Such a reader will say: "Either this writer does not realize how strong the arguments on the other side are—in which case the writer should not be arguing—or else the writer is dishonestly covering up opposing claims. In any case," the reader will continue, "I want to see the opposing claims dealt with, for only a writer who can refute them can prove the case and convince me."

In other words, if you cannot deal with the fact that an airplane can fly upside down, you cannot prove Vernoulli's principle (according to which it can't). If you cannot deal with the fact that the Soviet Union, starting about neck and neck economically with Latin America, has in about seventy years moved immeasurably ahead of it, then you cannot convincingly prove that communism is less successful than free enterprise. If you cannot deal with the fact that only unimmunized people contract polio, you cannot successfully argue that all disease is psychosomatic or that germs are simply scavengers rather than pathogens. If you cannot deal with the weight of contrary critical opinion, you cannot impressively argue that Dante was a greater poet than Shakespeare.

Note: *deal with*. It is not enough just to present the counterclaims; you must *refute* the other side to the satisfaction of your readers. "I don't think so" is not an argument. And I need not tell you that it will not be enough to argue that those who dispute you are crackpots or atheists, or that they are unpatriotic or subversive or "the cause of all the trouble we're having," or that they are dishonest, or that they are up to no good. If Mr. Jones maintains that both employment and unemployment are spirals, the question is not whether Jones is a communist, a compulsive gambler, a wife beater, a provoker of street riots, a

racist, or a moron; the question is strictly whether employment and unemployment are in fact spirals or in fact not.

Connectives in Argumentation

Once you understand the principle of clearly presenting the opposite side of
an argument, you next need to know how to do that without undermining your
own side of the argument. For even while you are presenting the other side (or
a random objection), your readers must be able to see instantly that it *is* the
other side, not yours (or that it is an objection you are going to refute, not part
of the point *you* are making). Sometimes, of course, the points on the other
side are true (though not strong enough, in your view, to win the argument as
a whole); then your signal to readers that you are presenting the other side of
the question will be an introductory expression like *true, I grant, granted, admittedly, of course, naturally,* or even *now.* (You may want to review our discussion of these words in Chapter 8.)

Sometimes, however, you will think that the arguments on the other side are
erroneous, in which case you will of course not introduce them with an expression like *true.* You will, instead, use an expression like *Marxists contend, some
people believe, students sometimes mistakenly assert, it has been falsely claimed,
once it was believed,* or *there are those who declare.* But in either case you must
use *some* connective; otherwise your reader is liable to become quite confused.

Equally important, if your reader is not to become confused, is a signal that
shows you have finished (at least for the time being) with presenting the other
side and have now come back to argue on your own side. The very best signal
for this purpose is the word *but* (though *however* will also do well for this
purpose). Immediately after the word *but* you must show (a) that arguments on
the other side, though true, do not destroy your argument; or (b) that arguments on the other side are false (or at least unproved).

Thus, to use a brief example, "*Lay people often believe* that you can help the
mentally distressed by being willing to listen to them. *But* psychiatrists warn us
that if the mentally distressed are giving voice to their illusions, we reinforce
those illusions by giving them an opportunity to express them."

X, 1, 2, 3 Again

A special matter in argumentation is the arrangement of your facts. Of course,
sentence X must be an assertion of the point you are arguing: "Psychiatrists are
best able to deal with our mental and emotional problems"; "Our schools benefit
from centralized rather than local control"; "Learned Hand deserved appoint-
ment to the United States Supreme Court." Most of your sentences 1, 2, 3 (and
4, 5, . . . , depending on the length of your theme) will of course support that
point. But somewhere you will want to insert, *in a paragraph (or more) of its
own,* the case for the other side. Do not confuse your reader by mixing your
side and the other side in the same paragraph! Immediately following the paragraph (or paragraphs) stating the other side, of course, comes your refutation
of it, in a paragraph that starts with *but.*

The placement of the paragraph giving the other side is not crucial, as long as you make sure that it does *not* come first or last, because that is where the reader will expect *your* views. In a three-paragraph theme, then, the other side will have to come in paragraph 2, and your refutation of it in paragraph 3. Sentence 1 could assert that you have evidence or proofs to offer, and paragraph 1 could offer them; paragraph 2 could present the case for the other side; and paragraph 3 could then present your handling of the other side. (Your final sentence should contain some reaffirmation of your original contention in sentence X.) But three paragraphs is uncomfortably short for an argumentative theme; it means that one-third of the theme will be the other side, and another one-third your refutation of it, so only one paragraph (the first) is left for you to present your own independent case. You will find that at least four or five paragraphs give an argumentative theme better balance.

As for the order of your own arguments in a theme that is longer than three paragraphs, put your second best argument *first*, your very best *last*—in the positions of emphasis—and the rest in between. But this rule is secondary to the one about not beginning or ending with the other side. Begin and end with your own views, even if it means starting with your third best argument.

The Goal of Argument

Finally—and I'm afraid this most important point is the hardest for students to realize and make their own—remember, always remember, that we argue not to win an argument, but to get at the truth. To win an argument without having won the *truth* for yourself and others is an empty victory indeed. It's like winning a lottery and finding you've won only play money. Cultivate the habit— *win* for yourself the attitude—of being pleased to see your opponent win if the opponent is right, and always be prepared to recognize when the opponent *is* right. After all, if you have won your argument that the capital of the United States lies farther south than any European capital (ignoring Lisbon and Athens), what does that make you? No, there is no particular glory in having won an argument. There is genuine glory, instead, in possessing the truth. Whether it is won by you or by your opponent, in the end it is possessed by both of you. Truth is at once your greatest glory and your best friend. Strive for it above everything.

If you keep in mind, then, the real goal of argument, you will understand more clearly than before the strongest practical point of this chapter. What is it? That your argumentative theme is worthless if you haven't shown *the other side* in its *best* light—in its most persuasive form—and then dealt with it *convincingly*.

ASSIGNMENT

Here are some exercises that your instructor will probably not want you to do all in the same day.

1. Go to the library and leaf through a number of articles in magazines like *The New Republic, Commonweal, Christian Century, Commentary,*

National Review, Harper's, and *Atlantic Monthly.* Look for about half a dozen instances of arguments of the *true . . . but* or *it is claimed . . . but* variety.

2. In a newspaper find an editorial that is an argument. See how it conducts the business of arguing. (Perhaps it leaves rival papers to present the other side.)

3. Write an argumentative theme. To avoid the pitfalls that have been pointed out to you in this chapter, perhaps your most honest, most successful, and best supported argument will be one you actually had *with yourself.* Mind you, I say honest. Describe a choice over which you really debated and that you had some difficulty making up your mind on; a choice about which you actually weighed arguments on both sides (not just changed feelings for no well-defined reason). If you never had such a debate with yourself, ignore this suggestion; don't write about your choice between taking a job and going to college or between dropping out of high school and getting your diploma if actually there was no question whether you'd go to college or stay in high school.

Answer to puzzle at end of Chapter 12 (page 140): What is the difference between *but* and *though*? The answer: *but* is always followed by the *point*—the conclusion, the contention, the determination, the main statement; *though* (or *although*) is always followed by something *other* than the point—something that is not true, or not relevant, or at least not as important as the point. Thus, in "I decided to go, *but* it was raining," the writer indicates, by using *but*, that the rain dictated the final decision, and that the writer did *not* go. In contrast, in "I decided to go, *though* it was raining," the writer indicates, by using *though*, that the determination to go outweighed what might be considered the deterrent fact that it was raining, and that the writer *did* go after all. (The reason behind this answer is that a clause following *but* is a main clause, whereas a clause following *though* is a subordinate clause. A main clause is the place for your main point; a subordinate clause is the place for a subordinate, or secondary, point.)

Chapter 16

THE
REAL WORLD

We are coming to the end of our lessons together. You may not now be the equivalent of an Olympic swimmer, but if you have followed my instructions (odd though they may have seemed) and done the exercises (unnecessary though they may have appeared), you will have a skill in writing that will impress the people you write for in the future—your professors, your employers, your clients. If they ask where you learned to write so clearly, cohesively, and persuasively, I hope you won't mind telling them.

But before you take your first unaided steps beyond this book, I must give you a little more instruction on how to make the transition to the "real world." You have been preparing for the real world all along, of course—that is the reason almost all colleges and universities go to the expense of hiring so many English teachers and making a composition course a requirement in the freshman year—but there still is a shock in leaving the safety of the English classroom, where the instructor understands your difficulties and helps you with them, and encountering the real world of a history course or a contract proposal, where you are expected to get it right without help on your writing. Looking ahead, I know of certain difficulties you will encounter, and I will take the rest of this final chapter to give you some practical advice, born of long experience, on how to overcome them.

Longer Themes

First of all, we need to consider how to stretch our short three-paragraph theme when circumstances—or an assignment—require that we write something longer. It should be possible in three paragraphs to establish that my grandfather is neat; but the causes of the Reformation or the reasons for relocating a plant in Duluth are likely to need more room. For such assignments

179

you should *not* turn your back on the six Steps you have painstakingly learned, any more than you would ignore what your tennis class taught you about the overhand serve when you go out to play a match on your own. But to make use of our Steps you will have to extend the principles you have learned for writing short themes.

Naturally, to write a longer theme, you could just increase the number of paragraphs from three to six, or to a dozen, or to whatever number you wish. In many instances, however, you may find you can think more clearly, and present your material more clearly to your reader, if instead you do the following:

Make your sentences 1, 2, 3 (or more) into the beginnings of *sections*. Then treat each of the sentences 1, 2, and 3 as a little sentence X (strictly related, of course, to your *big* sentence X at the very beginning), and follow each little sentence X with three or four or more Step 2 sentences of its own (call them A, B, C, and so on to avoid confusion with the previously numbered 1, 2, 3). Since this involves the same principles you have been learning all through the course—sticking to the point and going into detail—you will have difficulty only if you try to do something different. No, this is just more of the same. Follow this procedure and your longer themes will preserve the same orderliness, logic, and clarity you have learned to achieve in short themes.

In addition to extending the length of your papers, you may want to extend their depth. You have just seen how to increase the *number* of paragraphs; you may also want to increase the *size* of paragraphs. This kind of extension, too, does not require learning new rules, but simply following the principles you have already learned—in this case Step 4. Just carry Step 4 another stage or two further. What do I mean? Here is a simple example. In the following version of a paragraph I'm going to follow the topic sentence with three additional sentences making the topic sentence fairly specific:

> On your deposits in our bank the interest we pay will vary inversely with the availability of those deposits. On an open passbook account, interest will be lowest and availability highest. On a one-year account, interest will be higher but availability lower. On certificates of deposit to be held for seven years, there is the highest interest but, as "seven years" indicates, the least availability.

Now I'm going to increase Step 4 in that paragraph by adding to each of those three supporting sentences *another*, still more specific explanatory sentence. I'll put an asterisk (*) before each of these, so that you'll easily identify them. Watch:

> On your deposits in our bank the interest we pay will vary inversely with the availability of those deposits. On an open passbook account, interest will be lowest and availability highest. *That is, we will pay 4½% interest compounded daily on your remaining balance no matter when or how often you make withdrawals. On a one-year account, interest will be higher but availability lower. *That is, we will pay 5% interest compounded daily on sums left for a year. On certificates of deposit to be held

for seven years, there is the highest interest but, as "seven years" indicates, the least availability. *That is, we will pay interest that, compounded daily, will amount to 8% annually.

While theoretically there is no end to this process, I think that one more explanatory sentence added to each of the three just added will be enough for our example. You can identify the new additions by their double asterisks (**). Note, too, the final rounding-off sentence I add.

> On your deposits in our bank the interest we pay will vary inversely with the availability of those deposits. On an open passbook account, interest will be lowest and availability highest. *That is, we will pay 4½% interest compounded daily on your remaining balance no matter when or how often you make withdrawals. **For example, you can deposit your paycheck at the start of the month and withdraw it all by the end, and you will still earn 4½% annual interest on whatever is in the account each day in between. On a one-year account, interest will be higher but availability lower. *That is, we will pay 5% interest compounded daily on sums left for a year. **For example, you can save up at this 5% rate the money you need to pay taxes once a year. On certificates of deposit to be held for seven years, there is the highest interest but, as "seven years" indicates, the least availability. *That is, we will pay interest that, compounded daily, will amount to 8% annually. **Savings for a child's college education could fit in this more profitable category. In an emergency, of course, you can withdraw any or all of your funds from all three types of accounts, but not without a substantial loss of interest in the latter two.

Not a glamorous paragraph, not a gripping or an absorbing one, and a banker might criticize the lack of certain necessary Step 4 information. Still, the paragraph serves as a good example of expansion through orderly additions of relevant detail.

Some warnings: First, you must use only additional details that will add to your reader's grasp of the point; if adding a statement about the color of something does not add to reader understanding, such detail is humdrum, and worse, irrelevant. Second, your original sentence must be capable of greater development than "I live in Granite City." Third, once you have a sentence that does lend itself to fairly complex development, you may have to do considerable research. For naturally, the more extensively you know your material, the more really relevant and really specific details you are able to include in your theme. And the more relevant and specific details you include, the more successfully you use Step 4—and the more readably and usefully you will write.

Another important warning has to do with the length of the paragraphs that you produce by this process. A paragraph that is longer than a full page is too long! When it grows to that length (if not before), it needs subdividing, with each new subtopic becoming a separate paragraph. You will recognize that our sample paragraph about banking has three subtopics; if the paragraph grew much bigger, each of the three subtopics would properly make a paragraph of its own. How big would that need to be before you needed to subdivide? Well, remember that a paragraph in one of your themes needs at least *five* sentences; so if you find yourself with five sentences or more on one subtopic, give it a paragraph of its own. Please do *not* let your professor in another course blame your English instructor or Bill Kerrigan if you have a paragraph two or three pages long. That is *not* the intent of our instructions!

Finally, do you think our paragraph on banking would have been clearer if the three kinds of accounts had been enumerated: *One . . . Two . . . Three . . .?*

Introductions and Conclusions

Back in Chapter 6 (pages 76–77) I discouraged you (to put it mildly) from burdening your theme and your reader with introductory and concluding paragraphs. In a three-paragraph, 500-word theme, an introduction makes as much sense as flapping your arms three times before putting on your coat. At that time, though, I also acknowledged that an introduction and a conclusion *do* make sense if you're writing something several times as long; an essay of 2,500 words will seem well-proportioned with a whole paragraph of introduction and a whole paragraph of conclusion—provided the paragraphs are *to the point* and not too long.

Or perhaps, even in a shorter paper, your professor may insist on a full-sized introductory paragraph and a full-sized conclusion. Are you to tell your professor that Bill Kerrigan won't let you write them? No. I still know—and can demonstrate in the professional writing you read—that short expository writing does not need an introductory paragraph, and needs at most a single rounding-off sentence as a conclusion. Let me ask you to pick up today's newspaper to see for yourself: look at any of the shorter *news* stories (not the human-interest "feature" stories that use the structure of fiction writing) and see whether they don't simply begin with the point and end with details.

Still, your professor in another course may want you to write an introduction and a conclusion. This may be simply because once upon a time this professor's instructor declared that all student writing should have an introduction and a conclusion, and the professor-to-be didn't feel inclined to argue. More likely, though, your professor has a good reason for asking you to write them. The reason is this: in an introduction and in a conclusion you can practice relating the particular material of your theme to the general principles or setting of the whole course. In a course on Shakespeare, you will perhaps write about the character of the fool in *King Lear*; in a course on U.S. foreign policy, you will write about diplomatic negotiations with the Soviet Union during the Cuban missile crisis of 1962; in a course on principles of social work, you will study one disturbed child. Where does your particular study fit into the larger pattern? The introduction and conclusion can explain—the introduction leading the reader from the general situation to your particular concern, pointing out its importance; and the conclusion explaining the implications of this particular study for our understanding of the subject as a whole. If you were to concern yourself with these connections during the body of your paper, you would be distracted from giving specific attention to the particular topic you have chosen.

All right. But notice that this is *not* "tell them what you're going to say, say it, and tell them what you said"! No, this kind of genuine introduction and conclusion means *more work*—hard work carefully explaining the relationship of the part to the whole.

Let's have an example.

> In the theatre, the character of the fool takes on more importance than it ever did in the real life of medieval and Renaissance Europe. Shakespeare, in particular, sees the value of the fool as commentator on the action—a commentator who is free of the social and psychological pressures that limit the other characters, and thus one who can know and show the truth, both to the other characters and to the audience. We see the character of the fool as truth-teller from Shakespeare's earliest examples, in *As You Like It* and *Twelfth Night*, to Hamlet himself putting on "an antic disposition," but nowhere is the fool's role more central or significant than in *King Lear*. In *King Lear* the fool is the agent not only of revelation but of salvation.

The last line of that introductory paragraph you will recognize as the sentence X of the paper. But notice also that this introduction does *not* begin, "Fools are everywhere. Why, even my roommate is a fool. Shakespeare had fools too. One of them is in *King Lear*."

The conclusion of this paper might again suggest wider implications, but it will make sure that the point of the paper is clear:

> So the fool has been the means of turning the blindest of men, Lear, not only towards an understanding of his error—that was the easy part—but to acceptance and love of his daughter Cordelia, and to pity for the sufferings of all humankind. Lear learns, in fact, that true wisdom goes hand in hand with the humility of being taken for a fool, and he does the fool the ultimate honor of taking over his role himself, and at the end calling his beloved dead daughter "my poor fool." We have met this lesson before, in the New Testament, for example—"we are fools for Christ's sake," says St. Paul—but never in such a profoundly moving way as in Shakespeare's fable of proud King Lear.

Civilian Clothes

When you write for others, you must use the forms they are accustomed to. So you will have to camouflage the special X, 1, 2, 3 form I have insisted on throughout this book. To camouflage, you understand, means to keep it—but to keep it under wraps, to trade the uniform for civilian clothes.

Specifically, it means to keep the sentences X and 1, 2, 3, but to remove the letter X and the numbers 1, 2, and 3 from in front of those sentences. It means to continue writing your X, 1, 2, 3 first—but do it *for yourself only*, in the *draft* of your paper. In the final version that you hand in, *leave out* the broken line and the X, 1, 2, 3 that go above it. Your paper for the outside world should start with what appears *below* the broken line in our format.

I think you would probably like an example, so I will once more show you the little theme about winter that I last used to illustrate Step 5. As I have said before, it's much simpler than anything you'd be likely to write for another course, or for your employer. That is exactly why I put it here—so you can give full attention to what it would *look like* in civilian clothes. Compare the following version with the one in our standard format on page 107.

I dislike winter.

I dislike the winter cold. It makes me shiver. It chaps my lips. It gives me chilblains. It can even freeze my ears.

I dislike having to wear the heavy winter clothing that cold weather requires. I hate to wear earmuffs. I hate to wear galoshes. I hate to wear a heavy coat. I hate to wear long underwear.

I dislike the colds that, despite dressing for the cold weather, I always get in the winter. The colds stop up my nose. They give me a cough. They give me a fever. They make me miss school.

Please notice that this is the *same* theme as the one on page 107. Not a word is different! We have changed nothing, removed nothing except the letter X, the three numbers, a line, and the preliminary material that comes before the line. The theme itself is unchanged. Those letters and numbers, that broken line, and the preliminary listing of the X, 1, 2, 3 were set up to assist you in constructing your themes, just as construction workers set up a temporary scaffolding while they are putting up the walls of a building. Now that your understanding of the six Steps has been constructed, we can remove the scaffolding and look just at the sturdy, functional, almost handsome building itself. So remove the scaffolding; take off the uniform and put on civilian clothes when you send your writing out into the real world.

But make sure the body underneath remains well nourished and exercised! Let me tell you a story.

A young woman who had just started graduate school in the fine arts was given a job teaching in her university's large freshman composition program. She had been a capable writer as an undergraduate, but she was frustrated at the lack of progress her students made as they followed the assignments in the required writing handbook. Now her father had been successfully teaching with *Writing to the Point* for a number of years at the small college she had attended, so she telephoned in desperation and asked him what to do. "Just use the method of *Writing to the Point*, but don't tell them what you're doing," he advised. So she took out her old copy of the Six Basic Steps and began with, "Write a sentence."

The happy ending is that her class was delighted, and her students learned to write with a skill that mystified the other teaching assistants (she kept quiet about using a book that was not on the official list). That spring when the student newspaper published student evaluations of teaching, she was listed among the top instructors at all levels.

This true story is here to remind you of two things. First, you have learned a method that works! Second, what works is the method itself, not the particular form in which, for pedagogical purposes, we have embodied that method in this book. Do continue making a point, supporting that point, connecting your statements. Do *not* continue to use the letter X and the numbers 1, 2, and 3—as long as you remember to write a sentence X and sentences 1, 2, and 3 in their proper places anyhow.

X, 1, 2, 3 as an Abstract or Summary

In a paper or report written for another class or your business, you will find another use for sentences X, 1, 2, and 3 beyond their main function at the start of your theme and your paragraphs. They make up a simple *abstract* or *summary* of your theme. (*Abstract* and *summary* mean the same thing—a paragraph that briefly tells what your paper tells. In the academic world this is usually called an abstract, as in the publications *Dissertation Abstracts International* and *Chemical Abstracts*; in the business world the same thing is more often called a summary. A third term, *précis*, is used most often for a summary of *someone else's* writing.)

The writer who does not know our six Steps will have a hard time writing an abstract, because it requires saying in a very short space what the entire paper says. But that is exactly what your X, 1, 2 and 3 do already. So you simply put them into a single *paragraph* rather than on separate lines, and again *remove* the letter X and the numbers 1, 2, and 3. And that is all the changing you need to do; the words remain the same. Let me once again use the simple example of the theme on winter.

ORIGINAL THEME

X   I dislike winter.
1.   I dislike the winter cold.
2.   I dislike having to wear heavy winter clothing.
3.   I dislike the colds that I always get in the winter.

X   I dislike winter. . . .

ABSTRACT

I dislike winter. I dislike the winter cold. I dislike having to wear heavy winter clothing. I dislike the colds that I always get in the winter.

Notice: no X, no 1, 2 or 3; the sentences together in a single paragraph instead of on separate lines; but *the same words* as were previously above the line. (You will also make sure to find out exactly where your abstract should go—at the top of the first page of your paper, or on a separate preceding page, for example—and exactly how it should be labeled, Abstract or Summary.)

Notice also, however, that though this is as accurate a summary as could be wanted, the repeated phrasing of the four sentences is too monotonous when they come immediately after one another in the same paragraph. This is not a problem in the paper itself, where the sentences are separated by paragraphs, and where they in fact guide the reader to your main points by their repeated form. But in an abstract, such repetition is too insistent. So to avoid annoying your reader, you will want to rephrase the summary, perhaps putting several short sentences into one longer one:

ABSTRACT

I dislike winter for three reasons. I dislike its cold weather, I dislike the heavy clothing the season requires, and above all I dislike the colds I always get then.

In this more readable version, notice that the three Step 2 sentences have been combined into one, with pronoun (*its*) and synonyms (*the season, then*) substituting for *winter*, but keeping the repeated *I dislike* so the three main divisions will be clear. The *three* of *three reasons* connects with the three repeated phrases. The last of the three "I dislike" statements now begins with something other than the subject—the phrase *above all*.

In other words, having made the X, 1, 2, and 3 into a *paragraph*, I simply made it look more like a paragraph, using Step 6 and the rule about varying the length and beginning of sentences in your paragraphs. But the basic statements of the X, 1, 2, and 3 remain the same.

Now in most cases when you are asked to write an abstract or a summary you will have a paper with many more than three paragraphs. In that case, however, the principle is still the same: make a paragraph out of the sentence X and the principal paragraph topic sentences, in order. You may then want to combine sentences, as we have demonstrated above, and perhaps leave out some of the less important topic sentences altogether, to fit the length requirements of your abstract or summary; for no matter how long the paper, the abstract or summary usually must be kept to a very short length, perhaps as little as fifty or one hundred words.

The Research Paper

In the next few paragraphs you will not find me giving you complete instructions on how to write a research paper. That would take a book in itself, and you will undoubtedly be assigned a particular book to follow when you write a research paper. Follow it!

But here I want to give you some encouragement. Though a research paper may seem vastly different from the writing you have done for this course, it follows the same principles. What you have learned here will be of help and importance when you write your research paper. Again, it will just take some translation and camouflage.

Let us begin with research, as you must before you write your paper. Research simply means finding Step 4 material—specific facts and details—that you do not happen to know already. Usually you will be assigned to find these facts and details in books and articles you locate at the library, though sometimes the research will be experiments or interviews you conduct yourself. In any case, the principles of Step 4 remain in effect. Can you still recite Step 4 from memory? "Be as specific and concrete as possible. Give examples. . . ." Your specific details may be exact quotations from printed sources, or facts or statistics found there.

While you are collecting facts, you must continually review them to determine what *point*—what conclusion—they add up to. This is the hard part, but it is what makes the difference as you continue to search for further material, as well as when you sit down to do the actual writing. Do you remember, back in the chapter called "A Breathing Space," when I told the story of walking from the library to Mrs. Bradley's office and back again? Do you remember how pointless it was? If, in your research and writing, you have no point, you will not know what to include and what to exclude, what to take notes on and what to skip over. Are you going to write down everything you find about U.S.-Soviet diplomacy during the Cuban missile crisis? You can fill a thick notebook, but what will you do with it?

No, you need to know where you are going, and what is relevant and irrelevant. You must find a point, a conclusion to which all of your evidence leads. And the way you reach that point is to formulate a *research question*. Earlier we said that Sentence X can be phrased as the answer to a question. Now, even before you have all the evidence, and thus even before you know for sure what the answer will be, you need a question to guide your research. This will give a point to your research; you will look for evidence that supports one answer or the other, and you will ignore material that has no bearing on the question.

Does your evidence show that, in a crisis like that of 1962, the superpowers will take steps to avoid a nuclear war? Does it show the United States outmaneuvering the Soviet Union in keeping missiles out of Cuba, or the Soviets maintaining their strategic stronghold just off our coast? Maybe it will take some time and more research to decide which answer is correct. But at least you know what kind of evidence is relevant and what is not. You will not gather notes on the debates among President Kennedy's advisers on what the U.S. course of action should have been, nor will you bother with the speeches of Cuban premier Fidel Castro—because your concern is the interaction between the two superpowers.

Research done with a research question in mind is much harder than the vacuum cleaner approach that just sucks in anything about a topic, regardless of its relationship to anything else. But your reward for following a research question comes when you sit down to organize and write your paper. Then you have a sentence X—the answer to the research question—waiting for you. And with Step 2 in mind, you know what to do next: write the topic sentences for the paragraphs that support and explain your sentence X. (These sentences, suitably indented and labeled, can also serve as a *sentence outline* if your instructor requires one.) Steps 3 and 4 instruct you on selecting relevant supporting material from your notes to fill your paragraphs. You also know how to present, and deal with, the other side of the argument, as we discussed in the preceding chapter. Don't forget the proper connectives, and maybe a transitional paragraph or two.

A research paper also requires painstaking attention to detail—the detail of accurately using the material in your sources, and telling exactly what those sources are. The forms you are to use will be announced by your instructor and explained in your handbook. You will find them extraordinarily complex. Even your professors, who use these complex forms in their own scholarly writing, often are puzzled about the exact style for a quotation, a footnote, a parenthetical reference, a bibliography entry.

It is possible, however, to keep from drowning in a sea of bibliographic detail if you keep in mind that the detail has a purpose—a *point*, in fact. And a point helps make the detail clear!

This is the point of the rules about quotation: to make crystal clear to your reader when you are using someone else's words, and when you are using your own. When you use quotation marks, or indent a passage in a block, you are announcing to your reader that those quoted or blocked words are the words of someone else—exactly as that someone else wrote them. When you do *not* use quotation marks or an indented block, you announce to your reader that the ideas may come from someone else, but the words are entirely your own. (It is a matter of honesty to be careful about these rules. Violations of them are known as plagiarism, and sometimes entail severe penalties.)

The rules about *citation*—footnotes, or a name and a page in your text leading to an entry in your bibliography—have two points or purposes. The first of these is *acknowledgment*, that is, naming the person or persons who provided the information you are presenting. The citation is the answer to the reader's implied question, Who says so?

The second point of citation is *location*. Your paper should show your reader how to locate exactly the same source you used—the exact issue and page of a journal, for example, or the exact edition and page of a book. Depending on the system you use, this information will be contained in your footnote, or in the text of your paper with a reference to your bibliography. How do you know that your citation is complete? It is complete if your reader can go to any research library, order the exact materials you have used, and locate in them the exact passages you read and referred to in your paper.

So much attention to detail is required at all stages of a research paper that you may be tempted to forget that it is all supposed to add up to something. From this book, I hope, you will at least remember the importance, convenience, and effectiveness of having a *point*—in this case, a point to your paper, a point to your use of quotation marks, a point to your citation of sources.

Vocabulary

Though you might not dream it to read this book, I have perhaps as large a vocabulary as anyone else you will ever meet, and not just in one language but in several. (My most recent is Romanian.) In this book, however, I am writing not to show off my vocabulary but to teach a method of writing by the clearest means possible. So I would urge you too: unless your instructor specifically asks you to demonstrate your knowledge of technical terms, keep to language that you know the general reader will understand.

But I would not have been able to write this book if my vocabulary had not allowed me to do the necessary research for it—the *reading* that taught me the principles I have here explained to you. (Among the books underlying *Writing to the Point* are Euclid's *Geometry* and Cherubini's *Treatise on Counterpoint and Fugue*.) Nor could I communicate properly with the teachers and scholars who are my co-workers if I were limited to the vocabulary of a college freshman. So you will find, too, that as you grow more expert and more mature, your reading and vocabulary must mature, along with your writing. (I have a book on reading to recommend: *Reading for the Point* by William J. Kerrigan [New York: Harcourt Brace Jovanovich, 1979]. You will recognize some of its principles.) And developing your vocabulary, like developing your muscles, will require some systematic effort.

In your first half dozen years, to be sure, you acquired a vocabulary of several hundred words without effort, simply by exposure. And though your mind is less impressionable now than it was then, you can still acquire words by simple exposure—if you meet them often enough in the process of *regular reading*. Moreover, when you learn words through reading you learn also their *use* and their *connotations*. The dictionary, in contrast, tells you that *siblings* means brothers and sisters, but it does not tell you that our best writers never use the word (it belongs only in technical papers in the social sciences). The dictionary can tell you that *eerie* means "fear-inspiring, weird, uncanny," but you will learn the full force of the word only when a novelist uses it to describe the sound of a creaking door in a deserted house standing in moonlit countryside. I find it hard to teach students of literature the connotations (the suggestions, the emotional force, the overtones) of *desolate* and *forlorn* if they are meeting them for the first time in Keats's odes—and certainly a dictionary is no help.

I don't recall that I ever had a dictionary in any language until I was in my twenties, nor a dictionary in a foreign language, except for Latin and Greek (I'm a professor of Greek and English), until I was in my forties. Still, my English is not as exact as I wish you—with the help of a dictionary—would make yours. Look at the word *instance* in your dictionary and see the differences, the distinctions, the dictionary makes among *instance*, *example*, *case*, and *illustration*. These are distinctions of a kind I'm afraid I do not make; but it would be good if you (not so old a dog as I) could learn to make them. For another thing, if, because of not understanding a word, you cannot get the *point* of something you are reading, well, common sense will send you to a dictionary. (Still, if you are reading a Marxist essay and need to know the meaning there of *dialectic*, *alienation*, and *anomie*, you will not find the dictionary of much help.)

Again, if you are writing and are not sure of the meaning (or spelling) of a word you are about to use, you had better see what help the dictionary can give you. And by the way, you'll have to keep a dictionary right by you from the start, because experience will show you that you won't get up to get it when you need it, even if it's no farther than a few steps away.

For a different kind of help from the dictionary, begin to *notice* words. And stop occasionally to figure out, from the way a word is used, what it must mean: " 'A candidate, if unknown, will not be elected' employs an *ellipsis* of *he is* ('if *he is* unknown')." What must *ellipsis* mean in that sentence? Since *he is* is shown to be left out, doesn't it probably mean a *leaving out*? At this point, you'd look up *ellipsis* in the dictionary for confirmation.

Yet, finally, remember what I told you when I was introducing Step 6 (page 128). It may be nice to know the meanings of *sciolist*, *congeries*, *endemic*, *factitious*, *irredentist*, *leucomelanous*, *seriatim*, and *lemma*. But three things occur to me when I see vocabulary enrichment of that kind. First, students' trouble in reading is not so much with words like that, but with proper nouns—names— which writers frequently use to convey their impressions: the Rosetta stone, Rorschach, Freud, the Battle of Hastings, Queen Victoria, Falstaff, Don Quixote, Alice, Uncle Tom, the Parthenon, Linnaeus, the *Beagle*, Pythagoras, Walter Mitty, Mrs. Grundy, a Judas, a Moses, the Rubicon, and all the other references that students can learn only from diligent application in all their courses.

Second, I'd far rather see students at home with words like *get*, *set*, *hand*, *foot*, and *head* than in thrall to words like *naive* (which they often misspell), *intro-vert*, and *participatory*.

Third, let me say again—as I said in the discussion of Steps 5 and 6—that the real weakness in students' vocabularies is lack of knowledge of, and use of, the little words we think with, like *therefore*, *thus*, *whereas*, *although*, *however*, and *but*. Those are the words students should start with when they attempt to improve their vocabularies.

Variety in Expression

This has been a course about truth, not beauty. But since it has been asserted at least by a poet, John Keats, that beauty is truth, truth beauty—you may still be wondering whether you need to know more about making your writing more beautiful, in order to make it even more effective.

Of course. For if you now are able to write a clear, unified, coherent theme, you may want to know what you can do next to make your writing even better. It would be appropriate then for you to turn to the study of what is called *style*, which also is the subject of many books. I should warn you, though, that there is less agreement among experts on style than there is on the more fundamental matter of composition. Everyone agrees that a theme should have a point and stick reasonably close to it; that there should be some support for the point; and that statements should be connected with each other—the very lessons of our six Steps. Exactly what you should do to enhance the style of your writing, your way of expressing yourself, is quite another matter.

You will, for example, from time to time encounter readers who make special demands about the style of what you write—but their demands will rarely agree. Some readers will tell you never to use *I* or *me*; others will require that you avoid the passive voice ("The motion was passed") and use the active instead ("The delegates passed the motion"), no matter what, or that you never begin a sentence with *And*, or that *all of* must not be used to mean *all*. When they read or hear the commonplace word *hopefully*, some readers will react with shock and outrage—and others will not even notice it.

If you discover that the person for whom you are writing has a particular dislike (the rules are almost always negative), go along with it. You do not have to approve or understand—but you do have to get your point across, and you won't do it if you wave a red flag at a linguistic prejudice of your reader.

In this chapter I could not begin to list all the words that deserve special attention because of the reactions they provoke in some readers. There are whole books devoted to this matter of word usage, and they by no means agree with one another. But they are worth reading, if you wish to improve your style, because they all agree in conveying the message that words do matter; *every* word you use makes an impression on the reader, so you must choose *every* word carefully to make the right impression.

For a lesson on style that applies generally, rather than to individual words, I will here elaborate on a lesson I provided back in Chapter 5: the instruction to notice in your reading, and practice in your writing, a pleasing variety in the length and form of your sentences.

Sentence Length

First let's take *length*, since it is the simpler. The rule that used to be given to students was to vary a series of long sentences with an occasional short one. Today, when students tend to write short sentences, the rule has to be reversed: vary a succession of short sentences with an occasional long one. Practically, I have said (page 71), every third or fourth sentence should be noticeably longer than the others.

But how do you make a sentence longer? Just by adding more words? No. But I think you will have a sufficient number of longer sentences if you try to apply the following rule: do not put every idea in a simple little sentence of its own, but combine ideas into longer, more complex sentences. Take the following, for example.

"The Culture of Modernism" is one of the two or three best essays in Howe's book. In that essay Howe describes modern literature. By modern literature he means the literature of the past century and a half. He shows that it tends in general toward the solipsistic, the problematic, the nihilistic.

Some of those short sentences, surely, can be combined into long ones. Why don't you try your hand at combining them? Then I'll try my own hand at it. But you do yours before looking at mine. Well, then:

In "The Culture of Modernism," one of the two or three best essays in the book, Howe describes modern literature—that of the past century and a half—as tending in general toward the solipsistic, the problematic, and the nihilistic.

Several revisions of this short passage are possible, and yours may well be better than mine.

What if you reduce the number of sentences required by Step 3 when you combine short sentences? Well, you can apply Step 4 more vigorously. You can add sentences with more examples or further explanation. That way you will have improved your theme in two ways. And it could be argued that it's better to have fewer sentences with some variety in length than more sentences and no variety in length. (That's one reason why we had to change the phrasing of the sample abstract in the previous section.)

Besides length and variety, there is another reason for combining sentences—control. If you combine three short, simple sentences into one complex one, you will necessarily make one idea dominate the other two. Look at these: "She was sitting in the corner. She was facing the wall. Nobody realized that she was Barbra Streisand." Try putting them together in two or three different ways. Suppose you wrote this: "Because she was sitting in the corner and facing the wall, nobody realized that she was Barbra Streisand." You have not left it up to the reader to decide which of the sentences is most important; you have decided, by making "nobody realized that she was Barbra Streisand" the main clause in the new sentence.

Sentence Form

Variety in sentence *form* is the only other kind I will mention here. First, let me tell you that by combining some short sentences into longer ones, as described in the last section, you have already acquired a method that will tend to give variety to the form of your sentences.

You can go a long way, furthermore, by following the advice I gave you earlier in this book about varying the *beginnings* of your sentences. This is a simple matter of sometimes moving something from the middle or end of your sentence up to the very beginning. I have already suggested that you move your connectives up when applying Step 6. (But note one exception: don't apply this method of achieving variety to connectives like *however*, which go best in *second* place. Review pages 71 and 129 before you further practice varying the beginnings of your sentences.)

I'll give you some examples of varied beginnings. First I'll give each sentence unrevised, with the part to be moved in italics; then the revised sentence.

These scars will *eventually* disappear.

Eventually these scars will disappear.

Witches build their houses of candy *to entice children*.

To entice children, witches build their houses of candy.

I can be in Chicago within a few hours *by taking the morning flight*.

By taking the morning flight, I can be in Chicago within a few hours.

Do a little reading *whenever there is time*.

Whenever there is time, do a little reading.

The two sticks *joined together* will just reach the window.

Joined together, the two sticks will just reach the window.

Beethoven, *a revolutionary musician in his time*, now sounds quite orthodox.

A revolutionary musician in his time, Beethoven now sounds quite orthodox.

The prospects of easy profits were *gone*.

Gone were the prospects of easy profits.

Americans chewed a great deal of tobacco *in days gone by*.

In days gone by, Americans chewed a great deal of tobacco.

Extended Parallelism

A pleasing variety, then, enhances your style and is the single most important step you can take to make your writing *look* professional. But more fundamental than variety is unity, and for my last lesson before sending you out into the real world I will once again remind you of the value of *repetition*.

Earlier in the book, when I discussed the Seven Forms of Explicit Reference, I said that one—repeated sentence structure—is a form you would not often use. But I was not implying that repeated structure, called *parallelism*, is of little value in itself. Repeated structure (just look at the parallel lines of type on this page) is the basis of all art; it is actually the basis of Steps 1, 2, 3, and 4; and, as I have said, it can be useful in making obvious the connection between similar thoughts.

Although the basic idea of parallelism is, then, one you need to grasp, *extended* use of parallel sentence structure is a sophisticated device you do not need to know. But for the sake of completeness, before we close the book, I'll present it, in the form of the following rules for a paragraph embodying that device:

(A) The topic sentence is to have one form of arrangement, say subject coming first, and that form of arrangement is not to be repeated in the paragraph.

(B) Next, as we continue the paragraph, we write the three, four, or five sentences that give the several reasons, examples, effects, or whatever, that develop the topic sentence. Each of these is to be a sentence with an identical form of arrangement (but different from the arrangement of the topic sentence): gerund phrase first, adverb first, subordinate clause first, prepositional phrase first, or whatever.

(C) Then as we continue the paragraph, we may want to write sentences that stop to explain or comment on any of the three, four, or five sentences just named in B. Any such explanation or comment under C here is to be in a sentence differently arranged from those under A and B, and these under C are to be arranged just like one another, with an infinitive phrase first, or whatever.

(D) Any comments on the comments under C, if we choose to write them, would require still a new form, or set of identical forms, and so on endlessly in theory, though naturally there is a limit in practice.

In such a paragraph there is a minimum of logical connectives because the parallelisms do the work.

ASSIGNMENT

For those students who may wish to experiment with this form, I suggest four steps:

1. Examine the third (most expanded) form of the paragraph on banking near the start of this chapter. See whether it is arranged *exactly* according to the rules A, B, C, D just given.
2. If it is not, rewrite it to conform to these rules.

3. Write a paragraph of your own that follows these rules.
4. Try to find, in your reading, a paragraph that conforms at least fairly closely to these rules.

The Natural Way

"But doesn't a person just do that kind of thing naturally?" you may ask, as you go through the lessons in this chapter and this book. My answer is *no*. It's natural enough in itself, but you don't *do* it without thinking about it; so you'll have to keep your mind on it, either when you write or when you go over what you have written to add the finishing touches.

In fact, all I have set before you in this book is natural enough, something every instructor ought to insist on and that *you* ought to insist on. That your theme have a *point*? Naturally. But it won't if you don't force yourself to begin with a sentence X. That the paragraphs have topic sentences related to that point? Naturally. But they won't if you don't force yourself to write sentences 1, 2, and 3. That your general statements be backed up by plentiful facts and examples? Naturally. But they won't unless you deliberately set about to make them so. That your paragraphs be clearly connected with one another and that the role each sentence plays within your paragraphs be clarified by connectives? Naturally. But they won't if you don't remember to make them so.

And will your instructor, or any reader, insist that your comparisons and contrasts be properly matched up? Of course. But they wouldn't be if the need hadn't been called to your attention. That, in argumentative writing, your assertions be backed up by facts, not by theories or speculations? Of course. But they wouldn't be if you simply didn't think about it. And finally, that you continue to apply this method, and these principles, to the writing you do when this course is only a memory? Naturally. Just take a deep breath. . . .

Appendix I

The Six Steps

(Page references are to the first full statement of each step.)

STEP 1. Write a short, simple declarative sentence that makes one statement. (Chapter 1, page 6.)

STEP 2. Write three sentences about the sentence in Step 1—clearly and directly about the whole of that sentence, not just something in it. (Chapter 2, page 18.)

STEP 3. Write four or five sentences about each of the three sentences in Step 2—clearly and directly about the whole of the Step 2 sentence, not just something in it. (Chapter 3, page 31.)

STEP 4. Make the material in the four or five sentences of Step 3 as specific and concrete as possible. Go into detail. Use examples. Don't ask, "What will I say next?" Instead, say some more about what you have just said. Your goal is to say a lot about a little, not a little about a lot. (Chapter 4, pages 43–44.)

STEP 5. In the first sentence of each new paragraph, starting with Paragraph 2, insert a clear reference to the idea of the preceding paragraph. (Chapter 8, page 105.)

STEP 6. Make sure every sentence in your theme is connected with, and makes a clear reference to, the preceding sentence (Chapter 11, page 123.)

Appendix II

Checklist for Revision

In *writing* a theme, you are to follow the six Steps. In *checking over* the theme before writing or typing the final version, you will find it helpful to answer these questions. Answer them one at a time, and be honest in your answers, so that your instructor does not have to be painfully honest for you.

(Parenthetical references are to sources of information about each requirement.)

1. Does the theme make a point? (Step 1, Chapter 1.) Does that point follow the ten rules for sentence X? (Chapter 2, page 28.)
2. Do the paragraphs and their sentences keep to the point? (Steps 2 and 3, Chapters 2 and 3.)
3. Do the paragraphs support the point with specific details? (Step 4, Chapter 4.)
4. Do the paragraphs support the point with examples? (Step 4, Chapter 4.)
5. Does each new paragraph connect to the idea of the preceding one? (Step 5, Chapter 8.)
6. Does each new sentence connect to the preceding one? (Step 6, Chapter 11.)
7. Does the theme have a consistent grammatical subject? (Chapter 5, pages 68–70.)
8. Is every third sentence or so notably longer than the others? (Chapter 5, page 71.)
9. Does every third sentence or so begin with something other than the subject? (Chapter 5, page 71; Chapter 16, page 193.)
10. Is there a short rounding-off sentence at the end? (Chapter 6, page 77.)
11. Last of all, have errors in punctuation and spelling been corrected?

Appendix III

Seven Forms
of Explicit Reference

(See Chapters 11 and 12)

1. In sentence B (the second of any two sentences), repeat a word from sentence A. (Page 126.)
2. Use a synonym. (Page 126.)
3. Use an antonym. (Pages 126–27.)
4. Use a pronoun to refer to an antecedent. (Page 127.)
5. Use a commonly paired (expected) word. (Page 127.)
6. Repeat a sentence structure. (Pages 127–28, 193–94.)
7. Use a connective word:
   a. Identity (sameness)—*that is, that is to say, in other words, I mean.* (Page 133.)
   b. Opposite (contrary to)—*but, yet, however, nevertheless, still, though, although; whereas, in contrast.* (Pages 133–34.)
   c. Additional example or development—*and, too, also, furthermore, moreover, in addition, besides, in the same way, again, another, similarly, a similar, the same; first, second.* . . . (Pages 134–36.)
   d. Cause and effect—*therefore, so, consequently, as a consequence, thus, as a result, hence, it follows that; because, since, for.* (Page 136.)
   e. Indefinite connectives—*in fact, indeed, now.* (Pages 136–38.)
   f. Presenting the other side—*admittedly, I admit, true, I grant, of course, naturally* (Chapter 8, pages 110–11); *some people believe, it has been falsely claimed, once it was believed, there are those who declare.* (Chapter 15, page 176.)

Appendix IV

Seven Rules
for Contrast

(See Chapter 14)

1. Select for treatment differences that make a difference.
2. Contrast the same parts or qualities of each object or person.
3. Say about one person or thing the opposite of what you have said about the other.
4. If you mention something about one, be sure to mention the contrasting thing about the other.
5. Take up things in the order in which you first present them.
6. Use the words *difference, dissimilarity, likeness, similarity,* and *resemblance*—but not *a contrast* or *a comparison.*
7. To connect two contrasted statements, use *whereas* and *in contrast.*

Index

Theme (continued)
    form and appearance of, 32–33,
       106–107
    introduction and conclusion of,
       76–77
    length of, 3, 63, 179–80
    necessary qualities of, 30, 76
    sample, 33, 51, 52, 62–63, 107
    subject matter for, 79–81, 87–89,
       100–101, 121–22, 161–62, 171–74
Theme sentence, 56
  See also Sentence X
Theories, need validation, 79–81,
    172–73
Therefore, 136
  placement of, in sentence, 110, 140
These, 109
Thesis, Thesis sentence, Thesis
    statement, 56
  See also Sentence X
Thing, most general word, 39, 65
This, 109
Those, 109
Though, 134
  vs. *but,* 140, 178
Titles
  Step 1 sentences not, 5
  Step 2 sentences not, 72
Tone, consistent, 93
Topic sentence, 56
  See also Sentences 1, 2, and 3
Traditional names for Step 1 and 2
    sentences, 56
Transitional paragraph, 157–58
Transitions, 158
True . . . but, 110–111, 134, 176

U
Unity, coherence, detail, 76
Uses of Enchantment (Bettelheim), 119,
    166

V
Vague, vs. *general,* 37
Variety, in writing, 70–71, 191–93
Verbs, specific and concrete, 41–42
Verner's Law, 92–93
Vocabulary, 93–94, 189–91

W
Ward, Artemus, 110
Waugh, Evelyn, 99, 112
Welty, Eudora, 99
Where, in contrasts, 165
Whereas, in contrasts, 134, 164–65
While, in contrasts, 165
White, E. B., 112
Wilson, S. S., 168–69
Winter, sample theme, 33, 107, 184
Wonderful, in sentence X, 15, 115–16
Words, repeated, 68–70, 126
Writing, professional vs. student, 138
Writing in College (Kerrigan), 5
Written vs. spoken language, 81–82,
    131

X
X, sentence. *See* Sentence X

Y
You, use of in themes, 69